W9-DFH-143

❊ Praise For HAVEN ❊

"Thank you for this well-written, fascinating story, and for your critical work in directly affecting the lives of so many people. You are to be congratulated for shaping part of the history of a critical period and for setting it down so that generations to come cannot forget."

Harold Ickes, Jr., Deputy Chief of Staff
at the White House, son of Harold L. Ickes,
former Secy. of the Interior

"A never-before-told story which now takes its rightful place as one of the important events of that era. A beautifully written and inspiring book."

Peggy Mann, author, *"The Last Escape"*

"An important journalist's emphatic account of one moment of American redemptiveness in a time of wide indifference and hardheartedness."

Cynthia Ozick, author and playwright

"Ruth Gruber's engrossing and inspiring account of the famous 'Oswego refugees' from Nazi Europe shines like a beacon of light amidst the appalling tragedies of the Holocaust. This book is all the more marvelous because Ruth Gruber herself was an active participant in rescuing the victims."

Gerald Green, author of the *"Holocaust"* TV series

"Eyewitness/heart-witness account of one who was there. History made personal; a gripping story in rich detail, informed by compassion and totally unforgettable."

Bel Kaufman, author of *Up the Down Staircase*

"Those determined to find that only indifference and betrayal marked the attitude of the American government and Jewish leaders during the bitter Holocaust years should read HAVEN...a fast-paced, personal account of the author's involvement in a little known project to circumvent the supposedly immutable immigration laws."

Henry L. Feingold, author of *The Politics of Rescue*

"I found the stories of the refugees and their experience in the United States fascinating reading, particularly because it talks about the Holocaust from a totally different point of view."

Ernest W. Michel, Chair, World Gathering
of Jewish Holocaust Survivors

THEY FOUND A HAVEN IN OSWEGO, NEW YORK

They were all ages, from eighty to an infant born in a Jeep and dubbed "International Harry." Most were Jews, but many were Protestants, Catholics, and Greek Orthodox who had fled from countries overrun by Hitler. Among them were the cheerful Mathilda, who had run an underground rescue station; Leo, an opera star from Zagreb; beautiful Edith, who had fought with the Yugoslav partisans; and willowy Manya, who survived five concentration camps to become the group's first bride.

Helping them all was the courageous young American they called "Mother Ruth," who brought their stories to her boss, Secretary of the Interior Harold Ickes, and through him, to President Roosevelt himself. Most important, she took up their struggle to stay in America, and she tells us where they are today—in a story that's spine-chilling in its impact and unforgettable in its message to the world.

HAVEN

The Unknown Story of 1000 World War II Refugees

RUTH GRUBER

A SAFE HAVEN PUBLICATION
50th OSWEGO ANNIVERSARY EDITION

A SAFE HAVEN PUBLICATION
Fiftieth Oswego Anniversary Edition, 1994
Copyright © 1983, 1984 by Ruth Gruber

This is an authorized reprint of the editions published by the Putnam Publishing Group, Inc. (Coward, McCann, Inc.) 1983, and Signet New American Library edition 1984.

ISBN 0-930395-20-4

Printed in the United States of America.

1994 Edition addenda by Rivanne Advertising, Brooklyn, NY

To My Two Little Grandchildren

Michael Philip
and
Lucy Jennifer Evans

CONTENTS

FOREWORD

This is a true story.

Few people are aware, and those who knew have largely forgotten, that nearly one thousand refugees were brought to the United States as guests of President Franklin Delano Roosevelt during World War II.

Transported on an Army transport ship with wounded soldiers from Anzio and Cassino, hunted at sea by Nazi planes and U-boats, brought to haven in Oswego, New York, they were to know the exquisite relief of freedom from bombings and terror.

They were refugees from eighteen countries Hitler had overrun, who tried to rebuild their lives inside an internment camp on American soil.

As special assistant to Harold L. Ickes, Secretary of the Interior, I was sent by our government to escort them from war-torn Italy and to help resettle them in Fort Ontario, a former army camp on Lake Ontario.

Thus, I became witness and participant. I experienced their joys and pain, rejoicing in their marriages and love affairs, sharing pride in their children, mourning those who died by their own hands or by acts of God.

Stowed away in the bottom of filing cabinets were more than forty notebooks that I had filled during the eighteen months my life was interwoven with theirs. These notebooks, together with copies of the reports, letters and documents I had prepared for the government, were the major source for the events recorded in this book. Invaluable, too, were the diaries which Cabinet members frequently keep, made public by their heirs. Recently, the Ickes family opened Secretary Ickes' secret diaries to the world, and I spent fascinated hours in the Library of Congress discovering the personal, often intimate details of his years in office, his battles, both epic and small, and his discussion of the assignments he gave me.

In Hyde Park, I dug into the voluminous diaries of Secretary of the Treasury Henry Morgenthau, Jr., and the papers of

Eleanor and Franklin Roosevelt, all of whom played character roles, sometimes larger than life-size, on the Oswego stage.

Luck was with me. In the National Archives I uncovered the confidential log of the *Henry Gibbins*, the Army Transport on which I sailed with the refugees, and succeeded in persuading the government to declassify it.

Across the years, as I balanced my life as writer, wife and mother, I continued my friendship with many of the refugees, and within this last year more than one hundred of the original thousand have given me generously of their time and their memory. To all of them and to scores of others who have helped in making this book, I give my gratitude, among them Beanie Bach, the late Josiah E. DuBois, Jr., Henry L. Feingold, Gerold Frank, Russell Galen, Jetta Hendel Gordon, Arlene Greco, Walter Greenberg, Herman R. Gruber, Roberta Haynes, Joy Hyman, Dr. Nat Hyman, Joe Kanon, Dan Levin, Kathaleen Levin, Sharon Lowenstein, Golda Kaufman, Harold J. Kaufman, Peggy Mann, Edward B. Marks, Jr., Marie Mendelssohn-Bach, Adam Munz, Sylvia Mindlin, Sonia Sommerburg Rabin, Diane Reverand, Betty Sobel, Dr. Samuel H. Sobel, Helene B. Weintraub.

I have tried to write the story of the only refugees brought to America by the government during World War II with some of the humor I learned from the refugees, with anger and passion and honesty, and with love.

RUTH GRUBER

PART ONE
The Struggle in Washington

CHAPTER ONE

The words leaped at me from the *Washington Post*.

" 'I have decided,' President Franklin Delano Roosevelt announced, 'that approximately 1,000 refugees should be immediately brought from Italy to this country.' "

One thousand refugees.

Europe was burning. It was June 1944, the middle of the war.

For years, refugees knocking on the doors of American consulates abroad had been told, "You cannot enter America. *The quotas are filled.*"

While the quotas remained untouchable, like tablets of stone, millions died.

Suddenly, one thousand refugees were to be brought in *outside* the quotas, by order of the President himself. Until now I had felt helpless, frustrated, enraged. Noble speeches were made each day about saving refugees before they were swept into the fire. But the deeds belied the words. Our doors had been slammed shut. Now suddenly there was hope.

At my breakfast table, air-conditioned against Washington's summer heat, I continued to devour the article. The thousand refugees, I read, would be selected by the War Refugee Board, transported to America by the Army and housed in a "temporary haven," a former army camp called Fort Ontario, in Oswego, New York. The camp would be administered by the War Relocation Authority of the Department of the Interior. Only a few months before, the President had placed WRA, soon to be disbanded, under Harold L. Ickes, the Secretary of the Interior. I was Ickes's special assistant, his field representative for Alaska.

Ickes would know what lay behind this sudden humanitarian gesture.

At E Street I jumped out of a cab and looked up at the handsome gray stone Interior building with its great bronze doors and modern columns. Interior—the vast grab-bag department of Indians, parks, reclamation, public works, petroleum, mines, fish and wildlife, Alaska, Puerto Rico, Hawaii, the Philippines—would now be in charge of Europe's refugees too.

In my office, I telephoned Ickes's appointments secretary and arranged a meeting for eleven fifty-five.

Ickes sat behind a huge desk littered with papers. His head was lowered as I began the long walk across the huge blue-carpeted office. He was writing with the thick scratchy pen I had seen him use countless times.

"Sit down," he said briefly, and continued to write.

I sat in the armchair at the side of his desk. Behind him was a long table carefully stacked with books, newspapers, magazines. *The Nation* and the *New Republic*, to which he frequently contributed, were on top.

He finished his writing and buzzed for his secretary, who took the papers and disappeared..

Now he turned his full attention to me. "Yes?" he asked quizzically. "I understand it's urgent."

"It's about the thousand refugees that President Roosevelt is inviting to America."

He nodded. "The President sent me a copy of his cablegram to Robert Murphy in Algiers announcing it."

"Mr. Secretary," I said, "it's what we've been fighting for all these years. To open the doors. Save lives. Circumvent the holy quotas. What's behind it? How did it happen?"

He leaned back in his chair. His eyes looked weary. "It came up in a Cabinet meeting with the President. It seems that Yugoslavian refugees and others are finding their way into Italy at the rate of about one thousand eight hundred a week. It's a problem for the military in Italy."

Was it Army pressure, then? The Allied armies were just now pushing up the boot of Italy. The papers were filled with the bloody battles of Anzio and Cassino. We had lost thousands of troops in the hills of southern Italy. I could see refugees fleeing into Italy on the heels of the Army. Clogging roads. Needing to be housed and fed.

"Someone at the meeting," Ickes went on, "I don't remember who, proposed that refugees be brought to this country. The President was still in favor of finding havens for them in Europe, Sicily, or parts of North Africa like Libya. I suggested that if any were brought to this country, instead of coming to the mainland, they be sent to the Virgin Islands. There's plenty of room on the island of St. Croix, where the weather is mild, like southern Italy. Instead, they're putting the people in New York State, near the snow belt around Lake Ontario."

"But surely it's not only because of the Army that we're taking them in? It has to be more. It has to be humanitarian."

"Of course it's humanitarian." His eyes blazed through his gold-rimmed glasses. "And it's about time, too. We've been trying for years to open the doors to refugees. Look what happened to the Alaskan Development Bill we prepared here in the Department."

I nodded. In November 1940, a year before Pearl Harbor, a bill was introduced to bring ten thousand settlers to Alaska; half of them were to be Americans; the other half would be European refugees who would promise to stay in Alaska for five years. Then they would be allowed to enter the United States under the existing quotas.

The bill was to do two things at once—help open Alaska for settlers and provide a haven for refugees. But the opposition was so great, from Alaskans as well as from isolationists who wanted no refugees, that it died in committee.

"I'm sure there'll be opposition again," Ickes said, "the restrictionists on one side and the damn fools on the other who'll scream that one thousand isn't enough. They don't realize, with all the opposition to immigration in general, and Jews in particular, that you can't take in more than one thousand at a time."

I thought of the millions of Jews waiting to be rescued. There were frightening rumors that several million had already been murdered in Germany, Poland and other countries Hitler had overrun, though most of us still did not know how. But there were millions more—in Hungary, Rumania, Italy. Maybe we could rescue them—snatch them from Hitler's jaws.

Of all the Cabinet members, Ickes, who told me he had never met a Jew until he was sixteen, was the most passionate in denouncing the Nazi atrocities against Jews, and the angriest that the doors of America were sealed.

"Mr. Secretary." I heard the urgency in my voice. "These people coming here—they must be frightened, bewildered, coming to a strange land. Somebody has to be with them. Somebody has to take their hand."

"You're suggesting . . ." His eyes began to sparkle; the weariness was gone. "Of course. It's a great idea. I'm going to send you. You're the one to go over and bring them back."

Ickes was a man of instant decisions. He called his operator. "Get Dillon Myer on the phone."

Myer was the head of the War Relocation Authority; his agency would administer the camp.

"Myer," I heard him say, "I want to send someone over to

Italy to bring back those refugees. What? You've already selected someone? A man? You send your man, I'm sending her.
That's right. It's a woman. A young woman. What's that?'' His
jowls trembled with anger.

I felt my stomach knot.

"What has being young got to do with this job? Being young
didn't stop her from getting a Ph.D. in literature when she was
twenty—the youngest in the world. And she took it in Germany—
an exchange student from America. I know her capabilities.
She's been working for me now—"he turned to me—"how
long is it?"

"Three years." I could hardly hear my voice.

"Three years. With all kinds of jobs. And this one is right for
her. Those refugees are from the Balkans and Central Europe.
They probably speak mostly German. She speaks German and
Yiddish. There'll be a lot of women and children. She'll know
how to speak to them; she'll understand them. You better come
in at two-thirty today; I want to talk to you about her."

Midafternoon, I was summoned to Ickes's office. "Myer has
just left." he said. "I told him I couldn't think of a better person
to send."

I sat upright in the chair.

"I told him it's a unique job and you've got unique qualifi-
cations. You can communicate with the people. With your
background, they'll trust you."

I waited for him to go on.

"What's more, I assured Myer that you could be of great help
to us by writing and speaking about the refugees when you get
back. I told him how you are always asked to lecture on Alaska.
Also, your press contacts are important. I made certain he knew
that the *Herald Tribune* sent you to the Soviet Arctic. I told
him I have full confidence in you, that you understand these
people, and you can write."

He was still not telling me Myer's decision.

"It's not settled, then?" I asked.

Myer, I knew, was an old-school government offical who had
come up through the ranks of the Agriculture Department.
Instinctively, I sensed he would be dubious about sending a
woman to do this job.

"Myer says there are problems," Ickes went on. "Interior is
not in overall charge of this project. The War Refugee Board
is."

The War Refugee Board had been created by the President five months ago—to save war refugees.

"Myer will have to check with WRB to get approval for you. I told him to see you first before he checks with them. He'll see you at eleven tomorrow morning. I have to tell you—he's hesitant about you."

"He's never met me."

"I have the feeling he thinks you're a big buxom social worker."

I was neither big nor buxom nor a social worker.

"It's these bureaucrats," Ickes said. "They get in a niche and then they're afraid to do anything unusual, anything that takes courage and imagination. Come back tomorrow after you've seen him."

That night I replayed the scenes in Ickes's office. I walked to my desk and read again the President's message to Congress. It was dated June 12, 1944.

This nation is appalled by the systematic persecution of helpless minority groups by the Nazis. To us, the unprovoked murder of innocent people simply because of race, religion, or political creed is the blackest of all possible crimes . . . the fury of their insane desire to wipe out the Jewish race in Europe continues undiminished. This is but one example. Many Christian groups are also being murdered.

I leaned my head on my desk. There had been so many false starts to save them, so many conferences, so many hopes dashed. In July 1938 the United States had convened the Evian Conference in France on the shores of Lake Geneva. Thirty-two nations had sent representatives, most of whom stood up, one by one, to explain why they could not accept refugees. All that came out of Evian was a new committee, the Intergovernmental Committee on Refugees, which did little more than the League of Nations had done before to save refugees.

Meanwhile the two world leaders we loved, Roosevelt and Winston Churchill, made eloquent speeches about refugees even as they barred them. England closed the doors of Palestine, and the United States closed the doors of America. To be sure, individuals were brought into our country. Albert Einstein had been helped to escape; Thomas Mann had been invited as an honored guest. But now at last Roosevelt was inviting not famous individuals, but a whole group of "common" people.

For America, after World War I, had pulled back between its two oceans, isolationist, largely antiforeign. The idea of taking in large numbers of refugees—especially Jews—was unpopular. And the specter of anti-Semitism was in our country, to be evoked by any overt gesture. So FDR, along with many others, was careful not to show too much sympathy for beleaguered Jewish refugees. Besides, the time-honored distaste for Jews—if not outright hatred—was still a hallmark of the upper echelons of some government agencies, particularly the Department of State. I knew it firsthand working in Washington. Ickes was a different breed of high officialdom; there were not many like him.

That was why I was so excited, why Roosevelt's decision to bring in even one thousand seemed to me such a triumph. One thousand, out of the millions being slaughtered and more millions without homes or refuge.

It could be the beginning of a mass rescue movement, I believed. For a thousand people, it would mean life, not death.

At eleven the next morning, I entered the Barr Building on Seventeenth Street, a seedy, steaming-hot office building, and rode the elevator to the executive offices of the War Relocation Authority. Unlike the marble halls and broad corridors of Interior, the narrow halls and small offices seemed out of another era. I waited in the small room.

"Mr. Myer is free now." His secretary pointed toward the door.

My instincts were right. There was no warmth in his greeting. A tall man with steel-rimmed glasses and steel-gray hair, he stared down at me as I entered. He looked like the engineers I had seen on construction projects in Alaska, hard-driving men who seemed closer to machines and mortar than to people.

"So," he said coldly, "you're even younger than I thought."

I said nothing.

"I can't understand why, for such an important, unprecedented mission, Ickes should want to send a young woman. Do you realize what this job means? You'll be going over in the middle of war. You can be shot down. That's all we need, to have a young woman from our department shot down by a Nazi plane."

I wanted to tell him that I had been in the Aleutians when they were invaded, that I was a fatalist, that I would die when my number was up. Instead, I said, "It's a danger I'm prepared to face."

"Do you realize you'll be dealing with a thousand people—with men as well as women and children? Don't you see that after what they have gone through, they would have more respect for a man? They would pay much more attention to a man than they would to a woman."

In a corner of my mind I thought, Maybe there is validity in his arguments. Maybe refugees would have more respect for a man who was old and wise and experienced. I pushed the thought away, opened my purse and pulled out copies of the President's message to Congress and the cablegram he had sent to Ambassador Murphy in Algiers. I had underlined some of the President's phrases. I read them now to Dillon Myer: " '. . . *the Nazis are determined to complete their program of mass extermination . . . we have made clear our determination to punish all participants in these acts of savagery. In the name of humanity . . .'*

" 'In the name of humanity,' " I repeated the words. "Mr. Myer, what have age or sex to do with *humanity?*"

He stood up abruptly. "It's not up to me. I can't make the decision. I must speak with John Pehle; he's executive director of the War Refugee Board. I'll call you back after I've talked with Pehle."

Two hours later, my office phone rang.

"I've talked with Pehle." Myer's voice seemed a shade less cold. "He did some checking himself in Interior. You got some pretty good recommendations. Pehle agrees that you can go."

"Thank you, Mr. Myer," I breathed into the phone.

"You know, of course, I'm sending my own man over, Ralph Stauber. He'll be getting the statistics we need, where the people came from, et cetera."

I listened silently.

"You are Ickes's personal representative. But you can help us gain insight into the makeup of the people, so that we can develop policies. You must make it clear to them that they are coming here to live inside a camp where they will have food, a place to live in and enough to keep them warm."

"What about leaving the camp?" I asked. "What if they have relatives? Will they be able to visit them? Will they be able to go outside to work?"

"That's a policy decision to be made later, in thirty or sixty days after they arrive. Be very careful. *Don't make any promises we can't fulfill.* We don't want to raise their hopes too high. That happened in our other camps."

The other camps were the Japanese-American internment and

relocation camps where over 100,000 Japanese were then incarcerated under Myer's adminstration. After Pearl Harbor, after the "Day of Infamy" on December 7, 1941, the country had exploded with hysteria against the Japanese. Innocent men, women and children were pulled up from their homes, business men from their shops, farmers from their land. In one of his darkest hours, the President, describing them as "potential fifth columnists," ordered the Japanese segregated in isolated camps. They were fenced in with barbed wire, patrolled by soldiers. To run the camps, Roosevelt created a special agency, the War Relocation Authority, WRA, headed by Milton Eisenhower, who recommended Dillon Myer as his successor when he resigned. Two years later, in February 1944 the President ordered WRA transfered to Interior.

"This is something I distinctly do not want," Ickes recorded his reaction to his new responsiblity in his secret diary. "But I told the President that I would take it and do the best that I could."

Ickes was determined to close the camps down swiftly and resettle the internees as humanely as possible, a task Eisenhower and Myer had already fought to achieve. He held a press conference to announce his decision. Since he was the liveliest Cabinet officer they covered, most of the Washington corps of journalists and radio commentators filled the auditorium. They loved his quips, his sardonic wit.

Ickes revealed that 23,000 Japanese had already been resettled. He had even talked with Mayor Fiorello La Guardia about relocating them in New York. "La Guardia," Ickes said, "is perfectly willing to have the Japanese resettled in New York City, but not if they are still banned from the Pacific Coast." Ickes wanted the ban "lifted right away—the sooner the better."

Some of the reporters applauded. I joined in the applause, knowing that at last innocent people, whose only crime was the color of their skin and the slant of their eyes, were to be freed. I thought of the Jews that Hitler was murdering, whose only crime was that they were Jews.

Ickes looked up as I approached his desk. "Myer has agreed," he said. "I can tell from your face."

"The War Refugee Board gave the OK," I said triumphantly, and told him that Myer had admonished me to keep the mission secret and promise the refugees nothing.

"That's not bad advice," Ickes said. "But I don't want them to hamstring you. You're to feel free to do what you want, go where you want, see what you want, and report to me. I'm giving you full rein."

That was what I needed to hear. "Mr. Secretary, this is going to be the most important assignment you've ever given me—maybe the most important thing I've done in my life."

"I'm sure you'll do an excellent job. Myer is lucky to be getting you. You can reassure those refugees, make them feel better than some official just doing his routine duty. I know that this whole thing, saving refugees, means a lot to you, as it does to me. You're going to be my eyes and ears. I'm depending on you."

That evening I called my parents in Brooklyn. "I'm going to Europe," I said.

"What?" my mother screamed into the phone. "Are you crazy? Every day I read how they sink ships and shoot down airplanes. And my daughter has to go to Europe to get her head shot off."

"Mom, don't worry."

"Don't worry, she says to me. It's enough your brother Irving is in the Army and I pray to God every night that he should come home safe. He has to go to war, he's a captain. But you're no soldier. What do you have to go for? What kind of *mishegaas* got into you now?"

"I can't tell you, Mom. It's a secret. But it's very important."

"Important. It's always important. Ever since you were a little girl you started running. Do I know where you went? Germany. Siberia. Alaska. I never knew if you were alive. What normal girl goes to Siberia and Alaska? Now she has to go to Europe."

"I'll be all right, Mom. Don't worry."

My father, on the extension phone, said quietly, "Will you come home to say goodbye?"

I could see his handsome face, the wide-set eyes, the tall sturdy body, the father who always had faith in me.

"I'd love to come home before I go abroad, Pop," I said, "but I won't have time. I've got to go through a whole process of briefings before I go."

"Then I'll come to Washington to see you off," my mother announced.

CHAPTER TWO

I spent the next weeks in a maze of bureaucratic briefings.

The refugees were even now being selected in southern Italy. I had to reach them before their convoy sailed.

I was completely bureaucratized. At the War Relocation Authority, where my official travel orders had to be drawn up. At the State Department, waiting interminably for a special passport. At the Public Health Service, where a battery of doctors pummeled, stethoscoped, X-rayed and bled me and, with ominously prophetic voices, handed me a card with my blood type, "in case you're shot down and need a transfusion."

Typhus, typhoid, tetanus, smallpox and plague were shot into my arms, my buttocks, my stomach. I reacted with high fever and was told to stay in bed. I refused, hoping to speed up the briefings. It was useless. The bureaucracy in Washington moved on slow interminable wheels, each agency guarding its own authority, feeding upon its own red tape.

Marking time, I occupied myself trying to discover why Roosevelt was acting now, after all these years of a closed-door policy. I spent hours in the Library of Congress reading newspapers, and evenings talking with my friends in government, asking the question "Why are the quotas being circumvented now?" In restaurants and in the privacy of our apartments we told each other, "It's Congress and the State Department who bar refugees. Roosevelt can't act alone. He can't have his New Deal labeled the Jew Deal."

There were other factors too, we reminded each other. Long before Hitler, Europe was an anti-Semitic continent. In America the quota system, under the fitting racist title "National Origins Quota," had become law in the early 1920's, largely to bar Orientals and immigrants from Eastern Europe, many of them Jews.

Changes in the quota were unthinkable. The labor unions were opposed, fearing that refugees would take their jobs. The isolationists in Congress rode high. All this left the American Jewish community, with scarcely three percent of the population, powerless to save the Jews of Europe.

"Trust Roosevelt," one faction exhorted us. "Roosevelt has saved us from a Communist takeover during the Great Depression. Now he will save the world from Hitler. Don't make waves. Silent diplomacy is the safest route to rescue Jews."

"No. Silence is the enemy," a small group denounced silent diplomacy. Their leader was Peter Bergson, a young Palestinian; only an aroused public opinion, he insisted, could save refugees.

Ben Hecht, the brilliant playwright and journalist, wrote full-page ads with venom in his pen. One of his ads, a long ballad, carried the refrain

> Hang and burn, but be quiet, Jews,
> The world is busy with other news.

Even the Zionists, united in one goal, to open Palestine, were divided on whether this was the time to fight for a Jewish state.

In the end, it was clear that only the President himself had power to break the ironclad quotas and to begin rescuing Jews. Who had reached him?

"It was the cables," a friend in Treasury told me one day.

"What cables?"

"The ones that told everything—how Jews were being murdered."

"Why didn't we know about them?"

He shrugged and was silent.

"You mean—they were suppressed?"

"For two years."

Two years in which we were kept in darkness. Two years when public opinion might have galvanized our leaders into action.

Only now I can put together the pieces of the story that would lead from those suppressed cables to FDR's belated announcement, then to a shipboard odyssey and a haven in America, while war and Holocaust raged in Europe.

In the summer of 1942, a German industrialist, visiting Switzerland on business, brought shocking news. Hitler was planning to exterminate all the Jews of Europe with a new device—prussic acid, the deadly compound of Zyklon-B gas. The news was delivered to Gerhart Riegner, a thirty-one-year-old refugee from Berlin working for the World Jewish Congress in Switzerland.

Riegner, whom I was to meet two years later in Geneva, told

me, "At first I wouldn't believe it. Deportation of Jews—this we knew. Killing Jews, torturing them, shooting them in graves—this we knew." His eyes clouded over. "But this was a whole, total, embracing plan. It was *Vernichtung*."

Vernichtung. Annihilation.

"I had to verify it," he said. "I had to find out—were the Germans capable of total *Vernichtung?*"

Fair-skinned, blue-eyed, Riegner looked and sounded like the students I had known in Germany.

Riegner had promised the industrialist he would never reveal his name. He has kept his promise, even though research has now pointed to Eduard Schulte, a banker and industrialist from Upper Silesia, who loathed the Nazis. With friends in high places in the Nazi Government, Schulte was able to alert the Allies to Hitler's plans for annihilating Jews.

"I needed eight days to investigate the German industrialist and to convince myself. Finally convinced, I wrote a cable and took it to the American and British consuls, asking them to transmit it in code. In America it was to be sent to Rabbi Stephen S. Wise, who was president of the American Jewish Congress and was my boss in America. In Britain it was sent to Sydney Silverman, a member of Parliament and chairman of the British section of the World Jewish Congress."

The cable, dated August 8, 1942, read:

RECEIVED ALARMING REPORT THAT IN FÜHRER'S HEADQUARTERS PLAN DISCUSSED AND UNDER CONSIDERATION ACCORDING TO WHICH ALL JEWS IN COUNTRIES OCCUPIED OR CONTROLLED GERMANY NUMBERING 3½—4 MILLION [excluding Jews in the Soviet Union] SHOULD AFTER DEPORTATION AND CONCENTRATION IN EAST BE EXTERMINATED AT ONE BLOW TO RESOLVE ONCE FOR ALL THE JEWISH QUESTION IN EUROPE STOP ACTION REPORTED PLANNED FOR AUTUMN METHODS UNDER DISCUSSION INCLUDING PRUSSIC ACID STOP WE TRANSMIT INFORMATION WITH ALL NECESSARY RESERVATION AS EXACTITUDE CANNOT BE CONFIRMED STOP INFORMANT STATED TO HAVE CLOSE CONNECTIONS WITH HIGHEST GERMAN AUTHORITIES AND HIS REPORTS GENERALLY SPEAKING RELIABLE

RIEGNER

The cable was never delivered to Rabbi Wise. The State Department decided the information was "unsubstantiated" and summarized the report as "a wild rumor inspired by Jewish fears." Undersecretary of State Sumner Welles, one of the few

State Department officials considered friendly to Jews, signed the order to suppress the cable.

Three weeks later, Riegner was informed that Wise still knew nothing. "I went through the worst period of my life," Riegner told me. "There I was in my office looking out at the lake and Mont Blanc, and there was such peace in those snow-capped mountains. And the Jews were trapped in Europe."

Fortunately, the British did not suppress the cable to Silverman, in which Riegner had carefully inserted the words "Inform and consult New York." Silverman sent a copy of the August 1942 cable to Rabbi Wise by ordinary Western Union.

In New York, Rabbi Wise read the cable over and over. He knew Riegner well. He knew how cautious he was. It had to be true.

He rushed to Washington to see Sumner Welles. Had Welles seen this cable? Did he know these facts? Welles, of course, had seen the original cable weeks before. Now he prevailed on Wise to keep the cable secret until State Department representatives in Switzerland could confirm Riegner's charges.

Finally, in November, Welles telephoned Wise. "Come to Washington immediately."

Welles showed the rabbi documents and affidavits from his own men in Switzerland confirming everything Riegner had reported. He could no longer hold Wise to his promise of secrecy. "You're free now to release the information."

Wise released the terrible information. But three months had already elapsed. No one knew if the Nazis had begun their *Vernichtung*.

On January 21, 1943, Leland Harrison, our minister in Bern, ordered another cable from Riegner to Rabbi Wise coded and transmitted through the State Department.

It was Cable 482, a file number that was to become famous. In four horror-filled pages, Riegner described the terror that had been decimating Jews in two lands: in Poland, where the Germans had been killing 6,000 Jews each day; in Rumania, where 130,000 Jews had been deported to Transnistria in the Rumanian-occupied Ukraine. The clothes had been ripped off the refugees' backs; everything they owned was stolen. Of the 130,000 deported to the Transnistrian "reservation" for Jews, 60,000 had already died and 70,000 were starving to death.

Welles himself forwarded Cable 482 to Rabbi Wise. Wise immediately began arranging for a Stop Hitler Now mass rally to be held at Madison Square Garden in New York on March 1, 1943.

On February 10, 1943 the State Department sent an unusual message to Minister Harrison in Switzerland. It was Cable 354, and it opened by referring to Riegner's Cable 482:

YOUR 482, JANUARY 21. IT IS SUGGESTED THAT IN THE FUTURE, REPORTS SUBMITTED TO YOU FOR TRANSMISSION TO PRIVATE PERSONS IN THE UNITED STATES SHOULD NOT BE ACCEPTED UNLESS EXTRA-ORDINARY CIRCUMSTANCES MAKE SUCH ACTION ADVISABLE. IT IS FELT THAT BY SENDING SUCH PRIVATE MESSAGES WHICH CIRCUMVENT NEUTRAL COUNTRIES' CENSORSHIP WE RISK THE POSSIBILITY THAT NEUTRAL COUNTRIES MIGHT FIND IT NECESSARY TO TAKE STEPS TO CURTAIL OR ABOLISH OUR OFFICIAL SECRET MEANS OF COMMUNICATION.

In the strangulated language of diplomacy, this meant, "Stop sending any more messages about Nazi atrocities."

Sumner Welles again signed the cable. In Welles's defense, many people, including Henry Morgenthau, Jr., the Secretary of the Treasury, believed that he was too busy to inquire what 482 referred to.

For Minister Harrison and Riegner in Switzerland, Welles's cable was an enigma. Only two months earlier, the Allies had announced that Nazis would be punished as war criminals for their atrocities against Jews. America would need all the eyewitness accounts from Riegner to build its case against war criminals. Why now this order from the State Department to stop all information? And why specifically the order to stop further cables disclosing Nazi atrocities, when hundreds of commercial cables for private businesses were being transmitted?

Fortunately the cable to cease and desist was sent too late to halt the Stop Hitler Now rally.

It was a blustery first day of March 1943 in New York. The streets around Madison Square Garden were clogged with thousands of people. The Garden held 21,000 people, but at least 75,000 more were outside, unable to enter.

We kept each other warm, no longer strangers. We belonged together, a wall of Americans—Jews and Christians—shouting with one voice, "Stop Hitler now."

We listened to the loudspeakers as leaders pleaded with the Allied governments to act swiftly, before it was too late.

"The world can no longer believe that the ghastly facts are unknown and unconfirmed," Dr. Chaim Weizmann, the eloquent leader of the Jewish Agency, the shadow Jewish goverment in Palestine, declared. "At this moment expressions of sympathy without accompanying attempts to launch *acts of rescue* become a hollow mockery in the ears of the dying.

"The democracies have a clear duty before them." Weizmann's voice rang through the night air. "Let them negotiate with Germany through the neutral countries concerning the possible release of the Jews in the occupied countries."

Negotiate with Germany through the neutral countries to release the Jews in the occupied countries. Sweden was neutral. Switzerland was neutral. In fact, Switzerland was far more. It was a giant ear, the listening post for diplomats, provocateurs, spies, mysterious travelers. It was in Switzerland that Riegner was getting much of his information from German travelers.

"Let havens be designated," Weizmann went on, "in the vast territories of the United Nations* which would give sanctuary to those fleeing from imminent murder."

Havens! The word became symbolic in my mind. America had been one great big haven since its birth. We could have hundred of havens. If only we opened our doors.

Weizmann was pleading for a haven in Palestine. "The Jewish community of Palestine will welcome with joy and thanksgiving all delivered from Nazi hands."

A man near me shouted, "Tell it to Churchill."

But Britain, with a mandate from the world to turn Palestine into a homeland for Jews, was even now sending crucially needed warships to the Palestine coast, not to fight the Nazis but to prevent Jews from entering.

We heard Cardinal Hinsely, the Roman Catholic Archbishop of Westminster, denouncing both England's Foreign Office and our State Department. "We need cold deeds, and speedy deeds, not the *rhetoric* behind which governments are still hiding."

The air grew colder. More people kept thronging the streets around us, pushing, shouting, shoving, while the police sought to keep some semblance of order.

Now at last the voice we were waiting for swept over us. The President was talking from Washington. I could see the patrician face, the strong jaw exuding optimism and strength. The night air grew warm again, embraced by his words.

"The Nazis will not succeed in exterminating their victims . . ." He's talking now about the Jews, I told myself, he's going to tell us how he'll save them.

---

*The United Nations Organization was not created until 1945, but the term had already come into the language.

"The American people will hold the perpetrators of these crimes to strict accountability in a day of reckoning which will surely come."

Was that it? Were we to wait until the war ended? Why couldn't he act now? Open havens in the empty valleys, the hilltops, the deserts of America?

This was March 1943. Our soldiers were battling in North Africa. The Russians had driven the German Sixth Army back from Stalingrad, but Hitler still controlled most of Europe. I knew the argument; it was implicit in the President's words: First we must win the war. Then we will take care of the refugees.

But how many, I thought in despair, would still be alive?

"We have adopted a resolution," Rabbi Wise's voice rolled through the loudspeakers like the music of an organ, "a resolution which we will forward to Secretary of State Cordell Hull to protest against the continuing failure to act against the strange indifference to the fate of five million human beings."

I clutched my arms, shivering in anger and frustration. We were 75,000 people—and all we could do was send a protest to Cordell Hull.

No havens were opened. The doors to America and Palestine remained tightly sealed.

As the clamor in the country to save refugees grew into a groundswell, the State Department called a conference in Bermuda specifically to discuss rescue. The conference opened on the day the Nazis launched their final attack on the Warsaw Ghetto. It was also the week of Passover.

The Bermuda Conference was a fiasco. "Palliatives," *The New York Times* described it, "designed to assuage the conscience of the reluctant rescuers rather than to aid the victims."

Not one country offered to take in a single refugee.

Months passed. Hundreds of thousands of Jews were murdered. And still no havens were opened.

Then, late in 1943, the suppressed cables were discovered.

The World Jewish Congress in Switzerland had cabled Washington that they could ransom the lives of thousands of Jews in Rumania and France. They could raise the money themselves; they knew the officials to be bribed; all they needed was the license to send dollars abroad.

Both Treasury and State had to approve the license. Treasury agreed to issue the license immediately. State did nothing. Half a year was lost.

Outraged, Secretary of the Treasury Morgenthau called in

Josiah E. DuBois, Jr., a young assistant general counsel working with Treasury's Foreign Funds Control. "I want you to investigate the whole thing. Get to the bottom of it."

Joe Dubois was a large canvas of a man with a generous spirit, disheveled eyebrows and tousled hair. He was a young man on fire. He went through all the files to dig up correspondence with State. He found a copy of the cable to the State Department, dated April 20, 1943, from Minister Leland Harrison in Bern which opened by referring to Cable 354 (the cable of suppression). He telephoned the State Department. "Please send over a copy of your Cable 354."

"Sorry," he was told. "This cable does not relate to Treasury. Only a few people have seen it even in State. We cannot furnish it to Treasury."

"Knowing the State Department as I did," Joe told me later, "I became very suspicious. If State said it was none of Treasury's business, I was pretty sure it *was* our business. I decided I had to see it."

Joe knew the head of the Foreign Funds Control at the State Department, Donald Hiss. He telephoned Hiss asking for a copy of Cable 354. Briefly he told Hiss of Morgenthau's determination to get the license issued so that the rescue from France and Rumania could begin.

Hiss, sympathetic, promised to look for the mysterious cable.

Several times Joe called Hiss's office, only to be told, "Joe, I'm having a hard time getting that cable."

Finally, in desperation, Joe called Hiss at home; the cable was still missing.

On the morning of December 18, Hiss's secretary called Joe's secretary. "Please ask Mr. DuBois to be at our office at two-thirty this afternoon." No reason. No explanation.

Before two-thirty Joe was in Hiss's office. On the desk were two cables. "I've been warned," Hiss confided to Joe, "that under no circumstances should these cables be shown to Treasury. If anyone finds out that I'm showing them to you, I might lose my job."

Courageous and fearless himself, Joe knew that Hiss was risking his career to save thousands of lives.

"I can't let them out of my office, Joe," Hiss said. "I can't even give you copies."

Joe read of the terror in Poland and Rumania since 1941. "Can I copy these cables?" he asked.

Hiss nodded silently.

Joe pulled several small slips of paper from his pocket and

copied the full text of the cable of suppression and made notes of the longer horror cable.

Back in his office, he dictated a "memorandum for the files," and marked it confidential. For the first time it told the full story of the cables, "so shocking and so tragic that it is difficult to believe."

"I am physically ill," Morgenthau said when he read the memorandum. He then asked Randolph E. Paul, his counsel, to prepare a complete background paper describing the State Department's delays, subterfuges and suppression.

Paul turned the writing over to Joe DuBois. With the help of Paul and John Pehle, head of the Foreign Funds Control at treasury—both, like Joe, non-Jews—he began working on the report. He dictated drafts to his secretary during the day and worked evenings at home writing. He spent Christmas morning with his wife and family, then went back to his desk and continued writing. Finally, on January 13, 1944, he submitted his report to Morgenthau. Though it was signed "R.E.P." (Randolph E. Paul), Joe had written it out of his guts. He called it "Report to the Secretary on the Acquiescence of This Government in the Murder of the Jews."

It began with an impassioned denunciation of the State Department. "One of the greatest crimes in history, the slaughter of the Jewish people in Europe is continuing unabated." Officials in the State Department

> have not only failed to use the Governmental machinery at their disposal to rescue Jews from Hitler, but have even gone so far as to use this Governmental machinery to *prevent* the rescue of these Jews.
>
> They have not only failed to cooperate with private organizations in the efforts of these organizations to work out individual programs of their own, but have taken steps designed to prevent these programs from being put into effect.
>
> They not only have failed to facilitate the obtaining of information concerning Hitler's plans to exterminate the Jews of Europe but in their official capacity have gone so far as to surreptitiously attempt to stop the obtaining of information concerning the murder of the Jewish population of Europe.
>
> They have tried to cover up their guilt by:
>   (a) concealment and misrepresentation;
>   (b) the giving of false and misleading explanations for their failures to act and their attempts to prevent action; and

(c) the issuance of false and misleading statements concerning the 'action' which they have taken to date.

DuBois pointed the finger directly at Breckinridge Long, the assistant secretary of state who was in charge of the Visa Division, which decided who could enter the United States—in effect, choosing who would live and who would die.

Breckinridge Long, in DuBois's report, was the archvillain in our government's "acquiescence in the murder of Jews." The report quoted a speech by Congressman Emanuel Celler of Brooklyn. "Frankly, Breckinridge Long, in my humble opinion," Celler had told Congress, "is the least sympathetic to refugees in all the State Department. I attribute to him the tragic bottleneck in the granting of visas . . . It takes months and months to grant a visa, and then it usually applies to a corpse."

Congressman Celler blasted the misleading and fraudulent statements Long had made in testimony before the House Committee on Foreign Affairs. "We have taken into this country," Long had told the Committee, "since the beginning of the Hitler regime [1933] and the persecution of the Jews until today, approximately 580,000 refugees. The whole thing has been under the quota—except the generous gesture we made of visitors' and transit visas during an awful period."

Celler nailed that lie:

> In the first place these 580,000 refugees were in the main ordinary quota immigrants coming in from all countries. The majority were not Jews. His statement drips with sympathy for the persecuted Jews, but the tears he sheds are crocodile. I would like to ask him how many Jews were admitted during the last three years in comparison with the number seeking entrance to preserve life and dignity. . . . One gets the impression from Long's statement that the United States has gone out of its way to help refugees fleeing death at the hands of the Nazis. I deny this. On the contrary, the State Department has turned its back on the time-honored principle of granting havens to refugees. The tempest-tossed get little comfort from men like Breckinridge Long. . . . Long says that the door to the oppressed is open but that it "has been carefully screened." What he should have said is "barlocked and bolted." By the act of 1924, we are permitted to admit approximately 150,000 immigrants each year. During the last fiscal year only 23,725 came as immigrants. Of these, only 4,750 were Jews fleeing Nazi persecution.

If men of the temperament and philosophy of Long continue in control of immigration administration, we may as well take down that plaque from the Statue of Liberty and black out the "lamp beside the golden door."

Morgenthau read DuBois's eighteen-page report with mounting rage. He changed the title to the simpler "Personal Report to the President" and cut the document to nine pages, but kept most of its evidence and accusations, even adding his own charges:

There is a growing number of responsible people and organizations today who have ceased to view our failure as the product of simple incompetence on the part of those officials in the State Department charged with handling this problem. They see plain anti-Semitism motivating the actions of these State Department officials and, rightly or wrongly, it will require little more in the way of proof for this suspicion to explode into nasty scandal.

On a rainy Sunday morning on January 16, 1944, Morgenthau went to the White House with his young assistant John Pehle. Morgenthau had easy access to the President, who called him affectionately "Henny-Penny." On this Sunday morning, Morgenthau was no Henny-Penny. He had become a committed, anguished, passionate Jew. The suppressed cables had touched ancient roots. He told his friend the President that if these cables became public the whole world would know of the anti-Semitism in his State Department. The scandal, he said, could reach into the White House itself.

Six days later Roosevelt created the War Refugee Board, WRB, composed of the Secretaries of State, Treasury and War—Hull, Morgenthau and Henry Stimson. Of the three, neither Hull at State nor Stimson of the Army was enthusiastic.

Rescuing Jews was withdrawn from the sabotaging hands of Breckinridge Long and given to the War Refugee Board. Pehle, a slim, circumspect thirty-five-year-old lawyer, became its executive director. Cables would no longer be suppressed. Ships would be leased in Sweden to smuggle refugees out of the Balkans. Ira Hirschmann, an executive of Bloomingdale's department store in New York, would be sent to Istanbul to rescue, if he could, the sixty thousand still alive in the Rumanian concentration camp in Transnistria. Raoul Wallenberg, a young Swede of a distinguished family, would be sent to Hungary and single-handedly save seventy or eighty thousand.

But time was running out for nearly a million Jews in Hungary and another eight hundred thousand in Rumania. Letters flooded the White House. "Mr. President," a man in Los Angeles who signed himself "Not a Jew" pleaded, "do all you can to save the Jewish People of Europe. Establish rescue centers for temporary detention and care until we've knocked the Hell out of Hitler."

On March 6, 1944, Joe DuBois drafted a memorandum for the President urgently recommending temporary havens of refuge. Under his proposal the refugees would be treated "in effect as prisoners of war," for whom no quotas were required.

Peter Bergson and the young Palestinians who worked closely with the War Refugee Board began a massive propaganda campaign to establish temporary havens. "In the eleventh hour of the reign of death," they suggested, let "twenty-five square miles of rescue camps be set aside in five temporary mercy reservations in Palestine, Turkey, North Africa and some of our own abandoned military training camps in the United States." One of their full-page ads carried the headline "25 SQUARE MILES OR . . . 2,000,000 LIVES: Which Shall It Be?"

But bringing refugees into the United States outside the quotas was the political roadblock. How would the isolationists in Congress react? Samuel Grafton, the widely read columnist for the *New York Post* offered a brilliant solution. Free ports! Why not, he asked in his column of April 5, 1944, "have a system of free ports for refugees fleeing the Hitler terror?"

> Obviously we need a place where we can put refugees down, without making final decisions about them, a place where they can be stored and processed, so to speak, without creating legal and political problems . . . Of course, I am a little ashamed to find myself pandering to anti-refugee prejudices even to the extent of saying yes, pile the legal disabilities on them, give them no rights, store them like corn, herd them like cattle—but the need is so sharp, the time is so short, our current example to the world is so bad, that it is necessary to settle for whatever can be done.

In a cordial meeting in the White House, Pehle recommended that an executive order be issued establishing a free port as a temporary haven in the United States. Roosevelt seemed receptive, though he told Pehle he preferred the term "emergency refugee shelter'' to Grafton's "free port." The word "emergency" would show that it was temporary and shelter was "honest," since little more than shelter would be offered the refugees. Pehle, who had expected to rescue unlimited numbers, was startled when Roosevelt ended their meeting with the promise to consider opening one camp to rescue one thousand people.

"Roosevelt was a politician first," Joe DuBois told me later, "and then a humanitarian."

Still, one camp for one thousand could be the beginning. If the isolationists in Congress lay quiescent, then perhaps more camps could be opened and more refugees saved. At least this was what others and I hoped.

At a Cabinet meeting on May 24, Morgenthau introduced the resolution, drafted by WRB, proposing that one thousand refugees be brought from Italy to the United States. He admitted to the Cabinet members that the President was still "a little afraid."

Only Ickes expressed complete support. Ickes was now the honorary chairman of Bergson's "Emergency Committee to Save the Jewish People of Europe." Even Attorney General Francis Biddle opposed the resolution on legal grounds, though it was known he loathed Breckinridge Long's policies on refugees.

In Europe the trains roared toward Auschwitz. The Nazis occupied Hungary toward the end of March 1944. On April 27, 1944, the first transports of Jews were shipped from Hungary. Scarcely three months later, Adolf Eichmann had already packed 520,000 into cattle cars headed for the gas chambers.

On June 6 General Eisenhower issued his order of the day: "Soldiers, sailors and airmen of the Allied Expeditionary Force! You are about to embark upon the great Crusade . . . the eyes of the world are upon you." The invasion of Normandy began. At the same time seven members of the House introduced resolutions urging Roosevelt to open "free ports."

The time, at last, was right. On June 12, the President sent the formal message to Congress—the message I had read in the press—that one thousand refugees would be brought to a safe haven in Oswego, New York.

On Friday, July 14, Ickes called me to his office.

"The Army just phoned," he said. "You're leaving tomorrow. Are you ready?"

"I've been ready for weeks. The longest weeks of my life."

He swiveled his chair, turning his full face toward me. "You're going to be made a general. A simulated general."

"Me? A general?"

"You'll be flying in a military plane. If you're shot down and the Nazis capture you as a civilian they can kill you as a spy. But as a general, according to the Geneva Convention, you have to be given shelter and food and kept alive."

I laughed at the idea of my being a general.

"I'm coming in to work tomorrow," Ickes said. "Come see me before you take off."

CHAPTER THREE

I was packing my bag in the early evening when my doorbell rang. My mother, carrying a huge brown grocery bag tied up with a cord, burst in.

"Tell me the truth." She wasted no time as she walked into the studio apartment, headed straight for the kitchen and untied the cord around the grocery bag. She pulled out her nightclothes, then a roast chicken wrapped in wax paper, a small jar of gefilte fish and a larger jar of prunes marinated in my father's best scotch.

"The truth, now," she repeated, "do you really have to go?"

Before I could answer, she twisted open the cap of the jar filled with fat inebriated prunes.

"Eat one now." She jabbed a fork into the jar, speared a prune and put it into my mouth. "It will do you good."

Food, second only to her husband and her children, was intimacy, food was survival, food was the tribal memory of all the countries Jews had wandered through. Food, she was convinced, Jewish food, kept the family together.

Outside the window, dusk was settling on the Washington streets.

She looked at her watch. "It's nearly eight o'clock. Time to light candles."

I brought out my grandmother's brass candlesticks that she had given me when I moved to Washington. We walked to the raised dining area, placed a freshly laundered white tablecloth on the Swedish table and set it, with the candlesticks in the center.

My mother draped her hand-crocheted white silk scarf around

her mass of curly white hair, struck a match to the Sabbath candles and with outstretched hands drew circles over the flames. Then she covered her eyes and murmured the Sabbath prayer in the Hebrew she had learned as a child. In Yiddish she added a special message to God. I was sure she was begging Him to keep me safe. Sabbath magic flooded the white studio apartment.

"What do you need to go to Europe for?" she asked as we sat opposite each other.

I put my hands to my mouth, showing her it was so full of her delicious fish that I could not speak.

She waited impatiently for me to answer, her gray eyes penetrating and shrewd.

"I'm not going to have one night's rest all the time you're away. Honest, I can't figure you out, you have such a nice place here and you keep it pretty good." A rare compliment. In fact, so rare were her compliments that I knew she was desperate tonight.

"You have a good job. You could be, God forbid, killed."

I leaned across the table and took her gnarled, work-worn hands in mine. The sunset light and the burning candles softened the lines on her face. She was in her early fifties, but hard work from the time she was eight had grooved sharp creases in her face.

"Mom, remember when I went to Poland just before the war and I saw your relatives and Pop's relatives?"

She nodded.

"Remember I told you the story of how your cousin Yankel came to the railroad station in Warsaw to meet me, though it was midnight? He had a horse and carriage with hay. He made me lie on the hay and covered me with a big horse blanket while he whipped his poor horse like crazy."

Her eyes narrowed as she watched me.

"He was afraid someone would kill me. Bandits maybe. Even the gendarmes. The Poles were suspicious of any traveler—especially somebody like me, coming out of Russia and going into Germany. Both countries were Poland's enemies; besides, I was carrying a typewriter and a camera, and he was afraid the gendarmes would think that maybe I wasn't a journalist, maybe I was a spy."

She stared at me, pulling herself up in the chair. She was barely five feet tall, full-bosomed, wide-hipped. "What has this got to do with you going off—" she began.

I was determined not to let her interrupt. "It was two o'clock in the morning when we finally reached your shtettel. We drove into the courtyard. 'Wake up everybody,' Yankel shouted so loud you could have heard him in Brooklyn. *'Zie iss gekimmen* [she has come].' Suddenly I saw an elderly woman put her head out of the window. It was your Aunt Mirel screaming *'Gnendel's tochter iss du* [Gussie's daughter is here].' ''

In the Sabbath-filled room in Washington, I saw again the small brick courtyard coming alive with aunts, cousins, neighbors embracing me in the darkness, laughing, crying, drawing me into one of the little poverty-stricken wooden houses.

My mother's face grew animated. ''We thought you were crazy when you went off on that trip. We were so worried because you were going to all those dangerous countries, and there wasn't even a war then like now.''

''What I never told you, because I didn't want to scare you, is that about five o'clock in the morning two gendarmes knocked on the door with their nightsticks. They demanded to see my passport, opened my suitcase, held everything, even my underwear, up to the light, looking for something, examined my typewriter and camera and told me that if I didn't get out in an hour I would be arrested.''

''My God.'' My mother's face blanched. ''What happened?''

''Some of the relatives said, 'Don't pay any attention. They can't be serious.' But some of the others said, 'Leave right away. They could throw you in jail and, who knows, torture you, maybe kill you. Nobody like you ever came to our shtettel before.' I knew there was danger. I kissed all the relatives goodbye and climbed back into Yankel's wagon. The relatives stood wringing their hands, worrying. Yankel covered me all over again, this time even my face. Then he drove his horse like a madman back to Warsaw.''

''And we never knew,'' my mother said, shaking her head. ''They wrote us letters after, never telling us about the gendarmes. All they told us was how you left all your clothes with them, and how you went to Germany and then home with only the dress and coat on your back.''

A cloud of sadness darkened her face. She stared across the studio. ''Then the war started and we never heard from them again.''

Once again I leaned across the table to touch the gnarled hands. ''I might find your Aunt Mirel and your Aunt Sima and your cousin Yankel and their daughters.''

Tears formed in her eyes. ''I guess you have to go,'' she said.

* * *

Early the next morning we closed my apartment, put my suitcase in a cab and drove to my office, waiting for the call from the Army. It came just before noon.

"This is Captain Hester. Would you like to take a little trip this afternoon? Be at National Airport at three."

At two o'clock we entered Ickes's office, my mother still clutching her brown grocery bag. It was smaller now, with only her nightgown, robe and hairbrush.

Ickes stood up at his desk as I led her across the blue carpet.

"You look worried, Mother," he said, shaking her hand, his face crinkled into a warm, almost comforting smile.

"It's very dangerous, Mr. Ickes, what she's doing, flying to Europe in the middle of the war."

I was struck by the instant rapport between the short man of power and the short woman of Brooklyn, both self-confident, both unintimidated, both with jutting jaws.

"It is dangerous, but Ruth will come home safe," he assured her.

"I pray to God," she said.

He turned to me and shook my hand. "Good luck," he said.

He sent us down to the garage with instructions to his chauffeur to take me to National Airport and then drive my mother to Union Station. At the airport I showed her that I was carrying the jar of alcohol-soaked prunes in my handbag. "See, I won't get hungry on the plane," I tried to reassure her, and kissed her goodbye. "Don't cry, Mom."

"Who's crying?" she wiped her eyes. Then, unexpectedly, she asked, "Should I tip the chauffeur?"

"Mom, you don't tip a government employee."

Later she told me how she felt—a little woman with a grocery bag in the back of a limousine half a block long. "I gave the chauffeur a dollar. You should have seen how glad he was to get it."

National Airport swarmed with men and women in khakis, stiff whites, summer grays, olive greens, serious-faced civilians carrying briefcases, rushing to catch planes.

Exhilarated that at last I was taking off, I moved swiftly through the airport routine—passport control, currency control, baggage inspection.

"You carrying any letters?" a long-faced intelligence officer asked me as he examined my suitcase, my hatbox, my battered typewriter and purse.

"Letters?" Ickes had given me several letters of introduction to officials in Casablanca, Algiers and Naples. "Be sure to pay your respects especially to Ambassador Robert Murphy in Algiers," he had said. "Murphy is the President's personal representative. I want you to tell him how we feel about this project."

"Do you have a diary?" The intelligence officer was still interrogating me.

"Not yet. But I'll be starting one in the plane. I've got a lot of empty notebooks."

He waved me through.

A young second lieutenant in summer uniform approached me. "Sit down over there with those men."

Some twenty-five American and French officers, most of them one- and two-star generals with bands of colored ribbons on their breasts, sat in an open enclosure in the airport. They stared at me so curiously that I pulled my skirt over my knees and glanced swiftly to see if my blouse was buttoned. I had dressed carefully for the trip, with a blue silk suit, a small mauve hat with a mauve veil, and brand-new white gloves.

"Follow me." The young lieutenant shepherded us through the milling airport and up a flight of stairs to a small dark room with no windows and almost no air.

At one end of the room a panel of army officers sat behind a table; in front of them was a huge collapsed lifeboat.

"Gentlemen, I mean, lady and gentlemen," one of the officers began, "the first thing we are going to do is show you what to do if the plane is shot down over water and you ditch." He stepped forward and showed us step by step how to open the collapsible lifeboat, how to inflate the Mae Wests, how to operate the radio.

I listened intently, though I wondered how long anyone could survive in the shark-infested waters of the North Atlantic.

A Public Health officer moved among us teaching us how to apply a tourniquet if we were wounded. His voice became ominous. "You are going to be landing at a port in the Azores that has plague. You're never to go off the military reservation at the airport. There are rats outside; they carry lice that can infect you with Black Plague.

"There's malaria too," he continued the litany of peril. He walked around the table and handed each of us a bottle of mosquito-repellent fluid. "Use it constantly," he said.

A third officer passed out mimeographed sheets with the caption "Medical Briefing." "You're to carry this in every area you enter."

I held the sheet up in the dim light and read: "Eighty percent of the natives are infected with one or more tropical diseases. Avoid personal contact with them. Body lice, flies, mosquitos may infect you. Avoid personal contact with them too."

Army humor!

Capitalized words shouted at me:

> NATIVES in most countries FERTILIZE their fields with HUMAN FECES. They CONTAMINATE EVERYTHING THEY TOUCH. NEVER EAT UNCOOKED VEGETABLES OR FRUIT. Thick-skinned fruits can be eaten if they are soaked in Clorox (1% Hypochlorite solution) for thirty minutes.

My mind balked. Soak fruits and vegetables in Clorox! If the bugs didn't kill me, the Clorox would.

I forced myself to read on in the semidarkness.

> Venereal diseases are rampant in the tropics. Almost 100%. Staying away from all "Pick Ups" is your best insurance against serious venereal diseases. So-called controlled prostitutes are almost 100% infected with Syphilis, whereas with Gonorrhea, their annual rate is 40% to 60%. The natives of tropical countries are filled with all types of disease. *The women are human cesspools. Keep away from them.*

As our engines revved, I opened my notebook. "Six o'clock, Saturday, July 15, 1944, departing Washington."

The sturdy prop-engined C-54 flew over the great dome of the Capitol glistening in the July sun, past the stark obelisk of the Washington Monument, then, most beautiful of all, over the monument with the great brooding figure of Lincoln on whose steps I had so often taken refuge.

A bank of clouds enveloped us; about an hour later we were in the open, over my own city, New York, which looked like a toy town with miniature cars speeding on its highways. The light shimmered gray-gold; a ball of flame sank into the Hudson.

Boston, then Bangor, Maine, and now as the North Atlantic spread below us the captain's voice came through the loudspeaker. "We're flying north to Newfoundland. We'll be landing there to refuel and leave you. A new crew will take you on to the Azores, and from there to Casablanca."

I peered into the night sky. It was almost midnight when we landed at Stephenville on the west coast of Newfoundland.

An army bus drove us to a nearby army camp. In the mess hall, soldiers piled hotcakes and scrambled eggs in front of us.

But I could not eat, for around us were enlisted men, some sullen, some angry, some depressed. All were bandaged, several were without arms, those without legs were in wheelchairs, ready to be flown to hospitals in America. At eighteen or twenty, to be disabled, crippled forever!

One of the generals approached me. "May I join you?"

"Of course."

He was a white-haired one-star general with a leathery face and a Midwestern accent. "I'm an opera buff," he said, "and my favorite opera is *Aida*. Everytime I get to New York, I try to make the Metropolitan Opera."

I wondered why a general at midnight in Newfoundland would talk about opera. Still depressed by the sight of the wounded soldiers, I tried to listen, until I heard the general say, "We're all so curious about you. What are you doing on this plane?"

Heeding Dillon Myer's admonition, I said, "I'm sorry, General, I can't tell you. My mission is a secret."

"Are you Lily Pons?" he asked. Lily Pons, the Metropolitan Opera singer, and her husband, André Kostelanetz, the conductor, were touring army installations.

I assured him I could not sing.

It was midmorning Sunday in Washington, 1440 GMT, when we flew over the Azores, so low we could watch the ocean pounding the islands' cliffs.

A small contingent of American soldiers in shorts came running toward us as we landed, and some entered the plane. "You are not to go off the reservation," a sergeant commanded. "There's plague here, and it's bad."

I felt less hostile about the shots I had been given in Washington.

A stocky lieutenant whose walk and talk were straight off the sidewalks of New York escorted us to the mess hall with a rapid-fire patter: "This here's a secret base. We ain't here, see. We don't know from nothin'. The Krauts don't know we're here. Only the Portuguese know. They own the goddamn place. We don't even know there's a war. In France our guys are chasin' bullets. Here we're tracin' dust."

Back in the plane, we headed for Casablanca. I felt I would know it from the Humphrey Bogart movie, but from the air it was a giant, sprawling rock pile of white stone houses.

After we loaded into a bus, an army officer told us, "We're billeting you in the Atlantic Hotel, and you mess in the Excelsior."

I wondered for a moment why we couldn't mess and billet in the same hotel, but I knew better than to question the Army.

Unlike its name, the color of Casablanca in the early evening light was brown. The air was brown, the streets were brown, the people, the camels, the horses, the donkeys, the dust, all seemed brown and centuries old.

The next morning, I walked to the American Embassy. Arab men in white djellabas, Arab women, their bodies and faces hidden inside voluminous gray robes and hoods, peering at the world through narrow slits, moved in an aura of mystery, while not-so-mysterious women in tight Western dresses and frizzled hair clattered down the sidewalk on the arms of French or British or American soldiers.

At the embassy, I paid my respects to the consul general. "I'd like to get to Algiers and Naples as soon as possible," I told him. "Is there any way of flying out today?"

He pressed a button, asking an assistant to bring him the flight schedule. He shook his head. "I see nothing flying to Algiers today."

My spirits slumped. The refugee ship might sail without me.

"But you're in luck. There's a plane tomorrow morning at nine. It's probably all booked, with a long waiting list, but we'll get you on it."

"I do appreciate this."

He smiled. "Anything special you'd like to do today?"

"Yes, I'd like to see the Medina and the Mellah." The Medina was the ancient Arab quarter; the Jews lived in the Mellah.

"You can't go alone," he said. "It's not safe for a woman, especially a young woman like you. I'll give you a car and an English-speaking native driver."

Both the Medina and the Mellah were netherworlds of labyrinthine streets filled with the smells of poverty and dirt and goats and human beings. Maimed beggars pulled at my skirt. Naked children sat lethargically on stones, pus running out of their opaque blind eyes. Gaunt women showed me their babies, their little faces like masks of death. Bells clanged, donkeys brayed, camels moved past hovels with ten and twelve people crowded into a single dark, dank space. The smell of goats was everywhere.

"Had enough?" the driver asked me. "You look white. Why don't you go back to the hotel, get some lunch and have a rest?"

"Let's drive to the Anfa Hotel." Roosevelt and Churchill had met at the Anfa in January 1943 to plot the course of invasion.

This was a different Casablanca we were driving through, with spotless white streets, palm-lined boulevards, elegant shops. European men and women pedaled near us on bicycles; others sat at corner cafés sipping *café noir* from demitasse cups; water boys in colorful rags clanged little bells, hawking water which they poured out of sheepskin bags into a metal cup.

Surrounding the stately forty-bedroom hotel on a promontory high on the Anfa hill were luxurious white villas. The sweet smell of tropical flowers and the salt air of the Atlantic cleansed my lungs. I breathed the air deeply to wash away the dark smells of the Medina and the Mellah.

Tomorrow I would be flying along the very route our troops had wrested from the enemy, first Algiers, then Naples, where I would join the refugees.

Long before nine the next morning, I was already in the plane. The DC-3 with a five-pointed white star on its wings had none of the comfort and, I was sure, none of the emergency life-saving gear of the C-54. My American Army companions from our overseas flight greeted me like old friends. They told me they had spent most of yesterday swimming on the beach.

We sat on the tarmac in the desert heat, our motors roaring, but we did not move. Suddenly a small armada of fighter planes came out on the apron, tore down the runway and zoomed up in the air. The invasion of Normandy had already begun.

At ten-twenty Casablanca time we finally took off. Once again the city spread below us. In the morning light the houses had line and form and pattern, elegant white tier upon tier. But the odor of the goats was still with me. Casablanca would forever have a goat smell.

Algiers.

"Ambassador Murphy is expecting you." A young man ushered me to an American Embassy station wagon at the airport. "I'm taking you right to him."

Even the roads seemed to be boiling as we drove into town. I was sticky and queasy and apprehensive.

Ickes, suspecting that Robert Murphy, who came out of the State Department, might not be enthusiastic, hoped I could convince him of the importance of this first haven. It would be a message to the world that America was now assuming responsibility for refugees. A few countries—Sweden, Switzerland, England—had been taking in refugees, though, God knows, not enough. Now others too might follow our lead.

Murphy was the most important official I was scheduled to meet; Roosevelt's personal representative, he had limitless power in the Mediterranean theater of war. I expected a middle-aged, if not elderly, career diplomat. Instead, rising from a cluttered desk to shake my hand, was a tall, blond, youngish man with electric-blue eyes and an appraising smile.

"So you've come about the refugees."

I nodded and handed him Ickes's letter of introduction.

Murphy looked up from the letter. "You know, of course, we're building a huge refugee camp here in Algeria, in Philippeville, to house as many as forty thousand."

I nodded. The consul general in Casablanca had mentioned it.

Murphy began to describe the huge camp the United States was building east of Algiers, near the Tunisian border. I listened, wondering if he was trying, obliquely, to show me that a haven in America was unnecessary, that Philippeville, soon to be completed, could take in thousands of refugees without circumventing quotas.

I told him of Ickes's hopes for the haven in Oswego.

"It's a very important step and an excellent move," he said.

I was startled. Perhaps he was really convinced Oswego was a good step; perhaps we had all misjudged him.

"The first thing I did when Ickes gave me this assignment," I told him, "was to have the President's cable to you translated into twelve different languages. I plan to hang these cables all over the ship, so the refugees will be sure to read them."

Murphy looked pleased; his mouth broadened into a smile. But the blue eyes squinted and turned hard.

"I hope the refugees read that cable very carefully," he said, "especially the line that says they 'will be brought into this country outside of the regular immigration procedures and will return at the end of the war.' "

I said nothing. He had confirmed my suspicions.

CHAPTER FOUR

While I mulled over Murphy's words, a chauffeured American car drove me through the streets of Algiers to the Aletti Hotel. I wondered if Murphy was powerful enough, even at this late date, to stop the project.

The late-afternoon sun burned long shadows on the hot Algerian streets. Well-dressed Europeans, Arab men in burnooses, veiled Arab women walked down the broad French boulevards; the air was serene and peaceful. It was hard to believe that north of us, across the Mediterranean, tanks were clashing, planes were dive-bombing, human beings were burning to death.

The veranda of the Aletti Hotel looked like the porch of a resort hotel as people watched each other, studying newcomers. At the registration desk I was signing my name when a suntanned young man came toward me.

He held out his hand. "Pardon me. I'm Jimmy Saxon, Treasury Department representative in Algiers. Treasury alerted me to your coming."

"How do you know who I am?"

"I had a full description of you. Besides, not many American gals are floating around Algiers. Are you free for dinner tonight?"

"How soon?"

"In an hour."

An Arab in a djellaba and a red fez led me upstairs to a spacious room with a double bed, a huge tiled bathroom and French windows. I stepped out on the terrace and looked down at a geometric jigsaw of white Arab houses, flooded with sunlight. Back inside, I soaked luxuriously in the large bathtub and changed into a white halter dress with a white stole.

In the lobby, Jimmy looked approvingly. "You're a breath of America. Come on. We're off for the Allies Club."

The club was set in a tropical landscape of waving palms and sweet-smelling flowers. We sat in a tiled garden sipping a long cool drink, then entered the dining room crowded with American, French and British officers. Arab waiters set before us platters of fish and filled our glasses with chilled French wine, while Jimmy talked about how our Army and diplomats saw the refugees—a massive nightmare, clogging roads, blocking the path of tanks and troops, needing shelter, food, medical care.

"Lots of opposition to the whole refugee problem is being stirred up here," Jimmy said. "The British don't want them, never did want them, especially the British military, and the Colonial Office types are trying to keep them out of Palestine. Our own military don't want them, either. It was only direct pressure from the President on all the boys here—State and War—that got this whole Oswego thing started."

Suddenly he looked at me. "We're here making plans for after the war—what to do with the property of the Nazis, indemnities for the people who suffered, like the Jews. But you're transporting refugees right now, with the war on. That's some assignment. I wonder if I could handle it." He downed his glass of wine. "I don't envy you. You're in for some rough waters. Don't sink."

The plane for Naples was due to leave at two. I spent most of the morning at Allied Forces Headquarters with Major Sam Goldsmith, a small tense social worker I had met on trips to Chicago. Sam, scarcely a military type, his army uniform drooping on his slightly hunched shoulders, had been assigned to Philippeville.

"We hope to start with ten thousand refugees," he said, "but we're putting up enough housing for thousands more. Nobody here knows how many refugees we're going to have to take care of." Deep grooves etched into his forehead. "As soon as we liberate an area, we're overrun. The refugees have no papers, except maybe some false documents to help them survive. An order just came to establish another camp at Tripolitania. We're making plans to set up tents and huts, but we don't know who'll be living there—or how many thousands."

He stopped talking and stared out past the terrace as though he were seeing an avalanche of refugees. Then he went on. "Tomorrow another operation may start and uncork another area, and we'll be overrun with thousands of more stateless people. It's no good, I tell you. We're supposed to be working with the British on the refugee problem. But the snippety Britisher I'm to work with, Major Griffin-White, is disgusted with me, disgusted with UNRRA* for moving too slowly, disgusted with all these refugees, so that right now very little is being done. I hope you have more success in that camp in Oswego."

I listened to his foreboding as I had to Saxon's. "We don't know," Goldsmith said as though he were talking to himself, "how many tens of thousands, maybe hundreds of thousands, of refugees we may have to take care of. Right now it's still a trickle. Europe is bottlenecked. Jews especially can't get out. We don't really know what's happening to most of the Jews in Europe. All we know is that they were sent to Poland to build roads and fortifications—and died."

"But we do know more. The cables told us."

Goldsmith looked mystified. "What cables?"

It took me a few moments to realize that Goldsmith, a major in G-5 for displaced persons, working with refugees in liberated Algiers, knew as little about the death camps as did most

*The United Nations Relief and Rehabilitation Administration.

Americans back home. Even Army Intelligence had not been privy to the secret cables.

Briefly I told him some of the things I had learned in Washington.

"My God." The lines in his forehead etched deeper. "When will the country learn the truth?"

Broiling inside a life jacket and strapped into an iron bucket seat in a cargo DC-47A, I looked down at the turquoise water and the magnificient geography of the Mediterranean. Officers and soldiers sat silently, lost in thought. They were on their way to the Italian front.

Five hours out of Algiers, and Naples spread before us, a city of white rimmed with green water and green hills, with Mount Vesuvius penciled against the horizon. Naples was circled red on my map and in my consciousness. Here I would meet the refugees.

"Welcome, Ruth, welcome, welcome." Bob Neville smothered me in his huge embrace. He looked like a football player in army uniform. He was the editor-in-chief of the GIs' *Stars and Stripes*.

Bob helped me scramble up into the truck. "I want to hear everything—about New York, about Washington, about all our friends, everything."

But I could not talk. Naples, so beautiful from the air, was a lunar landscape. Buildings hung like rags. Whole streets were ripped up. Houses were sliced down the front, with staircases that led nowhere and curtains flying insanely in the wind.

"And people go on living," I murmured.

He nodded. "Without water, without plumbing, without food. Starving. The Germans blew up the water supply, even blew up the whole sewer system, before they ran."

He paused while the truck bounced over a giant crater. We were covered with ashes and dust.

"The Nazis blew up every hotel in Naples except the one you're going to, the Parco. They destroyed the whole waterfront. They mined the buildings at the port. They put a twenty-one-day bomb in the post office, so innocent people would get killed weeks after the Germans were gone. To add to the madness, they even emptied the prisons and insane asylums." I shut my eyes for a moment in horror.

The truck pulled up before the Parco, elegant and white. In the lobby Bob greeted American officers, while I dropped my bag in a huge room filled with massive furniture and phoned the Peninsular Base Section. My orders were to call military headquarters immediately on arrival.

An American voice with a Texas drawl answered. "We've been expecting you, ma'am."

I told him I needed to know three things. Where were the refugees right now? When could I see them? Were my orders to sail with them ready?"

"Sorry I can't answer your questions on the phone. Come in tomorrow morning. Do you need a vehicle tonight?"

"Not tonight, but tomorrow morning at eight."

"Yes, ma'am."

I hurried downstairs and climbed into the truck again to have dinner with Bob and his night crew. They were turning out *Stars and Stripes* in a once-luxurious complex of shops, arcades and opulent apartments. Their suite, the home of a Fascist judge, was high-ceilinged, with red lace curtains, heavily carved furniture, overstuffed sofas and armchairs upholstered in pink moiré. We joined the crew for a supper of turkey sandwiches and coffee, supplied and served by the Army. The men, having just put *Stars and Stripes* to bed, filled the judge's dining room with invasion fever.

Bob spread a map on the table to show me where the Allied troops were pushing north of Rome, battling Germans under Nazi Field Marshal Albert Kesselring. More areas would be liberated; more refugees would be on the run. I kept hearing Sam Goldsmith's words—"tomorrow another operation may start and uncork another area, and we'll be overrun . . ."

After midnight, I turned on the radio in my hotel room. The words bolted me out of bed. From somewhere in Germany an announcer screamed hysterically against "this assassination plot, this criminal attack against the Führer."

Hitler's voice, high-pitched, barked into the dark hotel bedroom. "We will catch these traitors," he raved. "Their stupidity is enormous. They plot for the slavery of our people. They planned a terrible fate which our people will live through." His voice and his madness felt like snakes crawling on my skin.

I stopped listening to the words, catching only the insane rhythms when I heard the announcer end, with a sob in his throat, "Long live our Führer. Heil Hitler."

I switched off the radio and lay in the dark Italian bedroom. What would have happened if the assassination had succeeded? Whole areas of Hitler's Fortress Europe would have been uncorked.

Hundreds of thousands of refugees would have raced to safety. We could be saving not one thousand, but millions.

The assassination attempt showed that not all the Germans were mesmerized by Hitler. Later we learned it was a young German officer, Colonel Klaus von Stauffenberg, who had plotted the attack at Wolfsschanze (Wolf's Lair), Hitler's headquarters in East Prussia. No one searched Stauffenberg's briefcase, in which he had hidden a time bomb; he was highly trusted; he had lost an eye and his right arm in the western desert.

Carefully Stauffenberg had maneuvered his briefcase next to Hitler and left the meeting. A suspicious officer kicked the briefcase away. The bomb exploded. Hitler escaped with a concussion, burns and shock.

Still shaken, and heavily bandaged, the Führer asked his aides to bring in Mussolini. The Duce had invited himself to Germany and had arrived at four o'clock that afternoon. Mussolini had left Italy in a state of depression and despair. The Allied armies and Italian partisans were routing not only his Fascist followers but the German divisions in the north.

Hitler's escape bolstered his spirits. "After this miracle," he assured the Führer and himself, "it is impossible that our cause should know defeat."

In Naples, food was the obsession.

"It's only because we have special privileges that we have powdered eggs," a young red-haired lieutenant assured me at breakfast in the Parco.

The eggs tasted like sawdust.

"This is a real delicacy," he went on. "The Allied personnel have been warned not to buy any food from the Neapolitans. First of all, there's damned little food, the Italians need it for themselves. But with no water and no sanitation, everything is filthy, and we can all pick up typhus. Even in the Parco, in all this splendor, we get little for supper except canned peas and beans. I'd give a dollar right now for a glass of fresh milk or one egg."

I lost my appetite and took off in the army car for the Peninsular Base Section. People were everywhere—in the alleys, in the rubble, gesticulating, screaming, laughing, weeping. Life was on the street in this ravaged city. Life was the one commodity you held on to with passion, with ferocity.

Most of the people were in rags, children were barefoot, but some of the Neapolitan women looked as lovely as Renaissance madonnas. Others had bleached their hair blond, and their dark roots were showing. For a while, Naples looked like a city of big-bosomed sexy women with two-colored hair and high platform shoes, a city that seemed to redefine itself in the bright Italian morning sun.

Now it looked like a military melting pot. Soldiers from the whole world seemed to be strolling down the rubbled streets looking the girls over, or standing at pushcarts buying up the city's meager rations of fresh fruit and vegetables. I had never seen such a hodgepodge of uniforms—American, British, French, Italian, Senegalese. There were Gurkhas from Nepal and black mercenaries from North Africa hired by the French, dressed in khaki GI uniforms, army boots and the dashing profile hats of Australia.

The Peninsular Base Section was a noisy confusion of men and women in uniform, opening and closing doors, rushing through corridors. Telephones rang. Typewriters clacked. Washington had been transplanted to Naples.

Captain L. C. Sutton, Jr., the assistant adjutant general, stood up from his desk as I entered. I had already learned from my chauffeur that Sutton was "a big wheel," in charge of all official correspondence, personnel records and the preparation and distribution of orders.

"Sit down." Sutton motioned to a hard chair opposite his desk. "I'll get your orders ready right away. Any questions?"

"The refugees? Where are they now?"

"They're aboard a troop ship in the bay."

Thank God. I said a silent prayer of thanks. Murphy had done nothing to abort the mission.

"When do we sail?"

"Tomorrow at five."

"Tomorrow! Can I go aboard now to meet them?"

"Once you're on the ship you won't be able to disembark again. If you have work in Naples, I recommend you do it today and go aboard tomorrow."

I was torn. A whole day and a half before I could see the refugees. But there were people I wanted to see and government officials I had promised Ickes and others in Washington I would call on.

"I'll go tomorrow," I said. "What kind of ship is it?"

"It's an Army transport," Sutton said, "and it's packed full. The thousand refugees are in the forward holds, and about a thousand wounded soldiers from Anzio and Cassino are in the stern. We use every inch of space on every ship to get those wounded men back to Stateside hospitals. A lot of them are in pretty bad shape emotionally. Battle fatigue. There are others too, doctors and nurses to take care of the refugees and the wounded.''

He stood up. ''And now, unless you have more questions, I'd like to get your travel orders ready.''

PART TWO
The Voyage of the *Henry Gibbins*

CHAPTER FIVE

The Naples sun streamed into the barren office, turning particles of dust into diamond sparkles, as Max Perlman came around the small wooden desk to greet me.

"What a stroke of luck to find you in Naples," I said.

I had learned that Max was one of the team that had selected the refugees. They had first been selected by Leonard Ackerman of the War Refugee Board, who, working day and night until he was no longer able to "go on playing God," had asked Max to help. Max was a natural, a representative of the Joint Distribution Committee in Italy. The JDC was the overseas arm of the American Jewish community, financing rescues through the underground, paying off officials to save Jews in Rumania and Hungary, and sending men like Max to rescue and feed homeless Jews.

"I was only a small part of the team," Max said. "Captain Lewis Korn became head of the group after Len Ackerman took ill; you'll meet Lew, he's already aboard the ship. Trying to select some of those thousand refugees for America was the toughest assignment of my life. Word of that invitation from the President spread like a brushfire. Day and night, people were knocking on the doors of all the offices taking applications in Naples, Bari, Rome. Women and men weeping, people fainting from emotion, parents holding their children up in the air so we'd notice them. It was a lousy job, Ruth. We were all playing God to a group of desperate people. Three thousand applied—"

"Three thousand!" I cried. "It would be so easy to bring three thousand into America!"

I remembered Joe DuBois's comment on the number of refugees. "It was the President himself," he had told me, "who fixed the figure at one thousand. He's a politician first and then a humanitarian."

Max leaned forward. "There's this tiny village in the mountains called Campagnia where Jews had been hiding out. I went up there by truck with Captain Moscovitz—he's with the Palestinian Jewish unit of the British Army. When the refugees saw our truck with the blue-and-white Star of David painted on both sides, they began embracing the two of us; they couldn't believe it—Jewish officers, one from America, one from Palestine.

"We went on to an old monastery built in the Middle Ages— the Fascists had turned it into an internment camp for about a hundred fifty refugee Jews. Some of them looked eighty; they were in their forties. I told them of the President's invitation to come to America. You can't imagine the excitement. Some of the men made whole speeches telling me how many years they had been dreaming about going to America. Others just wept openly."

His voice, usually a rich tenor, suddenly cracked. "They filled out the applications and then bombarded me with questions. 'When will we know if we're accepted? When will the transport leave for America?' I felt awful, leaving them with such anxiety. I couldn't tell them if they'd be accepted or not. These men were all alone; they had seen their entire familes wiped out."

His voice broke again. "Ruth, the pain in their faces is still with me."

My own throat went dry.

"But then there were things to make you happy. The best part for me was arranging the trucks to transport the people from Bari to the ship. I decided not to use British Army trucks, even though the British offered them to us. It's a long trip from Bari to Naples—five or six hours, crossing the mountains. I figured these people had been through so much that British military trucks might frighten them. I went back to my Palestinian friends, Major Bar Shmorak, a kibbutznik, and Captain Moscovitz, and asked them to lend us their trucks with the Star of David. Picture the sight. Refugees crossing Italy in a convoy of trucks with the Star of David painted on their sides, heading for a ship to America."

I stood up in the bare office, walked behind the desk and kissed Max's cheek. "I think these refugees will never forget what you did. Nor will I."

In Hungary, Jews were being selected for death. In southern Italy, a precious few were being selected for life.

Not allowed to board the ship until noon the following day, I decided to spend the afternoon and the next morning paying courtesy calls on the officials whose names were in my notebook.

At eight in the morning, the GI chauffeur stacked my bag and typewriter in the car. I had dressed for the protocol visits in a white suit, white gloves and a big red straw hat.

We finished the rounds and then sped down to the waterfront. Barbed wire barring unauthorized civilians and potential spies circled the entire port. A huge sign hung near the entrance gate: "KILL HITLER. KILL MUSSOLINI." The sense of war was in the water, on the docks, in the sky. Planes zoomed above us, army vehicles sputtered and choked, soldiers and sailors blocked already-snarled traffic.

In the harbor giant cranes lifted huge military equipment from cargo ships onto the docks. Young soldiers, some baby-faced, loaded with gear; marched down the gangplanks of troop ships, leaped into trucks and personnel carriers and headed north to the battlefront.

The GI driver took me to a launch where a young navy lieutenant in white uniform helped me jump into his motorboat. Soon we were chugging past wall-to-wall ships. Even the sun seemed to be searching for space in the harbor to cast silver shafts of light.

"There's your convoy." The lieutenant pointed to a flotilla of cruisers, troop ships, cargo ships, some sleek and elegant, some dowdy, but all riding high as if they controlled the water. They were anchored in the Bay of Naples, waiting like soldiers to begin a parade of war.

How many thousands, I wondered, are aboard those navy escort vessels—soldiers, sailors, gunners armed to the teeth? My nerves tightened with the sense of danger and the awesome beauty of this seawall of war.

"You'll be picking up more escorts in the Med," the navy officer was saying. "The Med is a bad spot with U-boats. Bombers."

I hardly listened. "Which is the ship with refugees?"

"Over there. It's an Army transport—the *Henry Gibbins*."

The ship, rigged with graceful steel cables, lifeboats, elevated tubs with gun emplacements, dwarfed our launch. Its decks were lined with people staring down at us, some waving.

The lieutenant stood up to signal the crew on the *Henry Gibbins*, who dropped a rope ladder down the side. A sailor in the launch held the ladder as I reached for the first rung. Suddenly the lieutenant stared at the white suit, the gloves, the big red hat as if he were seeing them for the first time.

"You can't climb the Jacob's ladder in that outfit. Not with a thousand refugees and a thousand wounded soldiers watching."

He ordered one of his sailors to go below. "Take off your pants and hand them up to me."

The lieutenant gave me the sailor's pants. I pulled them over my skirt, handed him my hat and once more began climbing the ropes. The ladder swung and pitched against the hull; I clutched each rung so tightly I could feel the rope digging into my skin. The water below looked menacing. Finally, near the top of the ladder, a sailor leaned over, placed his hands under my armpits and lifted me onto the main deck. The refugees crushed around me.

"It's Eleanor Roosevelt," a man shouted.

I laughed with relief.

Waves of bodies crowded around me, men in tattered shorts, naked to the waist, women in ragged and rumpled skirts and blouses, sad-eyed children in torn sandals or without shoes. Some of the people had cloth and newspapers tied around their feet. Several stared at me as if they were seeing an apparition.

A slender man broke through the crowd and extended his hand. "I'm Captain Lew Korn."

He was in army uniform, a thin bony man who looked sad even when he smiled, as though the weight of having selected most of these refugees was an enormous burden to carry.

"This is Miss Gruber," he introduced me to the refugees. "She's a representative of the government."

Two officers, army and navy, came forward, extending their hands. They introduced themselves, Major Judson W. Allen, transport commander, head of the army escort, and Lieutenant Donald M. Martin, commander of the naval armed guard.

"Captain Shea would like to see you on the bridge," Allen said. I recognized his Brooklyn accent.

The people opened a path on the cluttered deck. We entered the midship house and climbed a narrow steel ladder to the bridge deck.

Captain John Shea, a jovial Irishman in a spanking-white uniform, smiled broadly. "Glad to have you aboard. Feel free to come up here at anytime. If we can be of any help, don't hesitate. This ship has been in a lot of convoys in the Atlantic and the Med. But it's the first time we're transporting refugees."

It was a first for most of us.

"We've divided the ship," Captain Shea continued. "The refugees are all down in the forward holds, the wounded soldiers in the stern. They're not to have any contact. We're not looking

for trouble. Of course, you're free to go anywhere you like.
Nothing's off limits to you.''

He grinned, looking at the sailor's pants I was still wearing.
"I guess you want to get to your cabin."

I grinned, too.

"You have a few hours before we sail. We're weighing
anchor at five this afternoon."

He called to a midshipman to escort me to my cabin. There
two army nurses in summer uniforms lay on neatly made bunks
reading magazines.

"Hi, I'm Mary Toum." The attractive blonde put down her
magazine.

"And I'm Caroline Haltiwaner," said the other, a slender
nurse with a Southern accent.

I introduced myself while I pulled off the sailor's pants and
changed into slacks and a cool blouse.

"I know why Mary and I are on this ship," Caroline drawled.
"We agreed to take shifts in the ship's hospital, so we could get
home on rotation. What are you doing aboard?"

"To help with the refugees."

Mary lit a cigarette. "You've got your work cut out for you.
Some are already seasick down below, even before we sail.
They're going to need all the help you can give them."

I prowled the ship to find Ralph Stauber, the man whom
Dillon Myer had sent as his representative. I found him in the
wardroom, a chunky man with heavy eyebrows, thin well-shaped
lips and rounded shoulders. He was in a white short-sleeved shirt,
drinking coffee and writing on a long sheet of paper. The
wardroom was filled with army and navy officers talking across
wooden tables welded into the deck.

Stauber tried to rise.

"Don't get up." I put my hand out. "I'm glad to meet you."

He settled back, his manner correct. "Well, you made it. For
a while it looked as if the convoy would sail without you."

Later I learned that someone in the State Department in Naples
had sent a cable to Ickes that I had missed the ship.

"Am I interrupting you?" I asked Stauber, obviously a man
of paper and statistics. Even the yellow pencil he held tightly
seemed an integral part of his fingers.

"It's okay. I'm working up a statistical table on the number of
refugees, the countries they came from, their sex, religion and so
forth. Would you like a breakdown?"

I nodded.

"Number of refugees, nine hundred and eighty-two."

"I thought the President invited a thousand."

Three thousand applied.

"That's all that came aboard. I'll start with religion. Most people think all refugees are Jews. The greatest number on the ship, to be sure, are Jews, but this is by no means a Jewish project." His yellow pencil pointed to the figures. "Eight hundred and seventy-four are Jewish, seventy-three are Roman Catholic, twenty-eight are Greek Orthodox and seven are Protestant."

Roosevelt had cautioned that the camp not be known as a Jewish camp; he wanted refugees of all denominations.

"Here's the breakdown now by sex: five hundred twenty-five male, four hundred fifty-seven female. Lots of children and old people—the range is from an infant to an eighty-year-old man, Isaac Cohen from Salonika, Greece."

"And the countries they've come from?"

"Eighteen different countries."

I went back to the deck and began walking among the people. I joined a group sitting in a line on the ledge of the covered hatch.

"You haven't told us yet who you are," a slim professional-looking man said.

"I've been sent by the Secretary of the Interior—"

"The Secretary of the Interior! Are you a policeman?"

"No. In America the Interior Department has nothing to do with the police. It's not like Europe."

"Are you FBI?"

I put both hands to my head. "Me? FBI? Good heavens, no."

"To us, everyone in government looks suspicious," another voice came from the crowd. It belonged to a tall dark-haired young man about seventeen, with clear dark eyes and an air of strength even in his round adolescent face. His name, he said, was Adam Munz. "They don't tell us anything. Even when they invite us to come to America, they put us on this ship and they still don't tell us anything. You're not a policeman. You're not FBI. So what *are* you doing on this ship?"

More and more people left the spots they had staked out for themselves to join the circle around us.

"When we get back to America—" I began.

"If we get back," someone interrupted. "If the Nazis don't sink this ship."

I went right on. "I will have to report to my boss Harold Ickes—he's the head of the Interior Department—and he will report to the President, the Cabinet and Congress. I would like them to know who you are, what kind of people you are. What you've gone through to survive."

"You'll find out soon enough." Otto Presser spoke up. He was a smallish man, full of gestures that reminded me of Eddie Cantor. "We're all kinds of people. Big and little, some once rich, some not so rich, and now all the same—poor."

The people smiled at Presser, who was obviously a popular figure. Later I learned he had been a song-and-dance man in Vienna.

"I want to spend as much time as I can with you," I said. "People in America are just beginning to learn what Hitler has done to you. You will be the first group of refugees the people of the United States will see."

They were listening intently now. "You are the living witnesses. Through you, through the experiences you tell me, I can report to Ickes and he can tell the people of America what has been happening and surely is still going on now."

They sat in silence on the hatch-combing, staring far off into the sea. A few wiped their eyes.

"You're a woman," one of the men said. "How can I tell you the things they did to me—the dirty, filthy, obscene things?"

"Forget, if you can, that I am a woman. It's your story, it's your experiences, that are important—not how they affect me. Maybe if the world learns what you suffered, maybe we'll be able to rescue more people."

Tuck, the boatswain, a grizzly old tar with a rubbery face, followed by a few deckhands, made his way through the milling refugees toward the bow. We heard the clang of metal to metal and watched the huge chain come up through the hawse pipe to the anchor windlass.

"We're sailing," some of the refugees shouted.

We rushed to the rails. Some of the people hugged and kissed each other, some held up their babies to wave goodbye to the Italian shore. Several wept. The convoy was moving, ships were steaming white foam. Naples lay behind us golden in the afternoon sun as warships maneuvered around us in formation, ensigns flying. The Mediterranean opened wide and blue and fraught with danger.

CHAPTER SIX

A clanging bell announced dinner.

The sun was still riding high, dappling the water with silver. Leaving the deck, I followed some of the people into the galley and stopped at the door. Soldiers standing behind the steam tables were filling the refugees' aluminum mess kits with mountains of food.

Major Allen, the head of the army escort, joined me. "Anything wrong? You look startled."

"I never saw so much food dished out in my life."

Most of the refugees, unable to talk to the soldiers, pointed to the food they wanted—goulash, frankfurters, boiled potatoes, cooked onions. There were piles of salmon salad, long loaves of sliced white bread, platters of cookies, bowls of Jell-O. "Is this to make up for the years they starved?" I asked.

"Not at all. This is the way the Army feeds. Remember, an army moves on its stomach."

I joined him as he made his inspection.

"It looks like a lot," he agreed, "but by now they're pretty hungry; most haven't eaten anything since breakfast. We feed twice a day—seven-thirty in the morning, five-thirty at night."

There were no chairs, only long counters at which the people stood eating. Three little Greek girls had been propped up by their mother, who fed them first and then dug into her own mess kit.

I saw some of the children secrete frankfurters in their shirts and vanish. Was it hunger—or fear that there would be no more food?

A young teenager picked up a slice of white bread and eyed it curiously. "It's cake," he told the girl behind him. "Imagine eating cake with frankfurters."

"And what's this?" A young woman tasted the Jell-O. "Eekh, it tastes like horse glue."

But most of the people ate silently, wolfing down the food until their kits were empty.

A man whose pale skin seemed stretched across his protruding cheekbones caught me looking at him. "I still can't believe all this food. In the camp they gave us dirty hot water with something swimming in it, and they called it soup. What a country America is."

A few men walked out of the galley carrying mess kits. "That's for people too sick to come up," Major Allen explained. "Some were on K rations before they came aboard. They ate so much the first days while we were anchored in the bay, they had to be put back on K rations. Now they're eating regular, but they still feel so lousy, they can't come up from the holds."

I walked through the companionway and descended the narrow steep ladder to the first hold, clutching the iron rail. There was no air and only dim light. Stretching across the entire beam of the ship were canvas bunks squeezed together in tiers of three with narrow passageways.

An elderly woman with a wet handkerchief on her head called out to me.

"Can I bring you something?" I asked her.

She shook her head. "I can't hold anything." She put her hand on her stomach. "Maybe you know how long we will be on the water?"

"We don't know yet. It depends on how fast the convoy sails. It could be two weeks."

She moaned.

"Perhaps you'd feel better if you came up on deck. I'll help you up the stairs."

"Another day. Today my legs won't hold me."

By eight the next morning the people were already sitting and lying on the deck. They had breakfasted in the galley and now were staking places for themselves amidst the machinery on the deck.

Within minutes a group encircled me.

"Tell us what it is going to be like in America. How are we going to live?" Otto Presser, the song-and-dance man, assumed his Eddie Cantor-like expression of doleful laughter.

"I don't know what the quarters will be like. All I can tell you is that you are going to a former army camp."

"A camp in America!" Leo Mirković waved his arms in disbelief. A skeletal figure in once-white silk pajamas, he had been the premier baritone of the Zagreb National Opera.

"I haven't seen the camp," I said, "but I know it's being completely remodeled so that family groups can live together."

Presser put his hand on my arm. "*Liebes Fräulein*, don't tell me you're taking us to a concentration camp in America."

"Be realistic." A young man in his twenties limped toward us. He was Fredi Baum, from Yugoslavia. "They'll put us in a camp when we arrive and then we'll find out where we go from there."

"We *are* realistic," a middle-aged man with a sagging paunch, in black-and-white striped concentration-camp pajamas, shouted angrily. "We have a right to know. Are we or are we not going to a concentration-camp?"

"Why are we throwing all our anger at this young woman?" a bald man with broken glasses intervened like a judge. "Why do you jump to such terrible conclusions? The Americans are not going to put us into a concentration camp. I'm sure the Americans are doing this whole thing for the best reasons. To save refugees. But I think they are also doing it a little bit for publicity. We know they are geniuses at publicity. After all, this is a wonderful thing. We are the personal guests of President Roosevelt."

Mirković permitted himself a dimpled smile. "Maybe we are put on this crowded ship with no place to sit and those terrible bunks downstairs because somebody wants to embarrass President Roosevelt. My own feeling is that a great man like Roosevelt would want us to sail on a luxury liner."

"Oh, sure," a young woman interjected. "In Rome that Englishman who chose us—what was his name?"

"Sir Clifford Heathcote-Smith," I said. He had taken over the selection in Rome when Leonard Ackerman of the War Refugee Board fell ill.

"That's the one. He practically told us we'd have a swimming pool on the ship. Some of us even went all over Rome looking for fabric to sew bathing suits."

"There are always complainers." Manya Hartmayer, a young woman in a man's shirt far too large for her, shook her head. "After so many times close to death, to me this ship is better than the *Queen Mary*." She turned to me. "Don't listen to the complainers. They're just a few, but they'll make you crazy."

She stood before the group, her blond hair framing her face and falling to her shoulders. "Look how lucky we are. We are the chosen thousand."

Major Allen threaded his way through the refugees. "Can you come to the wardroom? I need your help."

I sat on the red banquette facing Allen.

"I worked up a list of orders for the people. I'd like you to translate them into German and announce them on the loud-speaker so everyone on the refugee deck can hear.''

We took his list to the radio shack. "Ladies and gentlemen," I said in German, "Major Judson Allen, our transport commander, has asked me to announce the orders of the day. Please listen carefully. If you have any questions, you can discuss them with me later.

"One, every one must police his or her own bunk and the area around it.

"Two, everyone must be out of quarters by nine A.M. or until such time as the daily Army inspection is over. It should be over no later than ten A.M.

"Three, Major Allen would like to have three men on each of the four holds, or a total of twelve men, to mop the four decks.

"Four, he would like to have eight or ten women to clean the women's latrines on D Deck, and five men to clean the men's latrines on C Deck.

"Five, he needs additional men and women to clean the public showers.

"All of this, cleaning your own areas, the decks, latrines and showers, must be finished by ten A.M. After that you are free to do anything else for the rest of the day.

"Six, we will have an air-raid drill every morning. Everyone must be on deck except those too sick to leave their bunks. Every bunk has a life jacket. Wear it each day for the air-raid drill. Curfew must be strictly obeyed. No one is allowed on deck after dark. If you even light a cigarette after dusk, the Nazis can spot us. You must be in your bunks from dark to dawn.

"Seven, the mess lines. Everybody who comes through the line with a meal ticket will get food. After you've had your food and the line is finished, you can come back for seconds. Provisions are ample for fighting men. They should be ample for civilians.

"Eight, in each section an army doctor will make morning rounds. The Army has assigned three army doctors and six army nurses to this escort: some are on special orders, some on rotation. We are also using refugee doctors and nurses who'll be working in the hospital.

"Nine, the Army has assigned three line officers just for this escort: Lieutenant Colonel Daniel Talbot, Captain Geher and Captain Lewis Korn.''

I had promised Ambassador Murphy that I would post copies of Roosevelt's cable to him that I had had translated in Washington.

I nailed them now on the walls of the holds, where the refugees could read the words in Serbo-Croatian, German, French, Greek, Slovenian, Polish, Albanian, Bulgarian, Hungarian, Rumanian, Yiddish and Czech.

Back in the wardroom, I joined Ralph Stauber and Captain Korn. We had decided to meet every day.

"What criteria did you follow," I asked Korn, "when you selected the people?"

"There were several," he said. "First, we tried to take people in family groups. Then we chose those in greatest need, and took as many as possible from concentration camps and slave-labor camps. Third, we took no families with contagious or loathsome diseases." He smiled a little. "Sometimes I think a cold is a loathsome disease. And, finally, we tried to choose people with a cross section of skills to make the Emergency Refugee Shelter as self-sustaining as possible."

Stauber pulled out his yellow pad. "You did get a cross section all right: doctors, dentists, pharmacists, opticians, artisans, merchants, bookkeepers, tailors, dressmakers, teachers, lawyers, singers, actors, painters, writers, sculptors, engineers and two rabbis."

It's a whole community, I thought, a microcosm of a small town.

"One of the first questions they ask me," I said, "is about housing. I guess when you've been on the run so long, when you've been homeless, housing becomes an obsession."

"What do they want to know?" Stauber asked

"Right now they want to know if they'll be put in houses according to their nationalities. The Yugoslavs especially seem to want to keep together."

"I'm getting the same question," Korn said.

"What do we tell them?"

Korn's sad face grew even sadder. "You have to tell them we just don't know."

"Education is another obsession," I said. "Some of the teen-agers haven't been in school for five years, and some of the ten- and twelve-year-olds have never been in school."

A shadow crossed Korn's face. "Housing and education are hard questions, but soluble. The toughest question of all is what's going to happen to them when the war is over. They all signed a release they would go back as soon as the war was over. But who knows if they believed it or not? What's more, I gather from the refugees who were selected in Rome that Heathcote-

Smith told them it was simply a form—to pay no attention to it."

"They better believe it," Stauber said. Anger edged his words. "That's the promise the President gave Congress."

CHAPTER SEVEN

A young American in a white undershirt and chinos approached me on deck. "My name is Abe Tauber." He thrust out his hand. "I'm with the Red Cross, assigned to the wounded soldiers on the ship."

His face was freckled, his hair copper red in the sun.

"We stood on the deck watching you as you came up the rope ladder in that fascinating and, I must say, highly unusual attire." He spoke with precision, each word rounded, before he sent it forth with a kind of Huckleberry Finn chuckle. "Every man on the ship wanted to know who you were, especially when the brass marched forward to welcome you aboard." He paused. "Now, my dear young lady, we know."

He handed me the ship's newspaper, a white mimeographed sheet called "Gibbins' Gab." My eye glanced down the page through the news summary.

His voice broke into my reading. "I'm sure the news fascinates you, a former foreign correspondent . . ."

I looked at him quizzically. How did he know?

"Turn the page over. You're on the other side." He pointed to the bottom of the page.

MEET YOUR (MYSTERIOUS) SHIPMATE

Comes out in a special launch while we ride at anchor in Naples.

Boards the ship, treated with great courtesy by full colonels!

Walks around in a daring red turban and GI pants, since changed to lovely red slacks, lugging camera and photometer. Confers with big shots and ordinary guys alike. MP's bow at her as she passes to and from the sacred portals forward and speaks to the folks in their own (7) languages.

Is she a psychiatrist? Obstetrician? Newspaper reporter? FBI man? Here's the lowdown.

The lady is Miss Ruth Gruber; she is here to help out with the movement of the civilian group. Special representative of Sec. of the Interior Harold L. Ickes whose department is handling the problem. A former correspondent with the NY *Herald Tribune*, traveler in pre-war Europe and Alaska. Author of many articles and a book on the Arctic. Nice gal, too—green eyes, soft voice, ready smile—and a good head.

Won't it be nice to get home to our own gals again??

Laughing, I reread the line "Is she a psychiatrist? Obstetrician?" I turned to him. "And what do *you* do?"

"I've just spent a year abroad with the Red Cross. Now I'm going back to teach the two subjects I love, English and speech, at the Bronx High School of Science." His freckled face grew serious. "If I can be of any help with the refugees, it would be an honor. A privilege."

I thanked him. I would need all the help I could muster.

Whatever skills I had acquired as a journalist seemed inadequate. A journalist sees, observes, stands apart, straining for objectivity, searching for truth. Now I would still strain for objectivity, search for truth, but I did not want to stand apart, nor could I. I wanted to feel as they felt, through every cell in my body.

They were the first witnesses coming to America in one single mass movement. Through them, through their faces, their bodies, their experiences, their fears, their bravery, their flight, their survival. America would learn at last the truth of Hitler's crimes.

Theirs would not be second- or thirdhand stories, nor even eyewitness accounts of trained observers. Their stories would be personal histories. They were the victims available at last to prove the crimes. I had to win their confidence without invading their privacy.

Pacing the deck, staring into the Mediterranean, I hit upon a scheme.

They talked in a babel of languages. We used German as the lingua franca only because the majority understood German or Yiddish. But there were many who spoke no German and no English. I would teach them English. I would set up classes on the deck. Even with a few words in English, we could begin to make contact with one another.

"Good idea," Major Allen approved.

"I'll need a blackboard."

"The bos'n will fix it up for you on the main deck."

On the loudspeaker I announced we would have a class in English in half an hour.

Tuck, whose face was screwed up like Popeye's, hung a blackboard above the covered hatch, and immediately a crowd of men and women left their places on the deck. They took positions sitting, even lying close together, on the hatch cover. The rest spilled over, sitting on the deck itself. I had expected a handful, perhaps twenty or thirty, but not hundreds who sat, faces uplifted, some smiling, some serious, all waiting for the lesson to begin.

"How do you feel?" I asked them, and then wrote the words in chalk on the board.

Those who spoke no English shrugged their shoulders. Others shouted, "Fine."

" 'I feel fine,' " I added the words to the blackboard. "Let's repeat. How do you feel?"

In unison, in all accents, they called out, "I feel fine." Some at the rim of the ship, clutching the rails, bending over in case they had to throw up, still mouthed the words:

"How do you feel?"

"I feel fine."

Most were smiling, laughing. We were making contact.

Abe Furmanski of Warsaw, a short, barrel-chested thirty-five-year-old man with the face and the muscles of a fighter, sat beside me on the cover of the hatch.

"You want to know our stories. I will tell you what the Nazis and the Vichy French did to us in France."

I opened my notebook. "Do you mind if I write your words down?"

His eyes narrowed. "You must write it down. The world must know. I hear people say that the things they did to us—it's all propaganda. Like the propaganda in the First World War. What I tell you is no propaganda."

I began to write in my own long shorthand. I could write while I watched his face. He looked like a man who would kill before he was killed.

"I was in France when Germany took it on June 16, 1940. A twenty-six-year-old German captain, his name was Captain Danniker—he was the Nazi commissar in Paris for Jewish affairs—sent for Rabbi Julien Weill, the Grand Rabbi of Paris.

"Danniker gave an order, 'Rabbi, I demand you set up a Jewish Council of seven men, French and foreign Jews, to collaborate with the Germans.' "

His face grew dark. "We did not collaborate. We sabotaged every way we could. All of us with Rabbi Weill were ready to pay, with our heads and our lives. And many of us did. We created our own underground and brought together all the Jewish political and religious organizations. It was the first time, I think, in history we all came together in our struggle. We began to smuggle Jews to the free zone in unoccupied France. But unfortunately most were captured by the Vichy French gendarmes. Whenever the Nazis caught one of us, there were terrible reprisals. Rabbi Weill was thrown into prison. I don't know if he survived the torture."

He stopped to light a cigarette.

"August 22, 1941. I will never forget that day. The Nazis took sixty-five hundred Jews—children, men, women nursing their babies—and threw them into the terrible concentration camp at Drancy, near Paris. Then they shipped them to Poland. There were some good French like the Gaullist groups who helped Jews flee to Spain and Switzerland and gave them false documents and money. But most of the French—" he puffed the smoke from his cigarette—"ugh. I cannot look at French people anymore. They built the concentration camp at Gurs near the Spanish border where they killed thirty to forty thousand Jews."

"I know Gurs," I said.

"You—you have been to Gurs, an American?"

"No. But Lion Feuchtwanger, the novelist, was in Gurs. He was one of the lucky ones who got out. He described it to me when he came to New York."

"One lucky man. A writer. In the underground we kept trying to get hundreds out of Gurs. We got out a handful." He ground his cigarette out on the sole of his shoe. "Then the worst blow fell. All of France was occupied by the Germans. The mass murders began."

He went on swiftly. "In trucks which were meant to hold twenty people, the Germans pushed one hundred and more. Quicklime was placed on the floor ten inches high. The doors were sealed tight so no air could escape. The people had to urinate—that started the lime cooking. The gas and fumes came up and choked them to death."

Abe stopped a moment, and his hands went to his throat. "The bodies were thrown into special ovens and burned."

I thought I could not listen anymore, but I listened.

"The Nazis said all the time, 'Kill Russians with bullets. Kill Jews with lime.' "

*   *   *

The noonday sun rode high over the convoy, the ships before us breaking foam in the green sea. My notebook lay open on my lap. I saw faces milling around me, but they were the faces of people in trucks, clutching their throats as lime turned into gas and fumes. I walked to the rail and clutched it, sucking in the air and the smell of the sea.

Had I heard enough for today? Could I absorb any more?

"Excuse me, but I think you must know what happened to us—in Yugoslavia."

I turned from the rail to see a distinguished-looking man. His open shirt revealed a wide gauze bandage on his chest.

"We Yugoslavs are not the majority on the ship," he said, "but we're about a third, there are over three hundred of us. I cannot speak for all the Yugoslavs. But my own story may give you some picture of what happened to us in March 1941 when Hitler issued his orders about Yugoslavia. I can hear them saying to each other. 'Beat them down as fast as possible. Destroy Belgrade from the air.' "

Pressing my notebook against the rail, I took down his words. He was like a man possessed.

"Yes. Yes, write it down. You have people here from eighteen countries, that Hitler captured, burned, tried to destroy. Get all our stories. Get all of the terror. We lived it. We will live with it for the rest of our lives. But you are the first one we can tell it to. Yes, write it down, so the world will know."

He interrogated himself for my benefit. "My name? Henry Macliach My age? Forty-four. My profession? Doctor of medicine. My rank in the Army? Major. My wounds?" He pointed to the bandage on his chest. "I am still not healed from the things they did to my body."

His hand trembled. "I tell you to write it. But no notebook and no pencil can describe what they did to us.

"Our Army could not resist the Nazis. Every day the Germans would line up the people who still had the courage and the strength to defy Hitler. Jews, nationalists, Communists, radicals, professors, schoolteachers, intellectuals, everybody was a suspect. Every single day five hundred people—I saw this with my own eyes—were shot by machine guns. Every day for six months! After the shooting they strung demolitions to each dead body and blew them all up.

"Maybe you do not believe this, young woman from America. And why should you? What do you, in America, thousands of miles away, know what the Germans did to us? Why should you believe that children not old enough to go to school were included among the five hundred? Why should you believe that in the hospital where I worked as a physician seventy men were locked for eight days in a tiny closetlike room without food or air? They did not need food or air when their bodies were picked off the ground."

I wanted to whisper above the noise of the ship and the milling people and the calm sea, "I do believe." But no words came.

"And what was the crime committed by two thousand men?" he asked. "They were selected in December to go out in the woods to cut wood for the Germans, to keep them warm. They chopped and sawed all day, and kept the Germans warm in that hard winter. In January, they were sent out in a terrible snowstorm, and not allowed to come back at night. Two days later, when the storm stopped, all two thousand were found. Frozen stiff in the snow. What was their crime? They were Jews."

He was a doctor now, examining my face. "I see in your eyes you are asking how did I survive? How did I survive? How did all of us on this ship survive when most of the Jews of Yugoslavia were shot in mass graves or riverbanks or deported to death camps?"

He spat out the words.

"We survived by running."

He turned on his heels and disappeared in the swarm of people.

I closed my notebook.

Now perhaps I could go back to my cabin, throw off the clothes sticking to my back, take a shower. Even the open-stall cold saltwater showers seemed like a luxury. But more people were pressing around me on the deck.

"Belgium. I will tell you what happened to us in Belgium."

The sun fell in slants on Samuel Silberman's ravaged face. It was a face of sorrow and nobility. His thirty-two-year-old wife, Breindel, stood silently at his side, clutching his arm.

"We have two children," Samuel said, "a boy and a girl."

"On the ship? With you?"

They shook their heads. Samuel began their story haltingly. Small, round-faced, with the thick, capable hands of an artisan, he had been a furrier in Tarnow, Poland. In 1928 they had moved to Brussels, where many Jews had settled, and in 1940, when the Germans occupied Belgium, they began the flight that was to take them ultimately to our ship.

"We tried to get out of Belgium when the Nazis came," he said. "We thought France would be safe. We left everything we owned, just a few things we could carry easily. We lost them too in the railroad station."

With hundreds of fleeing people, they reached Boulogne on the French coast, and hid in a cellar. For three days they were without food and water. Belgian soldiers escaping the Nazis with them brought them wine for sustenance. "That was the only thing our children had—wine." On the fourth day, Boulogne fell, too.

"I looked out of the cellar. German officers stood up in tanks and looked around in all the corners of the street with binoculars. Soldiers stood up in army cars pointing machine guns."

He shook his head. "We were so naïve. The Germans sounded so kind. They told us and the Belgian soldiers, 'Go home. Belgium is free.' We thought—imagine how stupid we were— the Germans have achieved such victories, maybe they'll forget the Jews."

They returned to Brussels to find that the Germans had already put in special laws against the Jews.

"Then in June 1942 the order came: All boys and girls between the ages of fifteen and twenty must go to the Malines to work. They were told to take work clothes, food for ten days, dishes. They were warned that if they didn't come, all Jews would be held responsible."

Breindel hugged Samuel's arm, as if she was hugging her only security, the core of her life. "We thought those children were going to work," she said. "But it was a lie. Malines was where they assembled the people and pushed them onto the cattle cars and sent them to Poland."

Samuel pressed his wife's arm tightly against his body. "Every day in the railroad station, a thousand beautiful young boys and girls came, carrying rucksacks, and every day five thousand adults came with them, parents, relatives, weeping at the departure of their children."

Breindel began to sob.

"Now the young people were gone," Samuel said, "the young men and women who could have fought against the Germans. Then the Germans began to snatch the older people. They closed the streets and pulled off every Jew they caught. The Jews began to hide during the day, so the Germans worked at night. They entered every house. The first night they took more than three thousand Jews."

Three thousand in Italy had clamored to come aboard our ship, to get to America. In Brussels, three thousand had been captured in one night.

Samuel was still talking. "Many of us Jewish men and women joined the Brigade Blanche to do underground work. We were very active, we broke into offices and burned documents with lists of Jewish names. We sabotaged trains taking raw materials out of Belgium to Germany; we assassinated Belgian collaborationists; we even made raids on the bureaus which printed meal tickets. Each month we got about two hundred thousand food stamps. We distributed them to the underground, to the resistance movement, to the Jews."

Samuel was standing tall now, like a resistance fighter.

"And your children?" I asked in a low voice.

"We hid them in a Belgian monastery. Most of the Jews hid their children with monks and nuns and peasants. Ninety-five percent of the Belgian people were very good to the Jews. But then it became hard for the Belgians. The Gestapo broke into their homes searching for Jews. Each day articles in an anti-Semitic newspaper, *L'Ami du Peuple,* said: 'Don't tell me where a Jew lives—just tell me his phone number; we'll get him and you'll be rewarded.' It became impossible for us to stay. We decided to try to escape. But the children were too small to run with us. They would never survive. We had to make the most terrible decision of our lives."

Racking sobs shook his body.

I could no longer write. I brushed aside the tears falling on my notebook.

"We had to leave our children—in the Belgian monastery. Will we ever find them again?"

The people were pressing forward now, some urging each other, "Tell her your story. Let her know what happened to us. Let her be our witness."

A man in prison pajamas made a path through the crowd for a buxom woman with a round, jovial face and dimpled cheeks; her contagious smile was illuminated by two stainless-steel front teeth. In her fifties, she wore her light-brown hair in youthful curls down to her shoulders.

"Mathilda, tell the American lady," the pajama-clad man said, "how you ran a whole underground station and saved over one hundred families, and how they caught you and locked you up and kept you in a cellar with ice for ten days with the ice dripping on you."

Mathilda Nitsch smiled, and it seemed to me all the faces around us began to smile, too.

"Why did I help all these people?" she repeated my question. "Why? Because I have belief in God."

The group shushed one another, eager to hear the story of this woman whose openness and obvious love of human beings seemed to embrace us all.

"I am a Catholic, a Roman Catholic. I could not understand why they killed Jews, who were innocent people, so I helped them escape. I stole false passports from the chief of police himself. You see, I had a boardinghouse in Sušak on the northern coast of Yugoslavia, though I am Austrian by birth and a Czech citizen because I married a Czech officer. But I have not heard from my husband since early in the war."

She stopped talking, no longer smiling. The people honored her silence. Then the smile returned. "I was very happy in Sušak. I lived there for fifteen years. Then the Nazis came and began to throw people into jail. That's when I decided to help them escape. I hid them in my boarding house, gave them the false passports I had stolen, and then I took them to other friends in Fiume."

"Fiume," she explained, "is right next door to Sušak in Yugoslavia, but it belongs to Italy. Most of the Italians—though not the Secret Police—are much better to the Jews than the Nazis. So at night, in Fiume, we put the people on boats, which took them across the Adriatic to other parts of Italy, where we hoped Italian peasants would hide them."

The people around us did not stir, wholly absorbed as this unlikely looking heroine spun her tale of courage and faith. The Mediterranean was lake-calm.

"Finally, the OVRA, the Italian Secret Police, caught me. That's when they put me in the ice-storage cellar for ten days to make me talk. There was no air. Ice-cold water dripped on my face and head and the ceiling and the walls. Water was in my shoes and over my feet. Ice water was all around."

Once again the luminous smile infected us. "The OVRA wanted to know who worked with me. Some of my friends were the police themselves in Sušak and Fiume. There were others too. We all worked together to help the people escape. I wouldn't give out their names. I wouldn't tell anything.

"Finally the OVRA saw they couldn't find anything out from me, so they sent me to the concentration camp in Ferramonte. I was there for four months, but I still didn't tell them anything."

"Brave woman," the gaunt man interrupted. "How many people are alive because of this one woman."

"I don't know much about politics," Mathilda said. "I am

here only because I saved others. I didn't want any other pay. God will see to it that I am taken care of in spite of the fact that I am so poor."

"God will help you." A small elderly woman embraced Mathilda. "God will help you because you saved people out of the goodness of your heart. You are a *gute neshuma*—a good soul."

Mathilda's light eyes were flecked with happiness.

"Now, going to America, my greatest hopes are being answered. Please—" she put her hand on mine—"please tell the people of America that I give them a thousand thanks."

CHAPTER EIGHT

Our greatest danger lay in the Mediterranean.

Nazi bombers and Nazi U-boats scouted the waters searching for convoys like ours.

The captain's orders, which I had read to the people on the loudspeaker, were rigidly adhered to. Each morning, the alarm bells rang through the ship for the air-raid drill. Swiftly we donned life jackets and hurried to our battle stations. After dusk, the *Henry Gibbins* looked like a ghost ship, with no lights, no people on the deck; even the officers stomped out their cigarettes before they emerged into the blackout. Only our engines kept their rhythmic pounding; we moved swiftly at fifteen knots.

More warships joined us. By our third day at sea, we were a flotilla of twenty-nine vessels—thirteen warships escorting sixteen troop and cargo ships.

"Those two ships running parallel to us—" the navy officer standing with me on the flying deck handed me his binoculars—"they're filled with Nazi POWs."

I felt a wave of revulsion. "Why are Nazi POWs in this convoy?"

"They're our protective covering," he said. "Any Nazi warships trying to attack us on the surface would have to attack those prisoner-of-war ships first."

"It's bizarre. Nazis protecting the refugees they created, the soldiers they wounded."

"It's a good thing the soldiers don't have guns. Those POWs might never make it to the States."

"But why do we have to bring shiploads of German prisoners to America?"

"There's a real labor shortage back home, especially on the farms. A lot of the POWs are keeping our farms and factories going. From what I hear, we've been bringing in over one hundred thousand POWs."

I blurted out, "We're bringing in Nazi soldiers who killed our boys on the beaches of France and in Italy. And no one complains—not one word. If I tell you—I have to tell you—" I was speaking incoherently—"we went through hell, we waited so long, millions died, before we could get even these one thousand refugees into the U.S. And Lord only knows what the isolationists in Congress can still do to us after we land."

I thought bitterly:

One hundred thousand Nazi POWs.

One thousand refugees.

Sunday night, our third night at sea, I woke up with a start. Bells were ringing. Orders were coming in rapid succession on the loudspeaker.

"Enemy planes overhead. Crew and gunners to battle stations. Civilian personnel and wounded soldiers don life jackets but do not move. Remain in your bunks. Repeat: Civilians and soldiers, don life jackets but do not move. Remain in your bunks."

The orders for civilians, I decided, were not for me. My battle station was with the refugees. I looked at my watch. It was two-thirty in the morning.

I jumped out of my bunk and pulled on a pair of slacks, a warm sweater and my life jacket. What do you save? flashed through my head. What do you take with you if the ship sinks? Passport? Ridiculous. Camera? Useless in the water. My notebooks, the most precious things I had—they would be washed out. No matter, the material in them was in my brain, my guts. The only things you save, I decided, are human lives.

Suddenly I realized, each person reacts differently to imminent death. Caroline lay back on her bunk wearing only her panties and brassiere. "Hell," she drawled, "Ah'm goin' back to sleep. Ah've been through enough air raids. If they get us, Ah might just as well be sleepin' as awake."

Mary stood up, her blond hair touseled. "Ruth, if they hit us with these damn aerial torpedoes, it will be bad. We won't have a chance. I've been in the hospitals after these raids. It's God-awful what happens to people who get hit. If it's torpedoes they'll get our boat, and they'll get all of us, bad.''

In another cabin, one of the older nurses sat writing her will.

I hurried through the narrow causeway, holding on to the wall of the ship, groping my way to the steep ladder that led down to the refugees' holds.

Could our ship withstand a direct hit? Army transport ships had taken a terrible beating in the early Lend-Lease convoys to Murmansk. Many had been dynamited in the frozen waters of the Soviet Arctic, in the Atlantic, in the Mediterranean. Could our thirteen escort ships protect us from bombers? Would the AA guns knock out the planes before they dropped their deadly fire on us?

Fear pulsed through my body, but I pushed it aside. No time for fear—everything in me was focused on the refugees. Were they in panic? What about the children, the women, the sick? I gripped the rail tightly as I sped down the ladder.

There was an eerie hush. In the semidarkness I looked out at the vast expanse of tiers of bunks squeezed together. The people lay in their life jackets, absolutely still. Even the babies seemed to sense something so dangerous they would not cry.

Army and refugee doctors moved up and down the tight aisles, here and there handing out sugar-coated placebos to those who lay frozen. A few men stood at the foot of the ladder, ready to rush up if they had to. But there was no hysteria, no panic.

I walked through the holds talking in a low voice to the people, patting some on the arm, taking the hands that some of the women stretched out toward me, stroking the foreheads of children who lay wide-eyed and still.

Manya, her long blond hair pulled back, stood beside her bunk wrapped in her life jacket. I heard her praying, ''Oh, God, please don't let us go down in the water. We're so close to America and so far. God, what it means to me, to be saved and brought on this ship from so horrible a time, those terrible years. Please don't let us go down in the water. Please, God.''

The sound of antiaircraft and machine guns ruptured the silence. Some of the people began to applaud. Rolf Kuznitzki, a sixteen-year-old, called to me exuberantly, ''Listen to those guns.'' Even in the dim light I could see his cheeks burning with excitement. ''They're shooting at the Nazis,'' he said. ''For years now, whenever they came over us we had to run or hide. I hope the gunners get every single one of them.''

Slowly, thick black smudge filtered down into the holds. The people began coughing, choking. A few cried out in panic, but they were instantly calmed by their neighbors.

Two MPs appeared, wearing gas masks.

"What's happening?" I asked

One of the MPs moved his mask aside. "It's a smokescreen. The escort ships have blacked us out. You know the orders—in case of attack, the warships have to close in, protect our ship first."

"That's to conceal the outside of the ship. But why the smudge inside?"

"Snafu. The boys who were supposed to close the intake vents must have panicked and run below. Now the smoke is coming through all our intake valves. We're trying to fix it, but you've got to tell the people not to move and to keep absolutely still."

They were still.

The MP added, "The rest of the ship is going crazy. Especially some of the guys who cracked up in Anzio."

I made my way back up the ladder to the deck. Gunners in the circular gun tubs pointed their weapons at the sky. I groped along the wall until I reached the ladder that led to the soldiers' holds.

At the top of the stairs, I heard men screaming, coughing. Someone shouted hysterically, "God damn those Jews. I made it in Casablanca, I made it in Bizerte. I made it in Anzio. Now I'm going to die."

Abe Tauber came toward me. "It's murder down here, Ruth," he said. "How is it with the refugees?"

"Absolutely calm."

"Stay here, Ruth. Maybe you can help."

Abe cupped his hands around his mouth and yelled as if he were on a football field, "Listen, you guys, listen to this."

I walked a few steps down the steep ladder, then waited. The men on the three-tiered bunks closest to me grew silent first. Then the silence moved in waves back through the blackout smudge in the hold.

"Fellows," Abe yelled. "She's just come from the front of the ship with the refugees. I've asked her to talk to us for a few minutes."

I began slowly. "I've just left—"

"Louder," a voice yelled in the distance.

"If you're all quiet," Abe shouted, "you'll hear her."

I raised my voice, trying to penetrate the hold.

"The refugees are scared—sure, all of us are scared—but

they're still. Even the children are still. Even the babies. They've been through hell—''

"Hell! Who's been through more hell than we have in Anzio and Cassino?''

A soldier beat his fist against the cast that imprisoned his leg. "It's because of these lousy Jews," he screamed. "That's why they're attacking us."

"But they're not all Jews," I said quietly.

I heard a few gasps of amazement.

"A refugee," I said, "can be anyone—anyone who's homeless, anyone who's displaced."

A young soldier leaned forward. "I'm Jewish and I'm damn glad you're bringing these people over. But it's true, isn't it, most of these people you're bringing to America are Jews?"

I was suddenly grateful to Stauber for his statistics. "Eight hundred seventy-four are Jews; the rest are Catholics, Protestants, Greek Orthodox. Let me tell you about one of them, a Catholic." Briefly, I told them Mathilda's story.

"Go on," Abe said, "We should know what these people have been through."

I told them of the hundreds of men and women crushed into trucks, choking to death from the lime. The Yugoslav doctor who had watched five hundred people shot each day. The thousand boys and girls in Belgium deported each day. Children hidden in monasteries, their parents lying so quietly now up front, anguished; were the children alive, would they ever see them again?

The hold was growing quieter. "This air raid is one more episode in their flight. Most of them have put their faith in God and in our AA gunners." The sounds of silence filled the hold.

I climbed back up to the deck. An officer told me, "We counted thirty planes over us so far."

"And they haven't bombed us?"

"Damn lucky. Looks as if they're on their way to another mission and don't want to waste their bombs on us."

The black smudge was disappearing. The guns were still. "Stand easy," came through the loudspeaker. I looked at my wristwatch. It was three-fifteen, just one hour since the ship's bells had rung.

CHAPTER NINE

No one slept.

In the morning we gathered on the main deck, talking, laughing, rejoicing. Some stretched out on the iron floor, watching the upturned bowl of cloudless blue. We were alive. One more miracle of survival.

Around us, the ships in the flotilla churned up pathways of white foam while we relived our escape from death.

"I was in the toilet when the air-raid alarm was sounded," David Levy, a dark-haired Yugoslav in his early twenties, said, half laughing, half still unbelieving his luck. "Somebody in the crew locked up all the watertight compartments, so I couldn't come out. I kept thinking, All these years everyone in my family was killed and I saved myself; now I'm going to die in a toilet."

The air raid gave the *Henry Gibbins* a new aura, like a maritime fortress on alert. The gunners sat tense in the elevated tubs, manning machine guns, watching for planes and enemy subs. Around us sailors tested the winches and practiced swinging lifeboats from their davits into the sea.

"If only we were past Gibraltar," the MP medic on the refugee deck told me apprehensively. A soft-spoken soldier, he had endeared himself to us the first day when he ripped the back off a wooden crate, lined the box with bottles of iodine and Mercurochrome, gauze pads and adhesive tape, and set up an outdoor clinic, bandaging children's cuts, dispensing aspirin, quinine and good cheer.

"Once you're past Gibraltar," he said, "once you're out in the Atlantic, you're still not home free but somehow you feel safer, there's more room out there to maneuver away from the U-boats."

In the sick bay, I walked toward a middle-aged woman nursing her baby.

"Did you give birth on the ship?" I asked Olga Maurer.

She laughed, "No, he was born in an American jeep."

"A jeep!"

"Yes, on the way to the ship." Her laughter was infectious, her words spilling over each other. "I never thought I would have another baby. I'm over forty," she chuckled. "It happened like this. We escaped from Vienna to Italy, my husband, my boy, Walter, and me. When the Nazis came, the Italians first hid us in a tunnel, then they ran with us to the mountains until some Canadian patrol soldiers came to tell us, no more Nazis. Such a celebration the Italians made for us in the moonshine! Such a honeymoon I had, at my age, with Leon! That's when I got pregnant."

Sitting up in her hospital bed, Olga told me how one of the men helping to select the refugees, charmed, I was sure, by her zest for life, accepted the Maurers' application to join the one thousand, although Olga was in her ninth month.

She was put into a command car and taken for the night to a women's hospital in Potenza. A doctor examined her and assured her that the baby was still high in her womb. The next morning she walked out of the hospital to see a convoy of trucks loaded with refugees from the Potenza area. They were the Palestinian Jewish trucks with the Star of David that Max Perlman had described to me in his office in Naples.

Palestinian and American GI medics made a bed for Olga in the back of a jeep, piling mattresses and khaki army blankets on top of an army cot. They joined the convoy for the hundred-mile drive across the mountains toward Naples. Sitting inside Olga's jeep were two GIs and a doctor in a British uniform with the Star of David insignia. Dr. Joseph Koehler, Olga discovered, had been born in her native Czechoslovakia.

"Doctor," she cried, "you are my *landsmann*. Until now I was afraid. Now it must go perfect."

As if on target, her labor pains began. "Doctor, Doctor . . ." she cried out.

"A few minutes," he pleaded. "Soon we'll be at the headquarters of our Palestinian unit. We have a camp there. We have supplies, everything to help you deliver. A few more minutes."

But Olga's baby began to push his way out of her body.

Dr. Koehler shouted to the driver, "Stop the jeep." It was twelve and church bells were ringing.

The driver pulled the vehicle to the side of the road, honking his horn to alert the other drivers. The trucks in front of him and behind him slowed down; the convoy came to a halt.

The people in the trucks jumped down. There were empty fields around them. "What's happened? Are we in danger? Is there an air raid somewhere? Are we turning back? What's going on?"

Dr. Koehler leaned out of the truck. "It's a boy!" he shouted.

The refugees embraced each other, crying, "It's an omen. It's a good omen. It's a new life on the road to the Promised Land."

One of the older men took out his prayer shawl and began to pray. Everyone grew silent. They wanted no disturbances as he offered his prayer to God. Then he turned to some of the people near him and said slowly, "Life—after all the dying. After all the murders and the shootings, after the burnings and the destruction. A baby boy, a Jew to take the place of a murdered baby, a Jew born on our way to freedom."

Together now the refugees recited the Shehehiyanu—the prayer of survival. "Blessed art Thou, O Lord our God, King of the Universe, Who has sustained us to this day."

Dr. Koehler, using the water from his canteen, washed the baby and mopped Olga's face. "Your baby is beautiful," he said.

He placed the baby on Olga's stomach. She lifted him up. He was beautiful, with full pink cheeks, large dark eyes and dark hair. She counted his fingers and his toes and stroked his body until she was convinced she had a normal child.

Outside the jeep one of the American GIs who had helped Dr. Koehler told the people, "We've named the baby International Harry, and we predict he's going to be a brigadier general."

I kissed "International Harry," then walked back through the ship to the yeoman's desk to type up Olga's story.

Her one request had been for orange juice. "I dream about it," she had said. A simple problem easily solved. But others had problems we might never be able to solve, raw wounds, deep scars.

I pulled the pages from the typewriter, folded them into my bag and went back to the deck.

Leo Mirković, the opera singer from Zagreb, surrounded by a bevy of beautiful young women, came toward me.

"I've been looking for you," he said. "I would like to sing opera in America. Will it be possible?"

Mirković's dark eyes peered at me. I judged he was in his sixties. I learned later he had just turned forty. He was medium height with dark balding hair. Deep ridges in his cheeks dimpled constantly as he spoke. He was gaunt and skeletal. "Do you think I can sing in one of your opera houses?"

"I can't make any promises," I told him, "they're making decisions right now in Washington."

"I will sing for anybody. Anytime. Singing is my life." He waved his arms as if he were on a stage.

Edith Semjen, a slender blonde with a husky voice, drew a pack of cigarettes from her pocket and lit one for Mirković and one for herself. "Leo," she teased, "why don't you tell her about your great love affairs in Zagreb?"

Before he could speak, another woman joined us. "Mirković," she asked, "do you want your pajamas washed today?"

She turned to me, explaining, "He came aboard with one pair of pajamas, good silk ones, and we women take turns each day washing them."

"Not me," Edith tossed her thick blond hair. "I'm willing to give him a cigarette, but that's it. Go on, Leo, tell her about your girlfriends at the opera."

Mirković laughed. Briefly, still circled by young women, he told us how he, like many of the Yugoslavs on the ship, had escaped to Split, on the Italian-occupied Dalmatian coast. Italian police arrested him, put him in a boat, then a train, where the prisoners were chained together. Determined to survive, he began to sing Italian songs, and he so enchanted the Italian guards that they unchained all the prisoners. They confined him in a little town called Zibello in the province of Parma.

"We had no women with us," he said, "so I wrote a letter to the Governor of Parma, 'We are all single men; we need women.' The Governor gave us permission to go to the whorehouse once a month. I tell you, the Italians are *menschen*—good human beings."

When the Nazis began deporting Jews from northern Italy, the Zibello chief of police gave him a bicycle to escape with and the names of people in Parma who put him on a train to Rome, where he lived as an Italian. He showed me his identity card. The face was Mirković's, but the name read "Ettore Testa."

"For a whole year I worked in the underground, bringing food to refugees and English soldiers that we were hiding out in apartments. We were waiting for you Americans in Rome. When you came, we were so tired, so hungry and sick, we couldn't shout, 'Welcome, Americans!' "

Once again he flung his arms out. "Now I can shout it. Now I can rest, I can eat, and maybe, in America, I will be able to sing."

He threw his head back and sang the words he could not sing in Rome.

"Welcome, Americans!"

CHAPTER TEN

"For me," Manya Hartmayer said, "the invitation from President Roosevelt came almost too late."

The noonday sun streaked gold through her shoulder-length blond hair. She was tall, painfully thin, her blue-green eyes sunken in her delicately boned face. But she moved with flowing grace.

"I was in five concentration camps. I tried to escape from one of them, but a prison guard caught me and kicked me in the back. For weeks I lay in the corner of the camp like an animal. I couldn't breathe."

"How old are you, Manya?"

The blue-green eyes looked weary. "I am young, but my heart is two hundred years old. I don't know where my family is—Papa, my brothers, Sigi and Willie. They're children—fourteen and fifteen. Will I ever see them again?" She stared into the Mediterranean as if she were conjuring up their faces from the water.

"See this shirt." A man's dark cotton shirt hung over her emaciated body. "It was Papa's. He gave it to me when we were still together in the concentration camp in France—in Rivesaltes. Every day there were transports coming and going. They put Papa on one of the transports. That's when he pulled off his shirt and gave it to me so that I would have something for the cold nights."

She turned her face away from me. "Then Sigi and Willie disappeared. Only Mama and I were still left, and then one day we were taken away, too, and we ended up in Camp de Gurs. I couldn't stand seeing the desperate faces of the people around me. So whenever I had a chance I started to sing to cheer them up. I sang all the songs I had learned and loved since I was a little girl, Yiddish, French, German. I even learned an English song—'South of the Border, Down Mexico Way.' Anything I knew. I had to stay alive! Every time a transport came in, we rushed to see who was on it. Every time a transport was sent away, all the people who were left cried. They knew they would never see those people again.

" 'Don't cry,' I said to them. 'We will make it.' And I sang more songs, and the Germans and the French went on deporting the Jews.

"One day a Frenchwoman walked through the camp looking for children whose parents had been deported. She had several permits to take them out. She had been in the camp before and heard me sing, and she knew me. There was one permit left, so she asked, 'Where is the girl who sings?'

"She told me a lot of money was being collected from French Jewish families to save some of the children and get them out of Gurs. She told me I would go to an orphanage in the *département* of Cantal. I went to Mama to tell her I didn't want to go; I didn't want to be separated from her. But she was very angry with me. 'Manya, if you stay, I can never escape. You must go!'

"The next day, it was still dark, I climbed into a truck with the rest of the children, my body shaking all over, I was crying bitterly. While I was in the orphanage, I got a postcard from Papa. He had escaped to the village of Saint-Martin Vésubie near Nice. Somehow he found out where I was. 'Manyele,' he wrote, 'the *leichter* are coming to you.' In Yiddish *leichter* are candles. It meant the fire is burning, the fire is destroying; so we called the Nazis '*leichter*,' the destroyers. It was our code.

"I was in danger again. The next day, very early in the morning, I disguised myself as an old lady with a babushka around my head. I went to the railroad station without any ID papers or any permission; I knew the consequences. I took the train to Nice, but I had to get off in Marseille to change trains. The next train was delayed, so I spent the whole night in the station wandering from one place to another, hiding in dark corners. My heart pounded like crazy when I saw a uniform.

"Finally the train arrived in the morning. When I was on it, I felt a little better. But pretty soon somebody came into the compartment and said, 'The Bosch are asking everybody for papers.'

"I pulled myself together and walked out heading for the lavatory. I locked myself in. Soon loud voices shouted, '*Aufmachen.*' Heavy knocks crashed against the door. I told myself, 'They will have to kick the door in. I won't open it. If they break in, I will jump out the window.' I got ready to jump out.

"The train was moving fast. Then all of a sudden I heard nothing. Whatever took them away from that door saved me. I found Papa and my brothers in Saint-Martin Vésubie in the mountains. We were together again. You can imagine what it was like to find each other, to be together.

"But Mama's girlfriend, Regina, wrote us that Mama was very, very ill. She contracted typhus. She lost her hair and had holes all over her body where they tried to squeeze out the pus. There was no way to help her. We prayed every day that she would get better, that she would be back with us again.

"Then we heard the Nazis were coming to Saint-Martin Vésubie. We had to escape over the Alps. . . ."

As Manya talked, a small group assembled around us, taking turns to tell me of an incredible trek from the southern-French villages across the Alps to Italy.

At the beginning of the war, Mussolini had resisted Hitler's demands that he attack the French. Then, just before France surrendered, the Duce acquiesced and attacked. As a reward Hitler gave him control of some of the French towns and villages along the Riviera. The villages, like Saint-Martin Vésubie, were filled with Jewish refugees who had escaped from the Nazis, from French gendarmes, from Poles and Ukrainians, and from Ustashi fascists in Yugoslavia.

Interrupting one another, the people on the iron deck talked of the climb. Young Adam Munz began the story as we seated ourselves in a small area in the bow of the ship. Manya sat beside me, listening.

"Our flight began September 8, 1943, the day Mussolini capitulated. The Italian soldiers took off and began to hurry home. The Germans knew that many of the Italians had been protecting us, given us false papers with Italian names. Though we had to report to the police every day, they let us live among the peasants who took us in. Most people don't know about the Italians. They had almost no food themselves, but whatever they had they shared with us.

"The Italian soldiers fled. We knew in our bones the Nazis would be coming immediately and they would either shoot us or deport us. Before dawn the next morning, all of us, all the twelve hundred in our village, packed whatever we could. We had baskets tied around with rope, knapsacks, suitcases, and we started to climb the Alps through the famous La Madonna della Finestra Pass, over six thousand feet high.

"We were a long straggly line of people. You can imagine how far back twelve hundred people extended. We looked like a string of ants scrambling up a mountain.

"That first day, we kept climbing and climbing until at last, exhausted, we reached a cow field. We were still in the French part of the Alps, afraid that the Nazis would be coming right after us. Still we had to stop. We couldn't climb in the dark for fear we'd lose our footing or lose some people. So we lit fires, wrapped ourselves in whatever clothing we had. My father gave me my first cigarette. 'It will help keep you warm.' ''

"We tried to sleep a little," Manya said. "Maybe Papa slept, but I didn't. I kept seeing Mama. Then early in the morning we began to climb again up the mountain, and each step I took was taking me farther away from Mama. I think I wet with my tears every stone I touched.

"There were fewer and fewer trees. When I looked back, a beautiful lake we passed glistened like a small jewel. I stopped momentarily and said to myself, 'Oh, God, so much beauty in this world and we cannot be part of it.'

"I lost the sole of my shoe. Somebody found a piece of wire and tied the sole back on. My feet were so sore, but I couldn't go barefoot on those stones. I had only summer clothes on and I was freezing. I saw the snow peaks high above us. I said, 'Papa, I don't know how we will make it.'

"We kept on climbing. I had to hold on with my hands. There were stones and rocks. We were at the head of a long line of people. My brothers, Sigi and Willie, went back down as much as they could to help other people up again. I saw them struggling on the mountainside, pulling older people and women and children with their bare hands."

Ićak Wajs took up the tale. Ićak, a huge man with a crescent face and pouches under his chin, had lost his entire family. He had attached himself to the Munzes. "You know how to survive," he had told Adam's father when he learned that the Munzes had escaped from six different villages, each time just ahead of the Nazis.

"People of seventy and eighty were climbing those walls," Ićak said. "If you tell this in America, people will say it is a fantasy, but it was no fantasy. Babies suckled their mother's breasts, and when the milk gave out they suckled blood. Rabbi Rothschild carried a Torah in one arm and a baby in the other."

Ićak pointed to Adam. "Adam took the baby and climbed with it. There was a man who had been crippled by the Germans. He had such terrible fear that he took his crutches and climbed with us. A pregnant woman began her labor and still she climbed."

He shut his eyes. "We climbed with fear. But it was more than fear. It was like the wind of God leading us—the *Ruakh Elohim*."

The midmorning sun blistered the iron deck. But no one moved.

Young Adam went on. "We were still climbing on the French side of La Madonna Pass. The Italian side would start at the summit. We had lost some of the people the first day. They were so frightened that the Nazis would be waiting on top of the mountain that they turned around and went back."

The ship's engines hummed as we plowed through the Mediterranean, keeping our place in the flotilla of speeding ships. I shut my eyes, blocking out the water and the rays of the noonday sun. I was climbing the Alps with Manya, Ićak and Adam, who had begun to speak again.

"We couldn't stop. We kept trying to reach the top of the mountain. We knew that the Italian border began there on the top with a military outpost. Finally, late in the afternoon on that second day, we reached the border. There was a large cement barrack; Italian *carabinieri* came out and greeted us. We were so happy to see them. We told them we were running from the Nazis. They understood. They knew that the Italian soldiers too were running. They told us to come into the barrack. We were shivering with cold. Hungry, thirsty, exhausted, we piled into the barrack on top of each other.

"During the night the pregnant woman gave birth to her baby, and the next day she climbed down with the rest of us. Descending was harder on many of the people than climbing up."

Adam stopped talking. There was silence. Then Ićak spoke.

"We descended into a valley. We had crossed the mountains alive. Famous mountain climbers sometimes can't make it. Not one of us died. It was a miracle. Everyone was so tired. Where should we go? We came into small Italian Alpine villages—only to hear something terrible.

" 'The Germans are here!' "

Nearly five hundred were captured by the SS. Many were picked up on the streets of the little villages by Nazi patrols.

"After such suffering and loss," Ićak said, "after climbing those terrible mountains they were deported to Poland—to die."

Manya took up the story of their new flight from the Nazis. "We were sleeping in a barn—Papa and the boys. We were together, all except Mama. As far as we knew she was still in Gurs. In the morning we heard someone yell, '*Die Deutschen sind hier.* The Germans are here.' We jumped up and ran back into the Alps. The Italian peasants were wonderful, but they were scared to death. They told us several villages had been burned because they hid Jews.

"So we hid out in the woods with no blankets, no food, no shelter. My father traded his gold wedding band for a piece of canvas, so we had some covering over our heads when it rained."

Manya put her hand over her eyes. A deep sigh rose from her body.

"We ran into the Italian partisans. They wouldn't take us, either; they said they didn't have enough food or ammunition. We kept wandering in the mountains until we knew it was too dangerous to stay together. We had to separate. It was a terrible decision. Somehow I ended up in Rome and wonderful nuns hid me in a convent for nine months. If not for them, I wouldn't have made it."

She stopped talking. Her forehead was wet with perspiration. "Why is it so emotional? Why can't I talk about it? In the convent there was hardly any food, only old chestnuts for breakfast, lunch and dinner, which the nuns shared with me to keep me alive. I don't know now where my father is. I don't know where my brothers are. I don't know if Mama is alive."

On the deck, I could hear behind us people talking. The MP medic was dispensing pills and cheer. Children were running, laughing. But our group did not stir.

CHAPTER ELEVEN

A sudden silence woke me.

The ship's engines, pulsing rhythmically day and night like the heart of a man, had stopped. The ship lay immobile.

I switched on the light over my bunk. It was one o'clock in the morning, just twenty-two hours since our first air raid. Were more bombers over us? Were more Nazi planes ferreting us out?

But this time no bells were ringing, no alarms sounding, no voices piercing the ship. Only the dead silence. Someone knocked on our cabin door. I flung on a robe. Caroline and Mary sat up, startled, in their bunks.

An MP stood at the door. "It's a submarine attack. You must go below and tell the refugees to be absolutely still."

I changed swiftly into warm clothes. In the silence of the ship, my heart pounded in my ears.

I raced down to the refugees' holds. Most of the people were awake, lying frozen in their bunks. I put my fingers to my lips to show them that we must not even whisper. Some lay staring up at the narrow ledge above them, their eyes glazed with terror.

In the weird silence, my mind conjured up a picture of a Nazi U-boat honing in on us with deadly missiles, piercing the welded steel, exploding into fire and smoke and chaos. I walked the narrow paths between the bunks hoping to allay their fears and mine with a squeeze of the hand, telling myself, Don't worry, with all the guns aboard and warships around us we'll survive the submarine just as we survived the bombers last night. I wasn't comforted. The ship lay motionless, like a cornered man playing dead.

After a while, my heart stopped thumping. Convinced that the refugees would remain silent, I went back up the ladder to the main deck.

The ships had formed a double column to sail through the Straits of Gibraltar. A searchlight from the shore now swept across our deck, then traveled down the water, east to west, lighting up the doubled column. A few minutes later, an airplane, burning navigational lights, flew low along the path the searchlight had paved. It was flying west to east, from the Atlantic to the Mediterranean. Was it a friendly British plane coming out of the airfield on the Rock, or a Luftwaffe plane flying out from Spain?

Our AA guns were frighteningly silent.

I climbed down the ladder to the soldiers' hold. They lay rigid. If there was panic, it was internalized.

We were like a ship of living ghosts.

Out of the stillness, a soldier in a bunk near the ladder hoarsely ejected the words "It's because of you and the lousy Jews."

Suddenly we heard the all-clear. The silence broke, the engines churned, pulsed, breathed. We were moving.

The hold came alive. "We made it. By God, we made it." A few of the soldiers wept.

I climbed back up and paced the deck. We had been saved again. But the soldier's words, mouthed in anger, rang through my head. Perhaps it was hysteria; perhaps the thought of dying now in a submarine attack had made him lose control. He needed a scapegoat.

I leaned against the rail, tormented. The fire of anti-Semitism

Hitler had lit in Germany was re-igniting brushfires in other countries. And one of those brushfires was right on our ship.

The irony of it. On this one ship we had refugees running from the Nazis and soldiers wounded by the Nazis. Both were victims. Both had a common enemy. But the angry soldier could not see that we were all in the same boat, in the same war.

Lieutenant Martin joined me at the rail. "I guess you can't sleep, either," he said.

"We had a pretty close call, didn't we?"

"How close we'll never know. Our sonar picked up propeller sounds. We're pretty sure it was a U-boat that caught the sound of our propellers. Thank the Lord, when we turned our engines off, the sub lost us."

Mirković's voice floated across the deck. Sitting in a circle of women and men, he beckoned me to join them. "Come sing with us."

I sat on the deck, next to him, looking at some of the young women, who were seductive enough to stop traffic on Times Square. Maybe if the soldiers could see them and hear them sing, maybe we could put out one little brushfire of prejudice.

"How would it be, Mirković," I asked during a pause, "if we got a group together like this to entertain the soldiers?"

"Entertain the soldiers! I'd love it."

"Do you mean it, Ruth?" Manya asked. "Would you really let us entertain the soldiers? We owe them so much."

"Wait here," I said. "I'll be right back."

On the bridge I found Captain Shea. "Captain, would it be possible to relax the rules against fraternization?"

He seemed disconcerted. "Do you realize what bedlam you'd create? You've got to keep the soldiers and refugees apart to run a tight ship. Some of those gals you've got are pretty . . . uh . . . uh . . . and some of our soldiers are . . . uh . . . uh . . . ."

"Captain, that's not what I mean. We've got some wonderful singers. Professionals. I'd like to see the rules relaxed so the refugees can go to the soldiers' deck and put on a show."

Shea's Irish face lit up. "Say, that's a first-rate idea. When can you put it on?"

"I can round the artists up right now. We can have the performance tomorrow."

"We'll give you all the help you need I'll watch it myself."

Elated, I went down the bridge to search for Abe Tauber. Standing in the doorway, I sat him in the midst of a group of wheelchaired soldiers. Some of the men were laughing. A few looked withdrawn, morose. I waited until the laughter subsided.

"Abe." I drew him aside. "I need your help."

It took less than a minute to tell him the plan. His enthusiasm was like an electric charge.

We hurried through the ship to the foredeck and beckoned the people to the area in front of the blackboard. I introduced Abe, who stood in his white undershirt, his freckled face eager and smiling. He was poised for action.

"I've asked Abe to help us put on a show for the soldiers," I told the people. "We're asking for volunteers—singers, dancers, entertainers. Any of you who would like to take part, please come forward right now."

The crowd moved to make an aisle for volunteers. Mirković came forward with Manya and Edith Semjen.

"Otto Presser," someone yelled. "Where is Otto Presser?"

"He's down below," someone else called out.

Two men went to the 'tween deck and soon returned with the small vaudevillian. Behind him came the composer, Charles Abeles, also small, pale-faced, with steel-rimmed glasses, and a sixty-two-year-old violinist, Samuel Landau.

More singers and musicians approached us.

Abe flung his arms out wide. "We have enough talent here to entertain a whole army. Let's begin."

We began the rehearsal on the deck, with the refugees themselves our first audience, applauding enthusiastically.

Someone handed Mirković a white handkerchief. He folded the handkerchief into a triangle, put it into the breast pocket of his silk pajamas and bowed to the audience. "One has to preserve the dignity of one's appearance at all times," he announced.

The refugees sat listening, their faces wreathed in delight, as he began to sing. The years of flight and hunger had not damaged his glorious voice. Yet there were some who sat hugging their bodies, so enclosed in grief that they seemed to hear nothing.

In the yeoman's office I typed an announcement of the performance and cranked it on the mimeograph machine. Then I climbed up and down ladders distributing copies in the pilot house, the mess hall, wherever I could find soldiers, passengers and crew.

Later that night I lay awake in my bunk. There was no air in the cabin. I knew we had talent and beauty. Still, I had no idea how the soldiers would react. Would the few who had shown their resentment to me lash out against the refugees? And how would that resentment affect the refugees?

Perhaps it would have been better to prepare the soldiers. Perhaps I should have typed up some of the case histories for distribution among the men. Let them know of Mirković's bravery, starving himself while he helped feed not only refugees but British airmen hidden in Rome.

In the dark, I shook my head. Case histories were scarcely the kind of reading matter wounded soldiers were looking for. They had suffered too much themselves. They might listen and even enjoy a few words about International Harry or the climb over the Alps. But as more people each day came forward revealing the whole fabric of pain and terror, of courage and survival, I knew I could not capture their stories on a mimeograph machine.

No, the soldiers had to *see* the refugees, *hear* them, *sense* them.

I finally fell asleep.

The next day dawned warm, the sea calm. We spent the morning with another dress rehearsal and at two-thirty assembled the troupe.

"Good luck. *Hals und Beinbruch*—break a leg," some of the refugees shouted as we left our deck, opened the watertight door and marched through the corridors toward the once-forbidden soldiers' deck.

Abe, in a fresh white shirt and chino pants, patted some of the performers on the back as he moved up and down through the corridor. "You're going to knock those GIs dead."

Through the hatch doorway, I looked out as the deck filled up with soldiers in wheelchairs, heavy casts imprisoning their arms or legs. Others hobbled out on crutches or canes, the walking wounded. Still others came, the battle-weary, the battle-shocked, the ones who, coming home with both legs and arms, would still carry the scars of war.

Behind them came pilots, navigators, bombardiers who had finished their missions, doctors and nurses, army and navy officers, and off-duty crew.

At the stroke of three, Abe stepped onto the improvised stage. Behind him, smiling radiantly as if they were on the stage of Radio City Music Hall, came six of our most beautiful young women.

Instantly the deck came alive with whistle calls, shouts. "Whoopee." "Hubba hubba." "Hey, good lookin'; what's cookin'?"

"Ladies and Gentlemen," Abe shouted, "our National Anthem."

Those who could stand rose to their feet, others pulled themselves tall in wheelchairs. The strong young voices filled the deck. Inside the doorway, I sang with them. The land of the free and the home of the brave had never seemed so precious.

Abe, master of ceremonies, began the program with a Bob Hope-like routine of off-color stories he had picked up in Italy from the troops. The soldiers laughed appreciatively even as they kept their eyes fixed on the six young women. Feeling the excitement they engendered, the young women waved at the men, who continued to wave frantically.

"Now, fellows," Abe said, his high-spirited voice ringing out across the crowd, "when you get back to the States—and we're all going to make it safely—" he waved at the warships in our convoy—"I just want you to remember one thing: that the language you used on this side of the ocean is not quite the same that we use on the other side, the American side. For example, when you're sitting with your family—and I hope you will soon—you don't say, 'Pass the fuckin' butter.' "

Some of the men slapped their white casts, laughing.

All eyes were on Abe. The afternoon sun burnished his red hair. "And another thing," he went on, "when you get back home, if someone talks about 'pro' they mean a professional, like a golf pro. They don't mean a prophylaxis station."

More laughter.

"Now," Abe ended his routine, "it is my pleasure to introduce Edith Semjen from Yugoslavia."

Edith stepped forward.

"Hubba hubba. Look at that tomato."

Edith motioned to sixteen-year-old Ernest Spitzer. Ernest pulled apart the bellows of his accordion for the opening bars as Edith placed her hands on her slender hips and in a husky cigarette-coated voice sang "You are my sunshine."

The soldiers screamed, "More!" They slapped their thighs and their casts. "Beat me, Daddy, eight to the bar."

Stretching her arms out toward the soldiers, Edith sang the refrain again.

The whistles and shrieks caromed off the deck into the sea.

More shrieks as Manya stepped forward, slender, graceful. A breeze from the water seemed to blow through her father's shirt. Poised and smiling as if she were in a Paris nightclub, she sang an aria from Franz Lehár's operetta *das Land des Lächelns—The Land of Smiles*.

The soldiers beat on their casts. "More. More. More. More."

"Before the war," Manya said, "before all the terrible things, I learned a Hungarian song in German called 'Pustalied.' It was from a musical comedy and we had the record. That's how I learned a lot of my songs—from records and the movies and the radio."

The soldiers listened, their eyes riveted on the tall young woman singing with a catch in her voice, as if she were singing of her own life, *"Mädel, so bist du.* Young girl, this is what you are."

This was truly what Manya was, I thought, watching the men smiling as I had not seen them smile before. How would they react if they knew that the pale, willowy young woman with the sweet soprano voice had survived five concentration camps?

The Atlantic was becalmed, our ship held its place in the convoy as Abe introduced the other entertainers. The afternoon was speeding as Otto Presser did an Eddie Cantor-like song-and-dance vaudeville routine. Livia Finger, a handsome star of the Budapest Opera, sang "The Last Rose of Summer."

Anny Pick, a young vivacious brunette, sang Yiddish songs, moving her hips and her rounded body with such infectious joy in life that the men guffawed.

Eva Bass stepped forward, as waiflike as Edith Piaf, with straggly black hair cut like a boy's and dark tragic eyes. In a shabby man's sweater and baggy pants she held the men spellbound.

Like Piaf she had been a nightclub singer in Paris. Fleeing to Italy, Eva had been thrown into prison, "a victim of politics, a victim of my religion," she had told me one evening as we sat on the deck, her baby Yolanda in her arms, her son Joachim at her side. His twelve-year-old body was that of a six-year-old, his face pinched and frightened. Carrying Yolanda in one arm and, when Joachim could no longer walk, carrying him in the other, she had trekked for sixty kilometers through the fighting lines to reach the Allies.

While Eva's voice pierced the deck, I slipped through the hatch door and walked toward the rail. I stared at the troop ship carrying the Nazi prisoners of war and, beyond the POWs, the convoy of warships escorting us to America.

Abe's high, hoarse voice came through the loudspeaker. "Now I have a special treat. The leading baritone of the Yugoslav National Opera. Mr. Leo Mirković."

Mirković, jaunty in his silk pajamas, drew himself tall. "Now

I sing,'' he said in the words he was learning in our English class, "Italian song.''

The soldiers sat absorbed.

He bowed deeply from the waist. "Now in Spanish I sing 'Lolita.' ''

Mirković was magic. "For end, I sing aria from *Barber of Seville,* by Rossini.''

Flinging his arms wide, raising his voice to the heavens, he punctured the air, the ship, the convoy, the whole microcosm of the war with the joyous words, "Fee-gah-ro. Fee-gah-ro. Fee-gah-ro.''

The soldiers screamed their delight. Mirković sang encore after encore.

"Another one, Manya,'' the soldiers shouted. "Come on, Edith.'' "Eva, come back.''

The afternoon sun was beginning to sink. Winds had come up; the Atlantic was growing choppy. But no one moved. Even the bell announcing dinner failed to convince the soldiers the performance had to end. They continued clapping, whistling, calling for more until Abe brought all the performers out to take final bows.

CHAPTER TWELVE

Euphoria and congratulations for the performers spilled over into the morning English class, where the people could talk of little else but the performance.

When the class ended, the people dispersed, some to write their life stories, others to sun themselves wherever they could find space. I walked toward Dr. Juda Levi, a distinguished-looking silver-haired jurist from Yugoslavia, who sat surrounded by several middle-aged men. Suddenly a little Polish boy raced in front of us, tripping over Dr. Levi's feet.

Levi shouted in Serbo-Croatian, "*Polako, polako!* Go slowly, go slowly!''

But to the Polish Jews on the deck the word *polako* had only one meaning—the denigrating insult *Polak.*

A Pole rushed forward and punched Dr. Levi in the chest. A Yugoslav tackled the Pole. From all over the deck, Poles and Yugoslavs converged, bloodying each other's nose, blackening each other's eyes. New fights and arguments broke out. People hurled insults at each other. MPs called to the deck, pulled the bruised and angry men apart.

At last calm was restored. Some of the women brought cloths to wipe the blood from the men's faces, though no one was seriously hurt.

During the air raid I had seen ugly prejudice among the soldiers. Now I was seeing ugly prejudice among the refugees.

Angry and disappointed, I went back to my cabin, hoping to be alone to sort out my feelings. The cabin was empty. I stretched out on my bunk.

Here they were, refugees fleeing murder and war, yet they were fighting their own age-old battles as patriots and even chauvinists of the countries that had tried to annihilate them. In the confines of our ship the fight mirrored the Balkanization of Europe.

Captain Korn, Stauber and I met for our nightly conference in the chaplain's cabin. This night we knew we would have to face the problem of nationality prejudice before it exploded even more violently.

We decided to set up three committees, one representing the Yugoslavs, one the Poles, and one the Austrians and Germans, the major nationality groups. Later we could have committees representing the smaller groups. Korn asked Fredi Baum, the multilingual young Yugoslav, to discuss the committees with the people and bring three representatives to meet with us in the morning.

Fredi ushered in three men who had already emerged as leaders: Dr. Juda Levi, representing the Yugoslavs, Dr. Artur Hirt, a judge representing the Poles, and Dr. Ernst Wolff, a well-known novelist who would represent the Austrians and Germans.

Dr. Levi spoke first. "Before we ask our questions, I would like to make a statement. I want to thank the three of you and the great President Roosevelt for saving our lives. Without your help, we would still be wandering, hungry, hunted, unwanted. We are deeply grateful to you for this noble act of humanity."

"Hear, hear," the Polish judge voiced approval.

Levi leaned forward. "Now you have brought us as leaders to discuss our problems. I would say our first problem is critical. How will you house us in America? Will we be thrown together, people from eighteen different countries, will it be the way we are thrown together in the bunks down below? If so, I think it would be a disaster. I strongly recommend that you keep us together according to our nationalities."

"*Behüte Gott.* Heaven forbid," shouted Dr. Ernst Wolff. He took his glasses off and wiped them with a handkerchief. "You keep us together by nationalities and what happened yesterday will be nothing compared to the fights that will break out. You'll have chaos."

"It is the only way," Dr. Levi argued. "I wasn't insulting that little Polish boy. It was a question of language. We don't speak the same languages. Put us all together and you will have a crisis every day. We are Christians and Jews, yet even the Jews among us don't speak the same languages. Many of the Ashkenazim who come from Germany or Eastern Europe speak Yiddish. We Sephardim, who come from the Balkans, speak Ladino. It's to Spanish what Yiddish is to Middle High German. Because we're the descendents of the Jews who were expelled from Spain, we have a Spanish background and Spanish culture. We have different values, different points of view. You can't put us together with people from Germany and Poland."

"But among the Jews there is a common bond," I said. "The bond of Jewishness."

"It is not enough," Dr. Levi argued, "to keep us living together under one roof. We can meet together in synagogue, in work, in schools, but living together under one roof—"

"Excuse me, but I disagree with Dr. Levi one hundred percent." Ernst Wolff turned toward me. "I agree with you there is a bond of Jewishness that links us all together. But I see our problem of housing in a different way. I speak as an Austrian, but I can't understand all the Austrian people. I believe you should put people together who have a similarity of interests and culture. Like writers and artists, doctors and lawyers."

Hirt, the Polish judge, curled his thin lips sardonically. "My dear lady and you two gentlemen from America, you should know you have two distinct groups here—the intellectuals and the nonintellectuals. You have the highly educated and the very simple. The wishes of one and the other are not the same. Here, packed like sardines, we are thrown into one kettle. But the two groups, I tell you, must be separated."

Anger was rising in my throat. I tried to keep my voice calm. "Gentlemen, for hundreds of years Europe has been torn by nationality rivalries. Should we be carrying these rivalries onto the ship, into America?"

"Look, madam." Hirt fixed his eyes on me. "You are the

government's representative. You are the father—no, forgive me, the mother figure on this ship. You represent the President of the United States. We are talking honestly and openly with you, because we feel you want to help us."

"I do want to help—with all my heart. But you make it difficult. Why all this squabble about how you'll be housed at Fort Ontario? Why bring Europe's sicknesses to America?"

"Because that's the way it's always been—and will always be. Madam, do you think you can change people overnight? You want peace in the camp, separate us."

"By nationalities," Levi shouted.

"By intellect," Wolff exploded.

Stauber's cheeks grew purplish red. "We cannot tell you now how the people will be assigned to their quarters. I can tell you this, however. You will be living in army buildings that housed troops in the past. They were dormitories for the most part. We are changing that. We are putting partitions in the houses so they will be like apartment houses and families will be kept together. Single people will still be in dormitories. So far that is all we know."

Word of the morning meeting spread across the deck. Dr. Rafailo Margulis came toward me and bowed as if he were still in uniform. He had been a lieutenant colonel in the Yugoslav Royal Army.

"My two sons want to study medicine," he announced. "They were already in medical school when we lived in Belgrade. They will make outstanding doctors."

His two sons were romantic figures on the ship. Rajko, at twenty-five, worked in the ship's dispensary; Aća, or Alex, at twenty-three, spent most of his time courting Renée Reisner, as if they were on a cruise ship. They had met in Aversa, the insane asylum—their assembly point—before boarding the ship.

"You must have the answer," Dr. Margulis pressed me. "You must know whether these young people, so hungry for education, will be able to go to school."

I shook my head, about to tell him I did not know, when the loudspeaker began to crackle.

Everyone stopped talking. Adam Munz was reading the news in German, then Yiddish, then French and Italian.

" 'Monday, July thirty-one. Thirteen hundred heavy U.S. bombers escorted by eight hundred fighter planes have attacked Berlin.' "

No one moved.

'' 'Fires are blazing all over the city. Oil storage tanks are shooting their flames into the sky.' ''

Someone murmured, "Dear God, I thank you."

'' 'On the Soviet front, the Red Army has reached the outskirts of Warsaw.' ''

Adam's voice rang out. "Warsaw is rising."

CHAPTER THIRTEEN

In the next days, while we steamed through the Atlantic, a change came over the refugees and the soldiers. Some of the young women, who had come aboard pale, frightened, haggard, were beginning to blossom as the good food rounded their bodies, and the sun and wind brought color to their cheeks. Soldiers found ways to circumvent the nonfraternization orders and came to the deck to talk and flirt with the girls. Some stood inside the waterproof doorway, bringing chocolate and cookies for the children.

The tension on both decks was beginning to relax. Each day Korn, Stauber and I, meeting with the committee leaders, helped calm the handful of angry men, while I made a discovery—that even in war and danger there is humor on the high seas. The crew of the POW ship were apparently jealous that we were the "glamour girl" of the convoy. Their captain flashed lights to the flagship that we were out of line in the convoy columns.

Commodore Blau, commanding the convoy, flashed us a gentle rebuke. "Have your men keep better watch."

Captain Shea flashed back, "Sorry. But after all we have a few distractions aboard."

"Any worthwhile?" the commodore queried.

The soldiers had indeed found several worthwhile. Romances grew as young American men made trysts with young women and found dark corners on the ship; even the lifeboats became retreats. Married couples, who could not sleep together in the open dormitory holds, made love under blankets on the deck. The sense that each day we were moving closer to the Promised

Land stoked fires that years of hunger and flight had cooled but never extinguished.

On the GI deck, a group of soldiers pelted me with questions.

"When y'all gonna bring those gals back here to sing again?" a Texan with corn-yellow hair and cornflower-blue eyes asked. "Some of them got better gams than Betty Grable."

Laughter rang across the deck. "My wife loves opera," a middle-aged officer said. "She would sure love to hear that opera singer. You think they'll send him to Detroit?"

"We'll only know after we get to the camp in Oswego."

"Hell," the Texan growled, 'y'all ain't set to lock those fillies up in a stockade? That's a waste of good stock."

"Maybe it's a good thing we're bringing in a thousand refugees to America," a paraplegic soldier in a wheelchair mused, as if he were talking to himself. "That show you put on—we saw real people, not some picture we got in our heads of refugees. We saw the kind of people Hitler's been trying to exterminate." He looked down at the stumps of his legs. "Maybe Hitler would like to do that to a lot of us Americans."

In the galley, the GIs who served the food adopted our three little Greek girls, Meropi, five, Stella, six, and Evangelina, four, and their mother, Athanasia Economou, a strong-faced woman dressed always in black, whose husband had been killed by a bomb. Nicknaming the children "the Dionne kids," the soldiers built a little table in the galley so that the Greek family could sit and eat while the rest stood at the counters.

Tuck, the boatswain, fixed a saltwater shower on the deck, and all day children ran in and out of the water laughing, racing each other. Major Allen then surveyed the space. "We gotta give these people a little more room. Let's swing two of these lifeboats off the deck." Tuck was still hoisting one of the lifeboats when a group of women came behind him, hanging their clothes on his line. I recognized Mirković's pajamas.

Time on a ship is different from time on land—especially wartime time. The convoy moved cautiously, scouting the sky and the sea for the enemy; but, for the refugees and the soldiers, time had two frontiers—breakfast and supper. In between were hours to be filled, days, perhaps even weeks. Despite the urgency of reaching a safe harbor, no one could pinpoint how much longer the journey would take. We had already spent a week at sea. The Luftwaffe and *Seebooten* helped chart our course. We filled the time with more English classes, one in American history run by Montgomery of the Red Cross, another in advanced English literature and composition taught by our chief gunnery officer, Lieutenant Don C. Martin. "If my students at the U. of Michigan," Martin told his overcrowded class, "were half as enthusiastic as you, I'd feel the way I feel on this ship. I'm teaching you, but you're teaching me."

One morning I was at the blackboard teaching English when Major Allen, in charge of the armed escort, stepped around the people and came toward me. "You must tell them," he said, "that the name of the ship is secret. And they must not tell anyone where we came from."

I told the people what Major Allen wanted, and then printed on the blackboard: "THE NAME OF THE SHIP IS SECRET. WE CAME FROM THE NORTH POLE." It was another joke we could share, like "How do you feel? I feel fine," when they were miserable with seasickness. Now, walking around the ship, I could hear people reciting to each other in all accents the litany of their first words of English, "How do you feel? I feel fine. The name of the ship is secret. We came from the North Pole."

The classes were made up mostly of adults and girls; the teenage boys had no time to learn English. They worked as part of the crew, the only refugees with access to the ship's giant-sized refrigerators and freezers. The boys had never seen so much food in their lives—crates of frozen chicken, turkeys, frankfurters, beef, all to feed the 2,200 people on both sides of the ship twice a day.

Each morning the boys took out the food the chief steward requisitioned and delivered it to the galleys. Food, once it left the refrigerators, could never be put back. Each evening, when the danger of Nazi boats detecting us through our garbage was lessened, the boys tossed the uneaten food and even unopened crates into the ocean. For teenagers who had been hungry for years, it was heartbreaking. They were compensated by going back to the galley, where they were given Oreo cookies, an American delicacy. Some wanted onions and lemons.

After each meal, the boys scrubbed the galley, mopped up the red linoleum floor. Then, holding twenty-pound sacks in one arm, they threw salt on the floor to prevent anyone from slipping. They had not seen salt since 1941.

The people could laugh and sing; middle-aged couples could relax under awnings the soldiers put up, and hold hands; the children could race around the deck. But the horrors of what they had gone through filled their days and nights.

"I am a refugee, just a single word," Dolly Sochaczewska, a forty-four-year-old Polish woman, told me as we found a corner on the ship where we could be alone. "The meaning of the word 'refugee' can be understood only by those who have heart and are willing to understand."

She had come one morning after the English class. "I am tired now," she said, "but I must talk to you when I'm rested, when my heart stops beating so hard. You are our witness. You are our hope in the new land. Can I meet with you later?" Now in the late afternoon we were talking.

"I am alone," she said. "I belong to the displaced persons. There is no road back to my country. This is why I had to talk to you. I have to continue my life. Until now I could not talk to anyone.

"Just before we came on the ship, I learned that my whole family, parents, three sisters, three brothers, and my fiancé were killed—tortured first, then killed. Poland, my escape, my life in prison, then in a concentration camp—these I'll never forget. But I am surprised what kind of jokes destiny makes with me. Whenever we were bombarded, I tried to help others. People told me that as a woman I was very brave. I am not brave. I wanted to help those who help life. But I could not talk about my own life without opening the wounds, without tearing off the scabs. My life is an open wound."

I searched for words of sympathy.

"No, don't talk. You have helped me—just by listening."

Each day as we moved closer to America, they brought me their stories of incredible survival.

All through the years of Hitler's occupation of the Balkans, people somehow found ingenious methods of escape. Some of them bought passage aboard unseaworthy vessels whose captains promised to sail them down the Danube, through the Black Sea, to Palestine. One of these vessels was the *Pentcho*, an eighty-five-year-old paddlewheel steamer. In charge were a captain and his wife who were both drug addicts.

Hans Goldberger, forty-seven, a former textile merchant from Bratislava, Czechoslovakia, described the voyage of the *Pentcho* one evening when rain had driven us off the deck. I invited him and his wife, Jolan, a dress designer, to my cabin. Mary and Caroline were working in the sick bay, treating the seasick as the *Henry Gibbins* rose on high waves, then fell into troughs.

But Hans and Jolan seemed unaware of the foul weather and the tossing, lurching, battered ship. They took turns telling me how the *Pentcho*, overloaded with 511 refugees, set sail down the Danube in May 1940. For four and a half months their ship lay in the Danube. No country would let them land. No country would give them food or water. They could see restaurants on the shores and hear music from cafés while they starved. They painted the word HUNGER in three languages on the ship, and still no one brought them food.

"Our equipment," Hans said, "consisted of only one anchor, and we had no lifeboats, no life preservers, no radio—in fact, nothing at all."

Rumanian warships finally forced the creaking boat into the open Black Sea. The captain, his mind besotted with opium, led them on a wild journey through minefields into the Aegean Sea. An engine exploded. They were shipwrecked off the Italian Dodecanese. They spent eleven days on an uninhabited rock island, and then were brought by Italian warships to an Italian concentration camp.

Of those who survived, twenty-four from the *Pentcho* were now aboard our ship.

The Goldbergers left my cabin. My notebooks and my brief-case were thick with case histories. I began to see a pattern, a refugee pattern, of flight across mountains, dangerous frontiers, mine-infested waters, of hunger and filth, of bombings, of hiding in caves, of capture, of imprisonment, of obscene torture.

The path of their flight was the path of Hitler's march across Europe. He came to Germany. They fled to Austria. He came to Austria. The Germans and Austrians fled to Czechoslovakia. He came to Czechoslovakia. They fled to Poland. He came to Poland. They fled to France, to Belgium, to Hungary, Rumania, Yugoslavia, to Italy.

They were a cross section of Europe's culture, Europe's occupations, Europe's nationalisms. Living with them on the ship made me aware that the most indestructible thing in the world is man. He survives the Gestapo, he survives the Vichy French, the Yugoslav Ustashi, the Poles and Ukrainians who helped in the slaughter. He survives hunger and wanderings and crippling torture. These people lived because they scratched and tore and hid and bought false identity papers, and never believed in their own death.

I realized that every one of them was alive through a miracle. But I began to see something far more profound. That every Jew in the world was alive through a miracle. That since Egypt's Pharaoh, persecutors had tried to do to Jews what Hitler was now trying to do in Europe. Before Hitler, I was an innocent, convinced that some day there would be no more nationalism, no more racism, no more anti-Semitism. Hitler had taught me I was wrong. I became a "Hitler Jew" with three thousand years of history.

Now I realized that even if we were born Jews, there was a moment in our lives when we *became* Jews. On this ship, I was becoming a Jew.

Like some mythical leviathan taking us farther and farther from the furnaces and hell of Hitler, the ship had become a journey out of darkness and fear, out of despair and death, to hope and life and light. From this voyage on, I knew, my life would forever be inextricably interlocked with Jews. I felt myself trembling in the Atlantic night, trembling not from the wind but from the revelation.

We had been at sea for ten days when Captain Shea announced to the crew, "Three more days we should be there. Any of you who have wives or sweethearts in America, speed the ship one knot."

On Tuesday, August 1, knowing it was to be one of our last nights in the Atlantic, we sat in little groups on the deck floor, singing songs in Yiddish, in Italian, in French, and popular songs in English. But Eva Bass, with her baby in her lap, seemed so drained she could neither sing nor smile.

Their lives, Dolly had said, were open wounds.

The waves were swishing against our hull. The moon lit up the deck, spreading gold over the water, over their faces and their ragged clothes. Were they thinking, as I was, that this same moon was shining down on the trucks with quicklime, on the Alpine mountains they had crossed, on the death camps?

I went below to the hospital. Six-month-old Elia Montiljo, the only child of Maria and Morris of Yugoslavia, was fighting for her life. Born in a concentration camp, malnourished in the first critical months of her life, little Elia had contracted pneumonia on the ship.

I sat holding the young mother's hand. "Make them keep her alive," she pleaded, her eyes filled with tears. "Don't let her die."

The refugee doctors hovered over Elia. They shook their heads. "She's gone."

I took Maria in my arms.

"She couldn't live," Maria sobbed. "She had to die before we reached America."

A ship's officer cut a white bedsheet and made a shroud. A carpenter built a tiny wooden coffin on white wooden legs. Little

Elia was placed in the coffin on a soft white pillow. Two candles were placed at each end of the little coffin. All night we held a vigil as friends came down to sit with the heartbroken father and mother.

Elia, we decided, should not be buried at sea. She would come to America, the guest of President Franklin Roosevelt, to be buried in a graveyard in Oswego.

PART THREE
The Oswego
Adventure

CHAPTER FOURTEEN

Thursday morning, August 3, our dark ship began to glow like a plain woman who becomes beautiful on her wedding day. Excitement built up in every corner—among the refugees, the wounded soldiers, the officers, the sailors giving the ship new spit and polish.

"Today," we told each other, "today's the day. Today we reach New York."

Only the weather was not cooperating.

Except for a few days, most of the voyage had been in warm, golden sunlight. Now we had storm warnings; a hurricane was moving toward us in the Atlantic.

By midafternoon the rain stopped, but the sky remained ominously overcast, so that we saw almost no land until we moved into the bay. Suddenly she emerged, the green mythic figure. The Statue of Liberty. The thousand refugees waved at her joyously, tearfully, as if she were a granite Mother welcoming them to the new homeland.

"The greatest day of my life," a bearded old man wept.

"Mine too," I said.

The people moved aside to let Rabbi Mossco Tzechoval come toward me. He could have stepped out of a Rembrandt painting, with a black beard framing his chalk-white face.

"With your permission, I would like to conduct a service now, while we are passing the Statue of Liberty."

"Of course."

The people grew silent. The rabbi knelt and kissed the iron deck. Then he rose and pronounced the Shehehiyanu. We joined him in the ancient Hebrew prayer, giving thanks that we had survived to this day.

The people listened, their eyes still glued to the statue, as he spoke.

"We must never believe the things the Nazis say about us— that we brought evil upon the earth. We did not bring evil upon the earth. Wherever we wandered, we brought the blessings of the Torah. The countries that have tried to destroy us have brought evil upon themselves."

His eyes swept across the silent faces on the deck. "As we enter America, remember we are one people. We must speak with one voice, with one heart. We must not live with hatred. We must live with love."

He held his palms outstretched, the thumbs joining, as if he were touching our heads in the benediction. "May God bless you and keep you and make His countenance to shine upon you and bring you peace. And may God bless this new land."

"Amen," we sang in unison.

I felt a surge of pride and patriotism. This was my city. My country. "Do you know what it says on the base of the statue?" I wanted the people to feel toward America as I felt. "It's a poem written by Emma Lazarus, an American Jewish woman. She was a Sephardic Jew, born in New York, with her roots in Spain. She wrote this about eighty years ago, after she heard the terrible stories of the massacre of Jews in Russia."

I pulled the lines of the poem out of my memory:

"Give me your tired, your poor,
Your huddled masses yearning to breathe free,
The wretched refuse of your teeming shore,
Send these, the homeless, tempest-tossed, to me:
I lift my lamp beside the golden door."

"When we tie up," Major Allen prepared me for our arrival, "army people will meet us. From here on, the refugees are under the Second Service Command—headquartered at Governor's Island. They'll be giving you the orders. The Navy is in the picture, too."

The navy chaplain, Captain Joshua Goldberg, had already come aboard with the harbor pilot. "What about the press?" I asked Allen.

"Press!" The Army won't allow civilians anywhere near us. It's wartime. Spies can pose as reporters. If they do allow photographers, they'll be carefully screened soldiers from the Signal Corps."

Sailors tossed our lines out at Pier 84. The sign over the green-patinaed shed read: "Hamburg-America Line." We had escaped the Germans only to come home to the pier they had once owned.

Wounded soldiers were carried down the gangplank on stretchers and lifted into the waiting ambulances. Behind the stretcher cases came men in wheelchairs, pushed by their buddies, then the soldiers on crutches, ambulatory men, the airmen, the Red Cross workers, doctors and nurses, all hurrying to make connections and get home.

Only the refugees did not leave.

The officers of the Second Service Command, in summer uniform, came aboard with new orders. "Tell the refugees," they told me, "they are to spend the night aboard the ship. Tomorrow morning we begin disinfestation and processing."

No one complained. The people stood on the deck, fascinated by the New York skyline and the frenzied activity on the dock.

I stayed for a while and then began saying goodbye.

Olga, holding International Harry, looked at me tearfully. "Ruthie, are you going to be like all the others? You'll leave us now, and we'll never see you again."

"I'm only going home for the night," I tried to reassure her. "My mother and father haven't heard from me for weeks. I've got to show them I'm really alive. I'll see you again, I promise."

"Come back soon," the people shouted as I followed a soldier carrying my bag down the gangplank. Was it only thirteen days since I had climbed the Jacob's ladder in Naples and begun this voyage?

On the pier crowded with army jeeps and trucks, I looked for the Signal Corps photographers. There were none. I clutched my camera bag with its rolls of precious undeveloped film. The only photos of the refugees on our ship were in this bag.

Dusk was falling as the yellow cab drove toward the Williamsburg Bridge. The bridge led to Brooklyn.

Off Bushwick Avenue, the cab turned into Harmon Street, its quiet one-family houses shaded by broad maples. We pulled up in front of the castlelike gray stone house with its stoop on which I had sat as a child reading books. I rang the bell under the stoop.

My mother came to the iron gate. "Thank God. Thank God," she screamed toward the back of the house. "Dave, she's home!" I bent down to throw my arms around her.

She bustled ahead through the hallway to the huge kitchen. "God answered my prayers. Did you eat? You must be starved. Let me look at you. I bet you never went to sleep."

I smiled. Her questions needed no answer.

My father hurried in from the backyard with a newspaper under his arm. He took my face between his hands and kissed me.

We sat around the kitchen table, my mother bouncing up and

down to bring more food. Now at last I could tell them what my mission had been. My father listened to the stories of the people, stroking his white mustache. His handsome face, framed in white hair, looked stricken; shadows of grief drew dark lines around his mouth.

"What's next for you?" he said.

"I don't know, Pop. I have to call Ickes first thing in the morning. Then I'll find out. Now I'd like to take a bath." I kissed them both good night, climbed the stairs, filled the pink bathtub and lay back luxuriating in the hot sweetwater. I could still taste the cold saltwater showers on the ship.

Relaxed and refreshed, I stretched out on the bed I had slept in since I was a child, wide-awake, my mind churning.

How could I tell Ickes the story of this voyage? How could I compress into the ten or fifteen minutes he usually gave me the life stories of a thousand people?

From the bookcase next to my bed I pulled out the well-worn, cloth-covered *A Thousand and One Nights*. A thousand. A thousand romantic tales to entertain a sultan and his harem. The stories I was bringing back to a small man in a blue-carpeted office would not entertain him. On the ship they had torn me apart. Some of the people, like Manya, were still bleeding. And I bled with them.

How could I tell this all to Ickes?

"I'm glad you're back." Ickes sounded cheerful on the telephone the next morning. "What did you find?"

"Incredible stories, Mr. Ickes. Of terror. Heroism. Survival."

"I want to hear them when you get back to Washington. But this is what I want you to do now. Dillon Myer has sent his public-relations chief, a man called Morrill Tozier, to New York to meet the press."

"But the Army says no press."

"Well, there's been such an uproar from the newspapers that the Army has backed down. Since you're the only one who knows their stories, I want you to help Tozier and his men. They're waiting for you in the Empire State Building."

"I'll get right over there."

"After that I want you to escort the refugees up to the camp and stay with them for a few days until they're settled."

"Fine." I could keep my promise to Olga immediately.

"Then come back to Washington and give me a full report."

*　　*　　*

At the Empire State Building, Tozier looked harassed. "The press is on our backs screaming, 'We want to see the first real live refugees.' Late today the Army is going to move the refugees to Hoboken by ferry and take them from there by train to Oswego. They've agreed to let the press meet the people inside the Hoboken railway terminal." He paused. "We'd like you to choose ten people and introduce them to the press. We'll meet you and the refugees early this evening in Hoboken."

I taxied back to Pier 84 and hurried up the gangplank. The threatened hurricane had given way to a balmy summer day. A Red Cross ship had come alongside the *Henry Gibbins*, and women in Red Cross uniforms were smilingly handing up to the refugees doughnuts, sandwiches, coffee and soft drinks. A military brass band sat on the main deck entertaining the people with an unending medley of popular songs.

The ten men and women whose stories I thought would most affect the press all agreed to be interviewed. I mimeographed their case histories and returned to the deck.

Sixteen-year-old Paul Arnstein stared at the towers etched into the sky. "I've seen this skyline so many times in the movies. It was always unreal. Now it's real, and I can't believe it."

"All night I stayed up," Zlatko Hirschler told me, "and I just looked at the electric lights. Do you know what it means to see a city lit up when you've lived in blackouts for more than three years? To know that planes won't bomb you. To know you won't be arrested by Nazi patrols for walking the streets at night. It was worth staying awake all night, just to feel that."

But many were distressed. Early in the morning they had been taken along the wharf to a Quonset hut, where the men were separated from the women. They were terrified. Separation in the camps meant death.

"We had to strip naked." Eighteen-year-old Margareta Spitzer was still pale. "We had to march in front of soldiers. Then the soldiers began to shoot us all over our bodies with DDT. They put our clothes through a gas chamber to disinfect them. Most of the clothes they put in that steam are ruined—burned or shrunk or full of holes. Anything in leather was destroyed."

"They sprayed us all over from head to toe." Rolf Kuznitzki ran his hand expressively from his head down. "But several parts of our body they sprayed especially. You know what parts I mean." With a touch of irony he added, "They don't want lice or insects coming from Europe—like us—without passports."

The refugees all had cardboard tags hanging around their necks or twirled around a button. In bold letters the tags read:

"U.S. Army Casual Baggage." Each tag had a number. It was their identity card, their passport to the Promised Land.

The sky was giving up its light when the Army lined us up, led us down the gangplank onto the wharf and transferred us to two huge harbor boats, each with the name of an army general.

Once again we were a swarm of humanity crowding one another in iron decks. Each crowd takes on its own character, its own meaning, its own dynamics. The throng of refugees, ferrying now across the Hudson, staring at New York's skyline as we sailed away from it, were radiant with hope.

Everything in me seemed to be focusing on one goal. I wanted the press to capture in a few minutes what had taken me days and nights to question and learn. I wanted the reporters to grasp, instantaneously, years of terror and running; I wanted them to understand, so that they could tell the rest of the country about human courage and heroism and man's will to live.

But there were pitfalls. I had been on both sides of press tables—interviewing as a journalist, interviewed as a government official. Reporters tried to be objective. But who was really objective? The most widely listened-to radio commentator in America was a Detroit priest, Father Coughlin, a vituperative anti-Semite. Would some of the reporters be Coughlinites?

At Hoboken, soldiers helped the refugees down from the ferries onto the terminal dock of the old Delaware, Lackawanna and Western Railroad. One hundred MPs, in full battle uniform, with several attractive young WACs, lined up at attention. Twelve army ambulances carried off more than a score of sick and elderly, and several pregnant women, to be put on the army hospital car. The rest of us were marched by the MPs into a blacked-out waiting room, cavernous, empty of passengers.

I stepped out of the line and waited to corral the refugees who were to meet the press. We kept together while the MPs moved the throngs of people to the tracks. Some of the soldiers lifted little children from their tired mothers' arms and carried them. Others picked up hand baggage; the grateful refugees hurried at their side, afraid to lose sight of the few things they had saved.

Zlatko Hirschler pleaded with an MP, "Please just let me telephone my sister in Tennessee. To tell her I'm alive—in America."

"Sorry. Our orders are, 'No contact.' "

"But it's my sister. What are you afraid of—Nazi spies? After what we've been through, you can't be afraid of *us*."

The MP was silent. Zlatko reluctantly stepped back into line.

"We've got to make sure," a WAC holding two children by

the hands explained to me, "that the refugees meet nobody and speak to nobody until they're safely in the camp. War precautions, you know."

War precautions had also turned down the lights of the waiting room; even the Tiffany-glass ceiling had been painted black. It was a forbidding setting for a press conference.

A long table had been set up in front of an arched stairway. The conference was to begin as soon as the Army had herded the people onto the trains. The refugees who were to meet the press waited behind the table with Tozier and me. Some looked frightened and bewildered.

"I'm so scared." Mathilda Nitsch's round body was shaking. "What will they ask me?"

"Just tell them the things you told me. Reporters are human, they'll have to be moved by what you went through. They have a job to do. They want a good story."

"But I don't speak English," Mathilda worried.

"I'll translate."

"Look at my clothes. They're full of holes. I wanted to look good when I arrived in America."

I hugged her ample body. "Mathilda, you couldn't look bad if you tried. They'll love you."

As the last of the refugees straggled out of the waiting room toward the tracks, a new crowd of reporters, photographers, radio commentators pushed and shoved one another toward the press table, their press cards protruding from their slouched hats.

Colonel Shaw of the Second Service Command gave the signal to begin. "The trains depart Hoboken at nine-thirty tonight." He looked at his watch. "You have thirty minutes."

"Thirty minutes!" a reporter with purplish jowls and a red bulbous nose spluttered. "How the hell can you get a story like this in thirty minutes?"

The colonel shrugged his shoulders and marched off toward the tracks.

Tozier opened the conference, reading a statement. He quoted the statistics Stauber had garnered on the ship, the number of refugees, the breakdown of the countries they came from. "In Oswego," he explained, "the War Relocation Authority will take over from the Army and administer the Emergency Refugee Shelter in Fort Ontario, one of the oldest military posts in America."

The reporters scribbled rapidly in their notebooks.

"The refugees," he went on, "will be housed there for the duration of the war."

"What happens to them when the war's over?" a middle-aged reporter, who kept studying the faces of the refugees, interrupted.

"They will be returned to their own countries. Every one of them signed a paper agreeing to go back."

"What if those countries are destroyed? What if they have no homes to go back to?" He held his pencil in the air, waiting. He had asked the key question.

"They signed a paper. They'll have to abide by it."

I clutched the edge of the table. I longed to give a different answer. To tell them, "The war's not over by a long shot. Let's wait until the war is over, then we can make that decision." But Tozier represented Dillon Myer and WRA. I could not undermine his statement; and the decision to send them back had been set by the War Refugee Board and the President himself.

A reporter held up a mimeographed sheet. "I have a press release. It's from John Pehle, executive director of the War Refugee Board."

"Read it," a young reporter shouted.

"I'll read this line. 'The arrival of almost one thousand refugees from Italy demonstrates this nation's willingness to participate in an international program to find havens for the survivors of Nazi persecution.' " He turned to Tozier. "Does the President plan to open any more such havens in America?"

I caught my breath. Would Tozier know?

"No plans," Tozier said, "to this date, have been made for the reception of any other such colony. And now," he said swiftly, as though eager to change the subject, "I would like to introduce the special assistant to the Secretary of the Interior who accompanied the refugees on the ship."

I had prepared a statement in my head; instead I said, "You can ask me questions later. But with the time that's left, I think you ought to meet and hear from the people themselves."

"That's right," the *Daily News* man said, leaning against the table. "Get going."

"Let me introduce Dr. Rafailo Margulis from Yugoslavia. He speaks English. You can question him directly."

Dr. Margulis, in a dapper blue beret, a necktie, and a gray suit that had somehow stayed miraculously pressed during the voyage, left the huddle of refugees. He walked upright toward the center of the table, adjusted his glasses, ceremoniously took some handwritten notes from his pocket, and began to read. His voice was formal, precise, as if he were addressing a detachment of troops.

"Allow me to introduce myself. I am a physician and a

lieutenant colonel in the Yugoslav Royal Army. I wish to extend my personal gratitude to the American and British armies who came to our country and are fighting now to liberate us from the Nazi yoke."

A short peppery reporter from *The New York Times* beat his fist on the press table. "Cut the crap, Doc."

Dr. Margulis stood erect and continued to read.

"Listen, Doc," the journalist punched his words across the table. "Thank the Army some other time. We're here to get a story about what the Nazis did to you and what they did in Yugoslavia."

Dr. Margulis seemed oblivious. The press was in an uproar. Irritated, red-faced, some seemed ready to riot.

My fears had been trouble with the press, not with the refugees. "Dr. Margulis,"I said in a whisper, "just answer their questions. They're not the enemy."

He stopped reading, took down his glasses and polished them carefully. Then he looked at the angry reporters.

"It is hard to tell you what the Germans did in Yugoslavia. I think, proportionately, of all the countries Hitler invaded, we are among the ones who lost the most. Of the seventy thousand Jews in Yugoslavia, so far less than four thousand have survived—most of them by fleeing the country."

A reporter, writing furiously in a stenographer's notebook, hardly looked up. "Keep going."

"In my city of Belgrade, there were twelve thousand Jews before the war. As soon as the Germans came, they rounded up all the Jews, put them in the city zoo, and then led them out, hundreds at a time, and shot them. Of the twelve thousand, less than nine hundred are left."

"What about concentration camps in Yugoslavia?" someone shouted.

He seemed not to hear. Once again he lifted his notes and began to read. His words were drowned out by the angry shouts of the reporters. An MP pulled him away from the press table and led him toward the train.

"We have a whole group here," I tried to talk over the din, "ready to answer your questions. You can see how nervous some of them are. Most of them have never met the press. They're tired not only from this long journey, but from years of running and hiding. I will introduce them to you one at a time. I'll try to give you whatever information I can. Then you can question them."

I extended my hand to a thin, frightened woman holding a

little boy close to her body. "This is Serafina Poljakan and her son Milan, who is nine. I will give you a copy of her story with all the others at the end of the conference."

"Just give us the gist now," a serious-faced reporter from the New York *Herald Tribune* called over the hubbub.

"Serafina," I said, "is thirty-six, a middle-class Jewish woman who lived near Zagreb. Her father, her mother and her eighteen-year-old brother were all murdered by the Ustashi, the Yugoslav fascists. She fled to Italy with her husband and little Milan."

"How did she escape? How did she survive?" The reporters threw a barrage of questions, interrupting each other.

Now the *Times* reporter shouted, "Quiet, you guys. Why don't you let her talk? Don't you see she's trying to help us?"

The dark waiting room grew still.

"In 1943, Yugoslav partisans came to the house where Serafina was hiding, searching for Nazi sympathizers. Her husband opened the door; the partisans mistook him for another man and killed him before her eyes. They admitted their mistake and took her and Milan with them into the mountains. For months she and Milan lived among the partisans, hiding. Once she and Milan spent ten days in the woods under pouring rain, unable to get food, while German soldiers were all around them searching for fugitives."

"Ask her how her little boy reacted," the *Herald Tribune* man said.

"Milan," I bent down toward him, "what was it like when you were hiding, with the Nazis around you?"

The reporters waited while Milan whispered, as if he were reliving the months in the mountains. "You always had to speak so low. They were always telling you, 'Shh, shh. The Germans will hear you.' "

Colonel Shaw returned to the press table. "You've got to terminate. We're already late."

"Come on, Colonel," a reporter protested. "We're just getting into the stories now."

The officer crossed his arms over his chest. "I'll give you a few more minutes."

"We'll speed things along," I promised him.

Mathilda was next. "Where do you come from?" a reporter asked her directly.

Mathilda understood his words. She had learned them in the English class on the deck.

"We come from the North Pole."

The reporters burst into laughter. I was beginning to relax.

They lost their hearts to the little Greek "Dionne girls," and roared at the story of International Harry's birth.

Hans Goldberger had just begun answering their questions about the shipwrecked *Pentcho* when Colonel Shaw shoved the reporters aside, lined his MPs up in front of the press table and shouted, "We're half an hour behind schedule. The conference is terminated."

Within minutes, I distributed the case histories. Some of the reporters and photographers, cleared by the Army, were making the night journey with us. On the dimly lit tracks, we jumped aboard the train. The doors closed instantly.

I walked through the dark coaches as the train pitched and jerked from side to side. Most of the children were curled up, sleeping, on the coach seats. Adults were talking in low voices. Through the open train windows came cool night breezes as the train hurtled northward.

A hand reached out to me in the dim aisle. "It's me, Manya. Sit with me a few minutes."

Manya's friend, Ernst Breuer, stood up. "Take my seat. I'll find another one while you're talking."

"I'm scared, Ruthie," Manya said. Over the noise of the wheels I could hear her agitated breathing.

"But you're safe now—in America."

"It's the train. Trains scare me. I know it's—it's not a cattle car, but . . ."

She was silent for a few minutes. Two MPs walked down the aisle. Then the words burst from her. "The soldiers—they aren't shoving us together. They aren't pushing us into those terrible trains, crushed up against each other. People died in them. Still—oh, God, I'm so scared."

"Manya, this is all behind you."

"I know. But I can't help the fear."

Ernst returned, hovering over her.

"Ruthie," Manya said, "go to your seat; you look so tired."

Leaning back in a coach seat, I shut my eyes. We were on our way to the first haven in America—where they were to find rest, surcease from running, time to heal pain, to obliterate nightmares. I should have been filled with joy. Instead, Manya's fear of trains and the key question one of the reporters had asked kept reeling in my head like the wheels of the train: "What happens to them when the war's over? What if they have no homes to go back to?"

CHAPTER FIFTEEN

Light was gently streaking the sky as the people began to stir and wake and peer excitedly through open windows at America's villages, towns and graceful dairy farms.

The train pounded toward Syracuse, then rolled north on a branch line to Oswego until, at exactly seven-thirty, the iron wheels ground to a halt at a railroad siding.

An MP waved his white gloves to the right. "We're at the camp. No one is to leave until we give the order."

The people on the far side of the train rushed across the aisle to gape through the windows for their first glimpse of Fort Ontario.

"A fence! Another fence!" a man gasped. His words, chilling, plunged through the train. For there, stretching as far as we could see, was a tall hurricane fence of chain links, topped with three rows of barbed wire.

Artur Hirt reached forward, rattling my shoulders. "How could you do this? In the free America! It's another concentration camp!"

The train grew ominously silent. "It's an old army post." I tried to dispel some of the fear. "All army camps in America have fences."

I knew my words had no effect. The silence persisted, awkward, nervous, disbelieving.

"The fence doesn't bother me one bit," Kitty Kaufman, a young Austrian traveling with her Yugoslav husband and young daughter, spoke up. "If you ask me, I feel safer behind a fence. Even in America."

The fence, I realized with a start, was a psychological symbol for refugees. For most of the people, the fence meant a prison, a concentration camp, a locked door, an end to freedom. To Kitty, the fence meant security. Her enemy could not enter.

A burst of activity temporarily deflected the anger and dismay of most of the people. There had been no food on the night coach. Milk and cookies were being handed up through the open windows, and children were eagerly munching and drinking, when the Army announced we could begin leaving the train.

The people gathered their hand baggage. I held little Joachim Bass's hand and climbed down the steep steps, suddenly aware that dozens of Oswego's citizens were watching us from the roof of a factory that made tanks.

More townspeople were hurrying out of modest wooden houses lining the street along one side of the fence. Reporters from New York, Chicago, Syracuse, Rochester and the local *Oswego Palladium-Times* swarmed around us. Photographers snapped their shutters, movie cameras rolled—catching the weary and frightened eyes of the elderly, the tentative smiles of teenagers, the lost look of children still without shoes, a violinist clutching his fiddle in a broken case, the knapsacks and torn boxes tied with rope in which many carried their most precious possessions, the flotsam and jetsam of the war, wearing their cardboard tags: "U.S. Army—Casual Baggage."

We straggled into the camp through a side gate at the railroad spur. It was a huge encampment of eighty acres that stretched from the town to the shores of Lake Ontario. A grassy oval parade ground filled the center of the camp, framed on one side by white wooden barracks in which the refugees were to be housed, and on the other, terraced up a small hill, by red brick Georgian houses with freshly painted white columns, the officers' quarters, where the director and part of the staff would live.

Beyond the brick houses was a gray stone rampart and a stone arch leading into the two-hundred-year-old fort itself. And, sitting behind a small table just inside the fence, Military Intelligence officers began the registration and identification, checking the people against a master list.

Multilingual translators flanked the officers; they wore armbands with the word DOLMETSCHER—"Translator"—printed in red ink. They had been sent to the camp by private Jewish and Christian agencies to help the government through these hectic days.

I listened carefully as the army officers began the screening. Would a few, like Artur Hirt, explode again? They had been screened when they were first selected in Italy, to keep out potential fifth columnists or spies. They had been screened again in Aversa, the insane asylum. Some had dropped out during the screening, one reason we had 982 instead of one thousand. Now they were being screened a third time. The questioning was sympathetic, benign. Name. Nationality. Country of origin. Name of spouse—if any. Names of children—if any. Profession—if any. Some were asked if they had firsthand information, photos, documents that could help our Army win the war faster. The screening became a two-way street, with the people offering eagerly to answer any questions to bring victory even one day closer.

"I'm Joe Smart." A small, slender man in an open-necked white shirt extended his hand to me. The director of the camp, he had open clear eyes and a serious face with deep ridges from his nose to his chin. At forty-three he had already had a colorful career, seven years as special agent in the FBI, regional director managing New Deal resettlement projects, regional director of half of the ten Japanese-American relocation centers, and assistant national director of the WRA. He had been working in Peru with the Institute of Inter-American Affairs when Dillon Myer, his former boss, telephoned asking him to take the job in Oswego. Now he was shaking hands, telling those who seemed terrified that perhaps they had come to another concentration camp, "Whenever there is a knock on your door, it will be a friendly one."

Ravenously hungry—we had eaten little all the day before—we were led to the white barrack mess halls, where long tables were stacked with pitchers of steaming hot coffee, bottles of rich cold milk, giant boxes of cornflakes, loaves of white bread, jars of peanut butter and bowls overflowing with hard-boiled eggs.

Manya, her mouth stuffed with one egg, reached into the bowl for another. "We never got fed like this in Gurs."

Customs inspection on the parade ground was fast and cursory. Some of the customs men were misty-eyed as they looked into torn suitcases that held nothing but newspapers, or family photos wrapped in frayed underwear or rags. A customs agent who found only one torn shirt in a battered bag copied the man's name from his tag, spent his lunch hour in a shop and bought the man a pair of pants, a shirt and a jacket.

By midmorning, there was an explosion of euphoria that caught me up in it. I accompanied some of the people to their homes in the two-story white wooden barracks.

"Such efficiency. Only America can do this." Olga Maurer stared at the entrance of her apartment. Her name and the names of her whole family, even International Harry's, were fixed on the door. "I feel already it's mine. My first apartment."

A tiny woman in her midfifties raced down the steps of her barrack near Lake Ontario. "Fräulein Ruth—" Elsa Neumann flung her arms around my waist—"this is more beautiful than anything in Europe. I have a villa by the sea." She sped off to share the news of her villa with others.

The morning sun shone down on the shady tree-lined streets and the huge grassy parade ground where once soldiers must have drilled and horses galloped. Now children were romping and rolling and tagging one another. Some of their parents strolled leisurely like tourists in a resort hotel.

"Come inside." A woman's voice called from a barrack window. It was Kitty Kaufman, who had found security in the fence. I entered her small partitioned apartment to find her stroking two cotton bedsheets. "In the caves of Italy I used to dream about bedsheets."

"And I used to dream about a mattress," her husband, Branko, a photographer, said softly. "How many years since we've seen a mattress?" He stretched out on the uncovered mattress. His face broadened into a smile that seemed to spread through his whole body.

The apartment had been furnished, GI style, with two metal cots, a small table, two chairs and a metal locker. "Please sit down," Kitty insisted. "I'm so sorry I have nothing to offer you to eat or drink."

The bedsheets were still in her arms when Margareta Spitzer called from the doorway of their apartment, "Come see how excited my mother is."

Her mother had opened the bedsheets and was fixing a cot ready for sleep.

"Bedsheets," her mother whispered in awe. Moses' Jews in the desert, I thought, must have whispered the same way as they watched manna falling from heaven.

She took off her shoes, lowered herself onto the precious bedsheet and turned her head to the wall so that we would not see her cry.

In a cab, I left the camp and taxied to the Pontiac Hotel, a three-storied white building set on a lawn far back from the street. It took only minutes to register and to drop my bag in a typical traveling salesman's hotel room. On a small writing table was a pile of stationery with an etching of the Pontiac Hotel on the letterhead and in the center the words "On Beautiful Lake Ontario Along the Roosevelt Highway."

I opened the window. Fresh sweet air rushed in. The Oswego River flowed swiftly below; the rear of the hotel sat on the river's bank.

Back in the cab, the driver took me through the town that had taken a thousand strangers into its midst. The warm sun fell on the busy main streets and the quiet residential avenues that seemed miles and millennia away from the war in Europe. It threw shadows on the churches and schools and the simple one-family frame houses shaded with thick trees. Oswego was smaller than a metropolis, larger than a whistle stop, plain and solid and peaceful and completely American.

In Washington I had read that its 22,000 people were a heterogeneous mix, descendants of immigrants who had come here in the late nineteenth and early twentieth centuries from Germany, Ireland, Quebec, Poland and Italy, and the majority were Roman Catholic.

Like many provincial New Yorkers, I had never heard of Oswego, but in Europe many people had learned about this town in central New York State on the easternmost lake of the Great Lakes. The Office of War Information had selected it as the "typical American community" and filmed a movie as part of OWI's wartime documentary services.

Its polyglot population, I thought as we drove through its tranquil streets, should bode well for accepting refugees from eighteen different countries; and the refugees too would find it charming. For it was part of the picturesque series of locks and canals that make up the New York State Barge Canal System.

It was a town surrounded by water. The Oswego River ran like a blood artery through its very center, dividing it into two equal halves. "Bridge" was the word I saw everywhere; of the two steel bridges flung across the river, one was even called the Bridge Street Bridge. The two main thoroughfares were East Bridge Street and West Bridge Street, and on each of them, flanking the river, were the shops and marts and emporia of American culture and commerce and trade.

The President's choice of Fort Ontario in Oswego was a stroke of timing. The Army had closed the camp in March, and towns-people had rushed to the White House and the War Department, pleading that it be reactivated; Fort Ontario was one of the mainstays of their economy. Thus, Fort Ontario was on the Army's mind when the search began for an available camp for the refugees. Only two campsites were suggested: Madison Barracks in Watertown, New York, and Fort Ontario. The War Refugee Board chose Fort Ontario, and in June the people of Oswego learned, most of them with delight, that the camp was to be reopened and officially designated the Fort Ontario Emergency Refugee Shelter.

I returned to the camp and showed my pass to the guard at the main gate. The only ones given passes were government officials, staff, representatives of the private agencies and the press. The people were to be kept in quarantine for a month, behind the fence.

"How can you have a fence in America?" those who were angry and obsessed again confronted me. But others, born survivors, had already turned the fence into their own bridge. Peering through the chain links, the refugees inside the fence talked and gesticulated in sign language to citizens of Oswego who were talking and gesticulating just as animatedly outside the fence.

Some Oswegonians sprinted home, armed themselves with clothing, especially with children's shoes, and tossed them like baseballs over the top of the fence. Others shoved cookies and candy through the metal chains. A sweet-faced nine-year-old, Susan Saunders, brought her Shirley Temple doll for a wistful little girl her own age. The reporters and photographers immortalized the scene.

Near the Fitzgibbons boiler plant next to the camp, Geraldine Desens, a tall, ebullient brown-haired waitress, braked her bicycle to a halt. Geri had never seen a refugee; these newcomers to her quiet town could have dropped in from outer space. Yet she felt strangely pulled to them.

She heard children shouting eagerly, words that sounded like "Beecycla. Beecycla."

She understood.

"Here, you guys, help me," she called out to three strong young men standing near her outside the fence. They raised her bike over the fence, then lowered it carefully to youngsters who caught it inside. "Go ahead, ride it," she pantomimed. The youngsters took off, careening around the camp.

Geri made a decision. Prowling along the fence, she searched for an underground opening she knew well. A mischievous grin spread across her face when she discovered the hole under the fence.

She raced home and changed into old clothes to look like a refugee. She knew the danger of being arrested for illegal entry. She hurried to the fence and wriggled on her backside through the hole. A woman neighbor gaping through the links shouted, "Geri, what in the name of all that's blessed and holy are you doing in there with all those Jews?"

Geri burst into laughter and walked off, shrugging her shoulders. Her neighbors would never understand. She waved delightedly at the teenagers riding her bicycle like cowboys in the Wild West. Strolling on the grassy parade ground, she stopped Edith Semjen.

"Hello," she said.

"Hello," Edith answered.

"I live here."

"And you're inside the camp?" Edith's eyes sparkled. "How did you get in?"

Geri led Edith to the hole. "We always got in this way; it's right opposite Big Rock, our swimming area; it's a shortcut for us."

"You got *chutzpah*."

"What's *hutz—?*"

"Army says nobody can come in. You find a hole—and you come in. That's *chutzpah*."

The two young women walked around the parade ground, Edith fascinated by Geri's bravado and warmth, Geri by Edith's wide-set brown eyes, her startlingly beautiful figure and her thick blond hair.

"I know a few Jewish people in town, but I never saw a refugee," Geri said.

"A refugee is no different than the rest of the world." Edith waved a cigarette at the people milling the parade ground. A few young women had settled on the grass, their faces upturned so that the warm radiant sun would tan them. "We're like everybody else, only maybe a little bit more tired."

"I guess you went through hell, though." Geri waited. "I guess we Americans can't imagine some of the things you lived through. We only see it in the movies."

"It was hell all right."

"Maybe you don't feel like talking."

"I'll talk. First my brother Darko disappeared. One day the Yugoslav fascists, the Ustashi, came to our house. 'We're taking Darko to a work camp for the summer. Pack a knapsack with work clothes.' We didn't think it would do him any harm. He was just two years older than me. He was a chemistry student at the University of Zagreb. They took him, along with two hundred fifty other students."

Edith lit another cigarette and began to talk rapidly. "We didn't hear from him. Then we started to hear horrible stories. That all the students were taken away and shot and never buried. My father wouldn't believe it. He had good political connections. He was a rich lumberman. He thought he could find my brother and get him out. He went to the Ustashi. They didn't know anything. He went to the Gestapo. They didn't know anything, either. Now *he* was on the list. A few days later they came for him. They took him away to the Yugoslav concentration camp in Croatia; it's a terrible place called Jasenovać. Christians who worked in the camp told us, 'The prisoners had to dig their graves and were shot.' One of them told us my father was hit on the head; he fell down, and they buried him alive.''

"My God."

A young boy whizzed past on Geri's bicycle, but Geri saw only Edith's father falling into an open grave.

Edith lit a new cigarette on the butt of the old one. "It didn't happen only to my family. It happened to every family. I was a rebel; I wouldn't obey army orders, curfews, anything. To save me, my mother sent me to Split. But the Italian Fascists threw me in prison."

"You—in prison!" Geri winced.

"From there they sent me to a concentration camp on one of the islands in the Adriatic. I escaped to the partisans, and I worked with them. I was a secretary, a teacher for little kids, I did whatever was needed. Then the Nazis came—in a big offensive—and I escaped again. To Vis, another island in the Adriatic, with my mother. The partisans brought us to Bari, and from there we came to America." Edith laughed. "And the first day I meet you, an American—another rebel, like me."

Geri looked at her watch. "I've got to go home and change my clothes. I wait tables in a restaurant. When I finish my shift, I'm coming back with the biggest steak I bet you ever saw in your life. And it'll still be hot."

At another part of the fence, Adam Munz drew a shiny dime from his pocket, a souvenir one of the soldiers had given him on the ship. He called out to a boy who seemed sixteen or seventeen, about his own age, "Can this buy a Ping-Pong ball?"

"I think so." The boy took the dime Adam pushed through one of the chain links. "Wait here, I'll be right back." He jumped on his bike and wheeled furiously down the street.

Adam waited. He had dreamed for years of playing Ping-Pong again. Prowling the camp, he had entered the recreation hall and discovered a new table complete with paddles and a net. But no balls.

A few minutes later, the boy, back on his bike and breathless, threw a brown bag over the fence. Adam opened the bag; inside were three gleaming white Ping-Pong balls.

"Thank you. Oh, I thank you. I thank you. What is your name?"

"Jim. What's yours?"

"My name is Adam. Jim," Adam smiled expansively, "you are a big ass."

Jim's face changed from a friendly grin to a puzzled scowl. Others outside the fence looked shocked.

Thinking he had been misunderstood, Adam repeated in a louder voice, "Jim, you are a big, big ass."

He saw the mood through the fence grow dark and threatening.

"What do you mean?" Jim asked.

Adam spreadeagled his arms, thrust his head forward like a plane zooming down on an enemy and spluttered, "Ack-ack-ack." Then he fell to the ground, the enemy plane destroyed. Looking up at Jim through the steel chains, Adam shouted, "The pilot, he is a big ass—just like you."

The grin returned to Jim's face. "Oh, you mean big *ace.*"

Late in the afternoon, I left the fence and the barracks to explore the encampment. Crossing the parade ground, I climbed a broad winding road toward the stone ramparts of old Fort Ontario.

It was the oldest garrisoned fort in the United States, built by the British in 1755. Its cannon and fortifications had protected the British from the French, the French from the Indians, Americans from all potential enemies. The stone wall was a pentagon of five "faces," five jutting points protecting the garrison from invasion.

Slowly I walked around the old fort, overgrown with grass, then left it to wander down toward Lake Ontario, blue-green, sparkling and seeming wide as an ocean. I stood on a cliff, looking out at the endless water, the lighthouse, the thousands of sea gulls screaming, challenging the air.

A sense of solace and refuge washed over me. Here, I thought, the refugees sitting on the banks of this great magical lake may find the peace they have so long yearned for.

Sunday afternoon we gathered for the official welcome on American soil.

Dillon Myer had arrived from Washington with several government officials. We sat with city officials and clergy on the speakers' platform, while the refugees stood on the parade ground.

"I welcome you all in English," Joe Smart, dressed formally in a tie and jacket, opened the meeting. "And Fredi Baum will translate. I know many of you speak other languages and may resent German. However, we are not at war with the German language, only with the Nazi oppressors. We will now sing 'The

Star Spangled Banner.' '' The people listened in silence, the words of the anthem unknown.

Myer read a personal message from Ickes: '' 'I hope that this haven from intolerance, suffering and persecution that you have undergone will in some measure ease your tragic memories.' ''

He paused to let Fredi translate, while Ickes's words etched themselves into my brain. *This haven from intolerance, suffering and persecution . . .*

'' 'I hope from my heart,' '' Myer continued reading, '' 'that the time you spend in this retreat will bring you strength and faith with which to face a future in which the dignity of the individual man will be recognized and assured everywhere.' ''

Would his word be prophetic?

Other speakers followed: Mayor Joseph T. McCaffrey, a large burly figure, offering the hospitality of the city, Anne Laughlin of the War Refugee Board, bringing greetings from John Pehle.

Dr. Juda Levy of Yugoslavia, speaking for the refugees, turned to the dignitaries on the dais. "There is not one single family among us whose members have not been deported and killed by the Nazis."

On the parade ground, the people's faces were a mingling of sorrow, memories, tears.

Then the Reverend A. S. Lowrie of the West Baptist Church brought greetings to the Christian refugees from the Oswego Council of Churches. "You have had a great variety of experiences, dangers and difficulties. These are now in the past, and a new life opens before you."

I caught Mathilda Nitsch gazing at him adoringly, though she understood not one word. "As Christian ministers," he said, "it is our desire to do all we can to make your stay here, in our midst, one you will always remember because of the Christian friendship, fellowship and goodwill extended to you by the people of the city. May God speed the day when war shall cease, when peace shall prevail in the world and all men shall dwell together as brothers in Jesus Christ."

A warm breeze swept across the parade ground, rustling the leaves. Rabbi Sidney Bialik, the rabbi of the Adath Israel Synagogue in Oswego, rose to end the program. "The Talmud says that silence expresses more than words. Your very presence here relates thousands of tragic occurrences, your countenances express numerous horrible experiences and travail at which words are senseless."

The people nodded. He was speaking their truth.

He blessed America, President Roosevelt and the United Nations, and then, joined by many of the refugees, intoned the El Moley Rachamin, the memorial prayer for the dead.

On Monday morning I spoke with Ickes in Washington. I told him of the euphoria, the unexpected beauty of the camp, the "villa by the sea." "Everyone wants to help," I said, "even the customs men. They found a nine-year-old-boy with only torn shorts and a ragged shirt on his back. They made a pool and bought him a whole outfit of clothing, and toys."

"It's good to hear." Ickes's voice suggested he was smiling. "Dillon Myer just left my office. He came back on the sleeper from Oswego. He says you did a fine job on the ship, and now in the camp."

I caught my breath. Dillon Myer—who had done his best to block me from going over.

"He asked me to let you stay on for another couple of weeks; at least until the refugees are settled. I suggest you stay up there for a while longer."

CHAPTER SIXTEEN

"Ernst and I want to get married."

It was early in the morning when Manya Hartmeyer and Ernst Breuer came to see me, speaking urgently. "We asked the captain on the ship to marry us," Manya explained. "But he refused. He said, 'Wait until you get to America.' "

Still wearing her father's shirt, she looked younger than her years, a tall green-eyed child-woman. Ernst seemed older, though he was just twenty-six. The high bones above his narrow cheeks, the pencil-thin mustache, the strong chin made him a dashing figure. In a different time and a different life, he could have been a swashbuckling buccaneer. Now, with haunted eyes, he had the long sober look of maturity.

"I want to protect Manya." He put his arm around her shoulders. "I want to take care of her for the rest of our lives. She's all alone in the world. My family's wiped out, too; only

my sister Lisa, who's here with us, is left. Manya needs me—
and I can't live without her.''

"I don't mind waiting," Manya said, "but Ernst would like
us married." She hesitated, then said slowly, "Today."

"Today!"

"It's not possible?" she asked wistfully.

"It takes time."

I would have to find out first if the War Refugee Board would
allow them to get married during the quarantine; then if New
York State would consider them residents and issue a marriage
license; and, finally, if WRB would give them permission to
leave the camp to register at City Hall so they could get the
license.

"How much time will it take?" Manya asked.

"I can't say."

Strips of light filtered through the vertical bars of my office. It
was the old army jail; when Joe Smart offered it to me
apologetically, I had laughed, "It's okay. Now I too am fenced
in."

Manya was crestfallen. "Can't the rabbi marry us?"

"Certainly, but only after you get a license."

"Don't tell me," Ernst exploded, "that we can't get married
in America."

"I'm not telling you that, Ernst. I'm telling you there are
obstacles because of your extraordinary legal status."

"It's pretty rotten, if you ask me. Why shouldn't two people
in love get married?"

"We'll have to get a policy decision from Washington." I felt
bleak and helpless. "They've got the lawyers. They decide how
to interpret the law."

Ernst's haunted eyes turned fierce. I imagined it was that rage
that had helped him survive. He had been a resistance fighter with
the French underground. His mother had been arrested with
thousands of other Jewish refugees and deported to Auschwitz.
Manya had told me how, with the Nazis searching for him in
Paris, he had escaped to Nice. But the Nazis continued to track
him down and found his hiding place. Once again he escaped.

"Ruthie," Manya said, "I don't like to see Ernst get so mad.
You think it will take long?"

"I'll call Washington today."

She leaned across the desk. "Before I came on the ship, I was
beaten on my body and in my soul. I felt I'm nothing, I'm
nobody. I'm a dirty Jew they're trying to take away from this
earth.''

Her green eyes were moist. "I was like a person falling into a big dark cave, deeper, deeper, nobody cared, nobody helped. Then they took us on the ship and a door opened, a light came through. And the light—that was you. We looked up to you with so much hope and happiness. You represented America to us— the land that was taking us in and shielding us from harm. It's that America that I believe in."

I reached for her hand and pressed it.

"Please, Ruthie. Ernst is my father, my mother, my brother. Please. He wants to get married right away. Help us."

She walked around the desk, pressed her wet cheek against mine, then grabbed Ernst's hand and ran out of the office.

The legal obstacles to their getting married mounted in my brain, a pyramid of nightmares—all because they had entered America outside the immigration laws. Even now, letters were going back and forth between government agencies, trying to define the people's legal status. The War Department wanted to register them as aliens under the Alien Registration Law. Then they would have both a legal and a political entity. The Department of Justice refused. "They cannot be registered as aliens, because they are not aliens."

POWs were aliens. Enemy civilians allowed in from Latin America were aliens. But the 982 refugees, "guests of President Roosevelt," were in limbo. Stateless, paperless, homeless. It was as if this camp on the banks of Lake Ontario were on another planet, isolated from the rest of America, spinning in space.

An American woman, smartly dressed with a straw hat and white gloves, entered my office.

"I am the president of the Rochester section of the National Council of Jewish Women," she introduced herself. "Our national office asked me to contact you." In her hand she held the special pass the private agencies were given.

She took the chair at the side of my desk. "I've been walking around the camp a little, talking to some of the people. God, what they look like. Some are like skeletons. All these years, we charitable organizations have been raising money to help refugees, but we never saw any—maybe one or two, but surely never a whole group like this. Wait until I tell my women. I've already heard that every voluntary agency in the country wants to help you. What can my Rochester women do?"

"Do they sew?"

Her face fell with disappointment. Perhaps she had expected

some lofty lifesaving task. She spoke dryly. "What kind of sewing do you have in mind?"

"We need curtains. Shower curtains especially. The showers are all together at the end of each barrack floor. The men's are on the first floor, the women's on the second floor, four open showers with no partitions, no doors. Some of the women have come to me, pleading, 'Can we have a little privacy?' After what they've been through, it's a high priority."

"A high priority." She leaned forward, her spirits lifted. "What about curtains for the windows? And perhaps bedspreads and tablecloths? They might make the camp a little more homelike."

"They certainly would."

"My members will have those showers and windows curtained by next week—the other things a little later."

"Can you get enough fabric, with the war shortage?"

"We'll get it if we have to beg, borrow or steal. I'm going right back to Rochester and call a meeting."

The telephone rang as she started to leave.

"Don't go yet. It's Flora Rothenberg in your national office in New York." Flora, an old friend, was the executive director of the organization. "Your Rochester president is here right now," I told her.

"That's good. You'll also be hearing from our Syracuse section soon. I want to know how we in National can help, too."

"We have twelve babies, Flora. We need twelve cribs, twelve baby carriages and twelve high chairs."

"My brother is with Gimbels in Pittsburgh. Between him and my organization, we'll rush them up to you. Talk to you again soon."

Two rabbis entered next, one middle-aged, heavily bearded and paunchy, the other young, pale-faced, with a Vandyke beard framing his chin. They wore black slouch hats and heavy black suits crumpled from the hot train ride from New York City. The young rabbi spoke English flawlessly in a singsong rhythm, as though he were rocking his body in morning prayers. They had come from Agudath Israel, an organization of ultra-orthodox religious Jews.

I extended my hand to the younger rabbi, expecting a hearty handshake. He pulled back as if my hand were foul-smelling, evil dirt.

Seeing my embarrassment, he explained. "We are not allowed to shake the hand of any woman except our wives."

He drew a white handkerchief from his pocket and held it before me. I touched the corner and flailed it awkwardly.

"Forgive me. I should have known. Gentlemen, please sit down."

Growing up in a traditional orthodox home, I had never encountered the ultra-orthodox. Silently I vowed to fill the gaps in my education.

"We have come about the children." The middle-aged rabbi stroked his graying beard. "Some have probably never been to school. It is a sin to allow children to go uneducated. We would like to take them to our yeshivas in New York. We have families who would be happy to board them. If you agree, we could take them back with us tonight."

"I appreciate your concern. But we are under quarantine. No one, not even a child, can leave the camp until September first."

"Even to be educated?" he asked in disbelief.

"Education is one of the problems being tackled right now. We don't know yet whether schools will be opened in the camp, or whether children will be allowed to go outside to local schools. But there is something you can do—right away."

"What is that?"

"One hundred sixty people have signed up to eat kosher. We've set aside a kosher kitchen and mess hall. But Rabbi Tzechoval tells me no one can eat in it because the dishes have been used before and therefore are not kosher. Can you get us new dishes right away?"

The two rabbis rose in unison. "You'll see." They hurried out, their black coattails flying.

The next morning a truck rolled up in front of the kosher kitchen, and out flowed two hundred sets of dairy dishes, two hundred sets of meat dishes, and assorted pots and pans and flatwear. Rabbi Tzechoval and the orthodox refugees rushed to the mess hall as the word spread, "Now we can eat."

Each morning, Manya appeared at the office. "Any word yet from Washington?"

I shook my head. "Not yet, a little more patience. We're pushing it."

Each day telephone calls came into Building 104, the administration building. The telephone, the lifeline to the outside world, outflanked the fence and the quarantine.

Joseph Flink, an army sergeant, called from New York. "I've just read the newspaper. My parents' names are on the list. Can I talk to them?"

His father and mother were victims of Kristallnacht, the "Night of Broken Glass," in Berlin, when the Nazis had smashed Jewish shops and beaten up Jews. Now his parents hurried to the phone, quivering with emotion.

"Miracles, miracles are happening," sixty-six-year-old Naftaly wept into the phone. "That I should hear your voice again, after six years."

It was 1938 when Joseph had left Berlin with a visa; he had become an American citizen and was now home on leave from the war.

"Maybe there will be another miracle," Naftaly breathed into the phone. "Maybe your sister is alive."

"Papa, because I hear your voice, for the first time I believe it can happen. When can I come to see you?"

Naftaly put down the receiver and asked someone on the staff, "When can my son come to see us?"

He returned to the phone. "You can't come. Not till the quarantine is over. A sergeant in the Army and you can't come through the fence!"

In a small apartment in New York's borough of Queens, a woman sipping her breakfast coffee read the list of 982 refugees in a newspaper. One named jumped at her. "Dr. Hugo Graner."

She shook her children. "Wake up—wake up! Daddy's in America."

She and their two children had sailed to America on the last ship in 1939. Born in Vienna, they had visas; there were still quotas for Austrians. But Dr. Graner, born in Hungary, had been denied a visa. The Hungarian quota was full.

She reached him by telephone. "Hugo," she cried. She had planned all the things she would tell him, how proud he would be of fourteen-year-old Otto and of Hildegarde, now eleven, how bright they were in school, how she had gone to work as a domestic to support them. There were a hundred questions she wanted to ask him. Instead she kept crying, "Hugo. Hugo. Hugo." She heard her husband crying.

Finally she said, "When can we come up to see you?"

"I'll go ask. Call me again in an hour."

He hurried across the camp to my office, hoping I could help. "When can they come?"

I shook my head sadly. "On September first. It's the first day visitors will be allowed."

"I don't know if Hildegarde even remembers what I look like."

"It's the quarantine—"

"But that's three weeks away."

I didn't trust my voice to answer. His shoulders sagged; he walked slowly out the door.

Screams of joy made me jump from my desk to the barred window.

"She's alive!" seventeen-year-old Miriam Weinstein called to her younger sisters and brothers. "Come quick. Mama's alive!"

I hurried outside, where a crowd was beginning to press in around the Weinstein children. Tears streaked down Miriam's cheeks. "My mother is in Switzerland looking for us."

She held us a copy of *Aufbau*, a German-language newspaper published in New York.

We had called the six Weinstein children "the Weinstein orphans." On the ship, Miriam, shy, soft-spoken, had told me how they and their parents had escaped from Belgium to southern France, where they hid for a few years. Then the rumors spread: "The Americans are in Naples, soon they will liberate all of Italy." A committee of Jewish leaders told the refugees, "Mothers with small children should try to get to Italy by bus; all the others should go by train." The Weinstein family separated. Mrs. Weinstein took her three youngest children on the bus; the father and the six older children went by train. The mother and the three babies disappeared.

"We were sure," Miriam had told me, "they were caught by the Nazis and were dead. Then, just before Rome was liberated, the Nazis swept up every Jew they could find in Italy, like a last gasp of hatred. They caught Papa and deported him to the death camps. And now Mama is alive."

While Rabbi Tzechoval blessed this latest miracle, assuring us, "God has arranged it," I went back inside my office and put my head on my desk. I was now working twelve and fifteen hours a day, waking at dawn, leaving late at night for my room at the Pontiac Hotel, spending hours with the refugees, acting as liaison with the Jewish and Christian agencies, sitting on committees, speaking with Washington.

The joyous scene outside my window left me elated and depressed. The Weinstein orphans were orphans no more. Their mother was alive. We would send her a cable in Switzerland that her children were safe.

But they could not be reunited. The children would not be allowed to leave the camp even after the quarantine was lifted—because they had come outside the quota. And, with the war, there was no way of sending them to Switzerland or bringing their mother to America.

They were in limbo.

The next days sped swiftly.

International Harry was circumcised. According to Jewish law, he should have been circumcised eight days after he was born. But on the ship Olga had insisted, "No doctor will butcher my baby. Only a *mohel* will circumcise him." A *mohel* was neither a doctor nor a rabbi, but a technician with a special knife for circumcisions.

The *mohel* was imported from New York City, and a mob of people squeezed into Olga and Leon's little one-room apartment. "We have to see how it's done in America."

Red-bearded, dressed in a white ceremonial kaftan, the *mohel* carefully placed Harry on a pillow, intoned a prayer and, while Harry screamed and Olga turned white, cut the foreskin.

"That *mohel* is as good as anybody in Warsaw, or Vienna, or Zagreb," the Brith Milah mavens approved. Leon poured wine for the guests, who toasted the proud parents. "He should bring you *nachas*. You should have a long life with him together."

Remembering the prophecy of the GIs who had helped deliver Harry, I asked Olga, "How does the brigadier general feel now, after his Brith Milah?"

"What brigadier general?" Olga, rapidly becoming Americanized, exclaimed. "He's going to be a doctor."

As the days passed, the people began to adjust to the life of eating, sleeping, walking, gaping through the fence and building friendships with visitors from Oswego and Syracuse who talked through the chain links. The young people had discovered an American delicacy, Eskimo Pies, and each afternoon those who had five cents bought Eskimo Pies from a vendor, marveling at a country that could put ice cream on a stick.

Most were still euphoric, but none more than the orthodox, who had been given a barrack near the lake for a synagogue. Jack Cohen, a short, dynamic businessman from Rochester representing B'nai B'rith, brought a Sefer Torah, the Holy Scroll, so that services could be held the first Friday night.

Meanwhile the need for clothing was critical. WRA decided that the refugees should be allowed to buy their clothing in town, to create good relations with the local shop-keepers. The refugees would be given a monthly clothing allowance of $4.50 for children under eleven, $7.00 for young people from twelve to seventeen, and $8.50 for those over eighteen. But until the quarantine was lifted no one could go downtown, and many still had no shoes.

A few volunteers went into town and bought hundreds of shoes for children, teenagers, adults, and distributed them from a warehouse. Manya found a pair of white kid pumps with low heels. "They fit," she shrieked. "I haven't had shoes that were fitted just for me for years. They're going to be my good-luck shoes."

But some of the people's feet had grown swollen and calloused; they could find no shoes that fit. And thus many were barefoot for the first Friday-night service in the orthodox synagogue.

All week men and women had scrubbed the barrack building until the floor, the windows, the walls glistened and smelled of scouring powder and soap. Carpenters had built an altar and an ark for the Holy Scroll.

The spirit of Shabbat settled on the camp at sundown. Men and women walked with their children down the tree-lined streets, past the post cemetery, its soldiers' markers casting long shadows on the ground, toward the synagogue barrack overlooking the lake.

Rabbi Tzechoval stood behind the altar, bearded like an Oriental prince, a white prayer. shawl encircling his shoulders and arms. The fortunate men who had little sons led them, like precious possessions, to the front of the synagogue as we joined together, reciting the prayers, singing the songs written hundreds of years ago, songs from the halcyon days of their childood.

The men in their ragged jackets, women in their patched and shapeless housedresses, children in torn sandals, joyously greeted the Sabbath:

> "O come, my friend, to meet the bride,
> O come and welcome the Sabbath queen."

The voices carried through the open windows down to the lake.

The next day, Shabbat morning, Joseph Langnas, having come of age at thirteen, born in Vienna, hiding and running for six years, celebrated his Bar Mitzvah. In a white silk prayer shawl, reading the Holy Scroll in the ancient tradition, he became a man.

Sunday morning, the Catholics celebrated Mass in the post chapel, followed by services for the Greek Orthodox and the Protestants. In the quiet afternoon, a long limousine drove through the gate. Tall, white-haired Rabbi Stephen S. Wise stepped out of the back of his car and entered my office. I remembered his impassioned speech at the Stop Hitler Now rally, and the terrible letdown when no action was taken by the government and millions more died.

"I would like to visit the camp. Will you show me around?" Rabbi Wise asked, his mellifluous voice rolling through the little office.

We drove around in the limousine. His wife, Louise Waterman Wise, famous for her work with orphan children, sat up front with the chauffeur, while the rabbi and I sat in the back. Word spread that the Grand Rabbi of America, *der Grossrabbiner Amerikas*, had come to visit. People crowded the streets to wave at him. Sitting like a monarch, he waved back.

That evening, in his honor, Mirković, Otto Presser, Anny Pick, Manya, the whole retinue of artists who had entertained the soldiers on the ship, performed in the post theater. At the piano Charles Abeles played three songs he had composed: "The Captain Korn March," "Miss Gruber's Slow Foxtrot" and "I Have a Girl in Springfield, Mass."

During the intermission, Manya came to the front row where I sat with Rabbi Wise and his wife.

"Any news about us?"

"Come to my office in the morning; I expect a decision tomorrow."

Early the next morning, Manya and Ernst pushed open the door. "Well . . . ?"

"Washington has told us, 'Follow all regulatory procedures.' "

Manya looked bewildered. "What does that mean? Is it good or bad?"

"It's good, Manya."

We wasted no time. Within the hour, Manya and Ernst were given blood tests in our camp hospital; the forms were sent to the Syracuse Department of Health. Then, with an escort, the couple were driven past the army guard at the main gate. They entered the office of the city clerk in Oswego, answered more questions, signed more papers, and received the legal document—their marriage license.

"Can we get married tomorrow?" Manya pressed me.

"I don't see why not."

She looked down at her father's shirt. "But, Ruthie, I have no dress . . ."

I telephoned my mother in Brooklyn. "We're having a wedding tomorrow, Mom. Can you come up and bring the cocktail dress I left in your house, and a veil for the bride?"

The *Henry Gibbins*, the ship on which the one thousand refugees sailed from Naples to New York. STEAMSHIP HISTORICAL SOCIETY COLLECTION AT THE UNIVERSITY OF BALTIMORE.

A typical day on the refugee deck of the *Henry Gibbins*.

RUTH GRUBER

The wounded soldiers came to the refugee deck to flirt with the young women and bring chocolate for the children. RUTH GRUBER

Some had little more than their prison pajamas. RUTH GRUBER

The last day on the *Henry Gibbins*; waving at the Statue of Liberty as the ship entered New York Harbor, August 3, 1944. RUTH GRUBER

Entering the camp at Fort Ontario; Eva Bass, a Piaf-like former nightclub singer in Paris, with Yolanda and Joachim, whom she carried on a sixty-kilometer trek through the fighting lines. ALFRED EISENSTAEDT, *Life* magazine © 1944 Time Inc.

Lining up for their first two towels and a bar of soap. Manya is second in the foreground; behind her are Ernst Breuer (r) and his sister, Lisa (l). ALFRED EISENSTAEDT, *Life* magazine © 1944 Time Inc.

The fence that encircled the camp. For some of the people, the fence meant a prison, a concentration camp; to others it meant security. LENI SONNENFELD

People milling in front of the barrack mess halls. LENI SONNENFELD

Dining, cafeteria-style, in one of the camp kitchens; Margareta Spitzer in the foreground. LENI SONNENFELD

The camp's high school students on the steps of the Oswego High School. Of all the schools the high school was the most pivotal in the lives of these young people, who brought with them a commitment and an eagerness for knowledge that were to penetrate the town.

Edith Semjen, "the blond bombshell," in her Yugoslav partisan uniform.

Eleanor Roosevelt, escorted by Joe Smart, director of the camp, visits the refugees in their barracks. "The First Lady of the world," the people marveled, "and she comes without police guards, soldiers or ladies-in-waiting. Who would believe this in Europe?"

BRANKO KAUFMAN

Manya and Ernst Breuer's wedding under the *chupa* on the camp-grounds. LENI SONNENFELD

Mathilda Nitsch, a Yu-goslav Roman Catholic, who ran an underground station and saved some one hundred families.
LENI SONNENFELD

"Would she . . ." Manya hesitated. "Would your mother give me away?"

I nodded swiftly.

Thursday, August 17. A gentle wind sighed off Lake Ontario; it was a perfect wedding day. Manya and a few of us raced around the camp picking flowers and leaves for her bridal bouquet.

In the barrack room, my mother and I helped Manya slip into the gown; ankle-length for me, it came to Manya's midcalf, swirling gracefully over her long shapely legs and her white "good-luck shoes." We angled a mirror so that she could see how the heart-shaped necklace framed her slender throat. The pearls my mother had thoughtfully packed made her white skin glow.

She turned and twisted to see the dress curving around her breasts and her slender hips. Her blond hair, brushed up into a French twist, lay in a soft wave on her forehead. My mother stood on tiptoes and, unfolding the gossamer white silk scarf she had crocheted, draped it over Manya's hair and shoulders.

Manya bent down and kissed her. "Maybe my mother is alive. Maybe God is keeping her alive. But today you are like my mother. I will always love you for this."

My mother's eyes filled with tears.

A little after ten o'clock Adam Munz's mother, Fradl, small, soft-spoken, entered the barrack. Manya had asked her if she would also accompany her to the *chupa*, the bridal canopy. Fradl took one arm, my mother the other, replacing the father and mother Manya prayed were alive.

The three women moved slowly past the crowd of refugees on the parade ground, then past the staff, most of whom had never seen a Jewish wedding under the sky, and finally past the corps of journalists and photographers recording the first bridal ceremony in the first government haven on American soil. Ernst, waiting solemnly under the *chupa*, stared at the beautiful young woman being led toward him. Their eyes met and held.

Fradl and my mother handed Manya to Ernst and stepped behind her under the canopy, and the ceremony began.

An American rabbi was needed to make the marriage legal. Rabbi Bialik of Oswego intoned. "May He Who is Supreme Power, blessed and glory, bless this bridegroom and bride." Holding a prayer book in his left hand and a wineglass in his right, he proclaimed, "The sanctification of all great moments in Jewish life is symbolized by the drinking of the wine."

He handed the goblet to Ernst, who sipped a few drops and then held the cup to Manya's lips.

"As you share the wine of this cup," the rabbi pronounced, "may you share all things, from this day on, with love and understanding."

Ernst slipped a gold ring on Manya's finger and in a strong voice repeated after the rabbi. "By this ring you are consecrated to me as my wife in accordance with the law of Moses and the people of Israel."

Manya looked at the ring for long moments, then, turning her face up to Ernst, recited the Biblical "I am to my beloved and my beloved is to me."

"Be thou, Marjam," Ernst spoke her given name, "my wife according to the law of Moses, I faithfully promise that I will be a true husband to thee and I will honor and cherish thee."

"And I," Manya answered just above a whisper, "plight my troth unto thee in affection and in sincerity."

Again the rabbi gave them wine to sip. "I pronounce you husband and wife. May the Lord bless you and keep you and cause His countenance to shine upon you and bring you peace."

Rabbi Tzechoval, partaking of the service, blessed them; then Rabbi Bialik placed a wineglass on the ground at Ernst's feet. "We break the glass, to remind us, even on this day of joy, of the destruction of the Temple in Jerusalem."

Ernst stamped on the glass, shattering it.

"*Mazel Tov! Mazel Tov!* Good luck! Good luck!"

Ernst reached for Manya and held her in a long passionate kiss. Manya clung to his body. He finally released her so that we could all kiss her—my mother, Fradl, the refugees, the staff.

As if it were a garden wedding, we walked in small happy groups toward one of the mess halls, where the chefs, forgetting the budget, had prepared a sumptuous wedding feast complete with a wedding cake. The reporters rushed to their typewriters. Late in the afternoon, a newsboy brought us copies of the *Oswego Palladium-Times*, the town's one daily.

"What does it say?" my mother asked. We had been walking the grounds, talking to the people. "Read it to me."

A small group assembled as I opened the paper. I read so that everyone could hear. ". . . The bride wore a gown of steel gray, fashioned street length, and a headdress of Spanish lace."

"Spanish lace!" My mother burst into laughter. "I finished crocheting it on the train coming up."

I read on, translating for those who spoke no English, "Her

flowers were roses of Sharon intermingled with ferns, in a hand bouquet.''

The reporter had written it up as if it were a Junior League wedding.

CHAPTER SEVENTEEN

Life came to Oswego.

"Refugees Arrive from Europe," *Life* headlined its August 21, 1944, lead article. In a myriad of faces, Alfred Eisenstaedt, *Life*'s ace photographer, captured the emotions of the first days, the bewilderment, the lines queuing up for two towels and a bar of soap, the people peering through the fence.

The photos were so moving, the article so sympathetic, that hundreds of readers wrote letters to the camp, especially to Edith Semjen, whose sultry beauty, set off by her partisan uniform, made her look as if she had stepped out of a Yugoslav version of *For Whom the Bell Tolls*. From New York to California, men asked her to marry them. Soldiers wrote that they were pinning her *Life* photo on their lockers. "Let me get you away from that fence and free you."

Edith carried a bagful of mail to my office. "What do you do in America? Do you answer every letter you get?"

"For a lonesome soldier, a letter from you could be a shot in the arm."

Edith lit a cigarette. "I'll get my girlfriends to help me answer them." She inhaled, then flicked an ash. "Maybe it'll help speed up the war." For the war was never more than inches away.

On the parade ground, Mirković rushed toward me. "Have you heard? Churchill is meeting with Tito. Maybe they'll be liberating Yugoslavia soon."

Waves of joy spread through the camp with the news that a thousand bombers had dropped their fire on German strongholds from Paris to the sea, and that the Seventh Army was landing in the very area from which so many had begun their trek across the Alps.

But fears for their relatives, especially in Hungary, hung heavy on the camp.

Until a few months before, Hungary had been able to stave off Hitler's plans for total *Vernichtung*. Admiral Miklós Horthy, Regent of Hungary, had insisted on his country's right to handle Hungarian Jews in its own way; Hungary was a co-belligerent, not an occupied or conquered land. Hitler, angry and irritated, attributed Horthy's actions to an unnatural sympathy for Jews. Horthy had a Jewish wife.

Then, on March 19, 1944, Hitler decided to wait no longer. German troops occupied Hungary. The mass extermination of Jews began. The Prime Minister of Hungary, Miklós Kállay, understood the Nazi action only too well. "The greatest enemies of the Nazis," he wrote, "the targets of their deepest hatred, were living unmolested in the very heart of the German sphere of power—a million strong. Was one little country, one man, to hinder the execution of their totalitarian plans?"

In the camp, we tried to bolster each other; there were ways now to save the Jews of Hungary. The War Refugee Board, which had created our shelter, was sending emissaries to rescue them. Perhaps more neutral countries would help. Perhaps the Vatican. Perhaps even the International Red Cross, never distinguished for its compassion for Jews. In moments of despair, we suspected that help would be too little and come too late. Eichmann, the great overseer of *Vernichtung*, engineer of the death trains, made sure the trains ran on time, rushing five and six thousand Jews each day to feed the ovens of Auschwitz. The guards in Auschwitz, with incredible callousness, were calling their newest victims "Hungarian salami."

Meanwhile, the day-to-day living problems, even the smallest ones, had to be coped with. "Those two slices of white bread they give us—" Abe Furmanski, short, rotund, sat in my office, gently complaining—"they're on one tooth. We want bread you can cut yourself with a big knife." He circled his left arm as if he were embracing a round loaf; then, with his right hand clutching an imaginary knife, he sawed through the bread, his eyes shut as if he could still smell the delicious aromas of the bakeshops of his childhood.

White bread versus black bread became a *cause célèbre*, picked up by the press. A columnist charged that we were starving the people "with uneatable white bread and undrinkable bitter tea."

"Would you look into this crisis," Joe Smart asked me, "before the papers make it sound as if we're having a riot?"

The budget for food was forty-five cents per day per person. The chefs, largely recruited from WRA, were serving the same menus, with the same two slices of white bread, that they had set before the Japanese Americans in their relocation centers.

After a few days I reported to Joe, "We've got a thousand people with a thousand different reactions. Some tell me they never ate so well and so much; one of them [it was Manya] still hides the bread under her pillow. But others say they're hungry all the time and whatever they eat is tasteless."

"Sounds like soldiers bellyaching in every camp."

"But, Joe, the yearning for black bread is different. Black bread is their oxygen, their culture. Why don't we establish a bakery on the grounds and bake black bread right here?"

"No problem."

The crisis was over.

"Washington wants us to set up an advisory council," Joe told me in his office. "I'd like you to help."

Flyers were sent around the camp in all languages, announcing the elections.

The leaders who had emerged on the ship now converged on Joe's office.

"The only way to elect these representatives is by nationality groups," Dr. Juda Levi of Yugoslavia insisted.

I expected a replay of the fiery confrontations on the ship, with Artur Hirt, the Polish judge, opposing him. To my surprise, Hirt agreed. "The nationality groups can be a bridge, helping the American staff understand us."

"Your arguments are well taken," Joe also agreed. "We will hold the election by nationality groups. The council will be made up of ten men. Two each will be elected from the four largest groups—Yugoslavs, Austrians, Poles and Germans. The final two will represent all the other smaller national groups."

Now it was Dr. Levi who protested. "That's not fair. We Yugoslavs are the largest group in the camp, we should have more representatives than all the others."

Hirt's face reddened. "There you go, you Yugoslavs. Always wanting more than anyone else. You suffered less than most of us. Some of you could even bring clothes with you. We have only the shirts on our back." He turned to me. "You didn't follow our advice about housing."

It was true. The staff, unaware of the confrontation on the ship, had assigned the barracks even before we arrived. Not nationality or intellect but the size of each family had been the criterion. The dire predictions had evaporated. In housing, at least, the frontiers of Europe had been washed away.

"I have to admit to you, Fräulein Ruth," Hirt said, smiling, "that we were wrong about the housing. But on this council, if you give the Yugoslavs more representatives than you give the rest of us, we will fight even if it starts a riot."

"The discussion is academic," Smart said. "Washington has approved a ten-man council."

The Yugoslavs held the first election. By six-thirty in the evening more than half of the 368 Yugoslavs in the camp crowded into the social hall. Arguments rose and fell, people yelled at one another, women carried out their sleeping children and returned to the fray. At midnight, the debate was suddenly halted. Ten men were elected, and they in turn chose two to represent them on the council. They were Dr. Levi and Filip Baum, Fredi's father.

In the next few days the other nationality groups met, until at last the ten representatives were chosen. Joe asked me to address the first meeting of the new "Temporary Advisory Council."

Building 3, an old headquarters barrack near the lake, was to become the parliament building, the mecca of democracy in the camp. The ten council members sat on hard chairs facing a wooden table at which Joe sat, flanked by Dr. Levi, the elected president, Fredi—the secretary and interpreter—and me.

Smart opened the meeting, greeting the council with the solemn dignity of a man cloaked in history. Thus, I thought, Washington must have addressed the Constitutional Convention of 1787.

"We meet," Smart said, "as a council on common grounds for a common cause, for the general good of the people in the camp." He waited while Fredi translated the words into German.

The basic policies of the camp, Smart explained, would come from Washington. "Over these policies I have no discretion. But other policies I can make, and these are the ones we shall be discussing in the days to come, changing them if they need to be changed, working together to implement them."

"The government's function," Smart outlined the spheres of influence, "is to provide food, shelter and clothing. Yours is to maintain spirit and morale."

He suggested that the councilors set up committees for such needs as housing, education and food, appoint a "house leader" for each barrack and meet with him every morning at eleven. The men then talked quietly among themselves. "We know this is a temporary advisory council," Dr. Levi said. "We would therefore like to suggest that after thirty days we have a general election for the whole camp. We would like to elect a council," he spoke slowly, emphasizing each word, "*not on the basis of nationalities,* but on the basis of barracks."

They were de-Balkanizing themselves!

"Mrs. Reid would like you to come to dinner this Sunday evening. Some of the guests may be helpful to you with the refugees."

For anyone connected with the New York *Herald Tribune,* an invitation to dinner at Mrs. Ogden Reid's was a kind of command performance. "Queen Helen," a national magazine had labeled her. Scarcely five feet tall, with delicate features and chinalike skin, Helen Reid was a publishing giant, owner of the most powerful Republican newspaper in the country. "Queen Helen" was herself a kingmaker, who tried and failed to make Wendell Willkie President in 1940 and would later succeed in helping to make Dwight Eisenhower President in 1952.

It was a warm August evening when I rang the bell of the Reid town house off Fifth Avenue on East Eighty-fourth Street in Manhattan. After the barracks of Oswego the house seemed more palatial than ever, with its marble foyer, its gracefully curved stairs, Persian rugs, crystal chandeliers.

Mrs. Reid, in a long silk gown, introduced me as the guests entered—politicians, foreign correspondents, industrialists and John Cowles, the senior member of the Cowles publishing empire, owner of the *Des Moines Register,* the *Minneapolis Tribune* and *Look.* After cocktails and hors d'oeuvres, we entered the dining room, lit with tall candles, festooned with fresh flowers. Seated at the head of the table, Helen led the conversation. The war. The Allied armies sweeping across Europe. The battles in the Pacific.

The talk swirled past me. I kept thinking, How can they help? Cowles's papers and the *Tribune* were the liberal vanguard of the Republican Party. They could create a climate of sympathy throughout the country. More refugees could be saved. More havens could be opened. Moreover, they could influence the townspeople of Oswego, for it too was a Republican stronghold.

After dinner we adjourned to the drawing room for demitasse. As the guests lit cigarettes and cigars, and sipped coffee, Mrs. Reid announced, "You all know, of course, about the thousand refugees who've come to this country at the President's invitation."

John Cowles and his wife, Betty, looked up from their coffee.

"Ruth brought them." Helen put her own cup down on an end

table and turned to me. "I wish you would tell us some of your experiences."

I told them of the three-day trek over the Alps, of International Harry, of Mirković and the beautiful young women entertaining the soldiers on the ship.

"Now we were on the train to Oswego," I was saying when Betty Cowles interrupted.

"What! You brought the refugees to Oswego!"

She leaped from her chair, her eyes dancing. "Oswego is my town. I was born up there. My mother's still there; they call her the Dowager Queen. When are you going back?"

"I'll be there tomorrow morning."

"The minute you get back, go to see her. I'll phone her to expect you. She can open every door you need opened."

The next morning I presented myself at Florence Bates's three-storied white mansion.

"Of course I read about the refugees in our *Palladium-Times*." She waved me to a sofa. "I even read about the wedding. Betty repeated some of the stories you told them last night. I've already decided. I'm going to help you." She was smiling. "Our town has needed something like this to wake it up."

However Florence Bates worked, she helped create the climate of goodwill we needed and opened innumerable doors, as did many others, merchants, educators, lawyers and religious leaders. Even before we arrived in the camp, Joe Smart had met with some of the town's leading citizens. Now they formed the "Oswego Advisory Committee."

Charlie Goldstein, the owner of Oswego's department store, addressed one of the first meetings in Joe's office. "On the whole," he reported, "the town reaction to the refugees has been nearly one hundred percent favorable. We've even started a 'fence club,' where the people make friends talking through the fence. People on the outside are getting a bigger thrill than the people on the inside. But, unfortunately, we do have, yes, anti-Semitism, and rumors are starting up against the camp."

"What kind of rumors?" I asked.

"That the refugees all have private bathtubs."

"Bathtubs! They don't even have privacy in the showers." The shower curtains from Rochester had not yet arrived.

"They're spreading other rumors—that every apartment has a refrigerator, and they're lavishly furnished, all at the taxpayers' expense."

"I'm not worried about rumors," said Ralph Mizen, a thin, tight-lipped attorney, who spoke with authority. He had just been elected chairman. ''I remember the furor that broke out in this town when the Associated Press notified us sometime around 1941 that Negro troops were being shipped here after they had shot up the town of Brownsville, Texas. Rumors were flying, 'Our women will be raped. They're going to rob us. Drunken soldiers will burn the town down.' But after they came, we found they were as good as any soldiers we had here.

''We felt the same way when the 'morons' were sent here,'' he went on. ''They were illiterate soldiers sent here for remedial work. Each group turned out much better than we suspected. Now it's our job to make sure that the town takes the same attitude toward the refugees.''

Turning to me, he said, ''Help us to understand the refugees better. What is their most urgent need?''

''Each day,'' I said, ''young people come to my office with one request— 'When can we go to school?' There are two Margulis brothers, Rajko and Alex. They were medical students in Belgrade. Most of their fellow students who were anti-Nazis or Jews were murdered. Their only dream now is to continue their studies. They're brilliant young men.'' I paused.

''I hope soon you will meet them. You will admire them, as I do. Young people, filled with a passion for learning.''

''What is the War Relocation Authority's position on schools?'' Mizen asked Joe Smart.

''The head of our agency in Washington, Dillon Myer, feels that government shouldn't have too much responsibility in education. There should be some schooling, to be sure. But the government doesn't want to make Americans out of them, because they aren't going to be Americans. They're going back to Europe when the war's over. We have two options. We can keep them in the camp and bring in teachers; the private agencies have already agreed to pay for them. The other alternative is to throw the Oswego schools open to them. The invitation must come from you.''

''I would think,'' Mizen said, ''we will have to discuss among ourselves some of the problems this raises. The smart thing to do—to use your name, Mr. Smart—is for the group to organize itself into an education committee and study this question.''

In the Pontiac Hotel, lying in bed, I listened to the rush of the Oswego River below my window. I had been in the camp for nearly two weeks. It's time, I thought, to go back to Washington. To report to Ickes.

Even in these weeks of quarantine, the people had begun

settling into a rhythm of life. Some of the adults and teenagers had started giving informal classes in English; the entertainers were putting their acts and skits together. Yet anxiety hovered over the camp.

"What will happen to us when the quarantine is lifted on the first of September? Can we leave the camp? What about jobs? Schools? Freedom to travel? Freedom in the land of America?" I had no answers.

Whatever power I had lay in Ickes's confidence. In the totem pole of Washington bureaucracy, the top man made decisions. But below him, his staff formulated recommendations, gave him options, fought, if necessary, for their convictions and, once the decision was made, carried them through.

Ickes had to know some of the problems before they escalated.

Friday morning I telephoned him. "Mr. Secretary, I feel I must come back to Washington."

"But I've just had a letter from Rabbi Stephen Wise, asking me to let you stay on for some weeks longer. He writes you've been so useful—"

"I must see you. There are urgent problems."

"Very well. I'll see you at ten on Monday morning."

Friday evening the beauty of the Sabbath once again spread across the barracks and the parade ground. The knowledge that this would be my last weekend in the camp, for a while at least, gave this Sabbath evening special poignancy.

Some still in their rags, others in the clothes that had been thrown over the fence, the people walked across the camp. A second house of worship was to be inaugurated this evening for the conservative and reform Jews, in the former army chapel. The chapel was used on other days for the Christian refugees.

In the late-afternoon sun, the army barrack where the orthodox were worshiping and the white wooden army chapel with its tall spire seemed like sanctuaries of peace. Inside the chapel, the altar had been covered with a white silk cloth, and the people sat on wooden benches in the glow of the Holy Torah and the Eternal Light.

Dressed in a black robe and a white prayer shawl, Rabbi Hajim Hazan led the services in Hebrew, Serbo-Croatian and Ladino, the language spoken by many Jews of the Balkans. Expelled from Spain in 1492, the Jews had created this Judeo-Spanish language; its base was Spanish, with a mixture of words from lands in which the Sephardic Jews had settled. Rabbi Hazan, who spoke almost no German, began his sermon in Serbo-Croatian. A young Yugoslav sitting beside me whispered,

"He's talking about the ones we lost—sons, brothers, husbands, wives, children . . ."

Behind me, two women began complaining in German. I turned and put my finger on my lip, hoping they would be silent. Instead one of them leaned toward me. "*Schrecklich. Ich verstehe nichts.* It's terrible. I don't understand a thing."

A few men stalked out of the chapel. Joe Smart, a devout Mormon, believing that the service was over, followed them.

When the Friday-evening prayers ended, I left the chapel, only to find a small cluster of men waiting for me.

"How dare he?" they shouted.

"Who?"

"Hazan! That he would give a sermon in a language not one of us understands."

An argument on Shabbat! When would these rivalries end? Seeing my dismay, an Austrian Jew explained, "Most people in the camp, even the Yugoslavs, understand German. But only the Yugoslavs understand the Yugoslav language."

A Yugoslav waved his fist at some of the Germans. "You are Germans first, then Jews. You want to inflict the German language on everyone. Remember, out of seventy thousand, the Germans have wiped out sixty-six thousand Yugoslav Jews. We want to kill the German language in our minds, in our hearts, in our souls. We have a right to our language. But in this camp the hated German language is constantly thrown at us."

Bitterness and resentment, stored up for generations, erupted. The Sabbath peace was broken.

Mr. Campbell, in charge of the camp guards, was called to the fray. He frisked the men and discovered a knife in an Austrian's pocket. He took the Austrian, and a Yugoslav with whom he had been arguing, to Joe's office. Joe was called from his home to determine whether the town police should be involved.

Joe decided to wait. He asked both Campbell and the leaders of the Advisory Council to investigate and report to his office the next afternoon.

In the evening, a few of the older men sought me out.

"Look what's happening to us," Ernst Wolff said. "That we can have a fight over such a little thing. There's a war against us in the world, and we fight among ourselves. It's a disgrace."

Fewer than ten people had been involved, but it needed only a few to poison the air. The men were soul-searching now, trying to understand the outburst and put it into perspective. The German and Austrian Jews had lost more than their homelands. They felt they were being reviled by the others in the camp because they were a constant reminder of the German madness that had darkened the earth. Victims themselves, they felt betrayed, rejected, hated. The sermon in Serbo-Croatian was the final straw.

Saturday morning, Dr. Margulis, a leader of the Yugoslavs, met me on the parade ground. "You must attend this meeting. We lay much weight upon it."

I had no intention of not attending.

Joe sat behind his desk holding a typescript in his hand. "I've had the report from Mr. Campbell. There were loud arguments, but there was no violence. One man had a knife in his pocket, not in his hand, and there was no evidence that he tried to use it."

"What about the Oswego police, will they arrest anyone?" Dr. Margulis asked.

"I would like to explain something to you about our country. The police in America are given considerable discretion; they decide whether to make arrests or not. Mr. Campbell has recommended that no one be arrested or tried."

Dr. Milorad Novović, a Serbian Orthodox lawyer, looked worried. "We hope this ugly incident will not be published in the newspapers."

"This is a free country, and not even the government can censure the press," Joe said. "I hope you members of the council agree with our decision to arrest no one."

The men nodded.

"I realize," he went on, "that I made a mistake by walking out. I have therefore written an apology, which I should now like to read to you:

> "I went to the service happy to worship in reverence, happy to worship a common God who knows no difference of language and nationality; and proud to worship with people I thought shared a common bond of humility and devotion. Racial or national and religious differences have no place in Fort Ontario or anywhere in America. I, of a faith different from yours, came to worship with you a common God; and I hope you will respect that difference as surely as you must the differences amongst yourselves which result from the many cultures represented."

The council members sat openmouthed; they had obviously never heard a man in a position like Joe's offer an apology.

"We are so impressed by your wisdom in handling this crisis,"

Dr. Novović said, "that we would like to translate your apology into all our languages for the whole camp to know."

Saturday night I took the midnight sleeper to New York. My mother and father were wide-awake as my taxi pulled up to the stoop early Sunday morning. Neighbors in their Sunday best were walking to church.

"I'm learning a lot about your work," my father said mysteriously. We were eating breakfast in the huge kitchen-dining room. My mother was in the alcove, toasting bagels.

"I guess Mom's been telling you about the camp—and the wedding."

"She told me. But I got a lot from the newspapers." He walked toward a stack of papers on the buffet. He was obviously saving every scrap of information about the refugees.

"Listen to this from Friday's *Forward*."

My mother called from the alcove. "Dave, don't you dare start reading until I bring in the coffee."

"You want to hear it again. You've only heard it twelve times."

"So I'll hear it thirteen times. All right, now begin."

He adjusted his glasses, stroked his mustache and began to read. " 'Darling and mother of the shelter is a young woman named Ruth Gruber . . .' "

My mother broke in, "You should have heard them—'*Unser Mutter Ruchel iss offgeshtanden.*'" (Our mother Ruth has risen.)

"Come on, Mom," I protested, "you didn't hear them say that."

"Would I make up such a lie? Would I know that women older than me are calling my daughter their mother?"

"You two can argue later," my father said impatiently. "Let me go on. 'She is an official of the Department of the Interior who was sent to Italy to accompany the refugees on their journey across the sea.' "

"Pop, we know all that."

He seemed not to hear. " 'During the thirteen-day trip across the ocean, Miss Gruber taught the refugees English, listened to their life histories and tried to help them with their personal problems. In camp, also, the refugees come to Miss Gruber with many of their problems and complaints.' "

"You should have seen how they came to her," my mother interrupted again. "Like she was a *rebbe*."

My father continued. " 'Frequently heard at the shelter is the phrase. "She is our guardian angel. Miss Gruber will intercede on our behalf; she will help us." And the smallish young Miss Gruber must listen to all the complaints, appeals and requests of the refugees.' "

"I don't know what kind of guardian angel I was; but anyway I'm bringing some of those complaints and appeals to Ickes."

On the four-thirty express to Washington, I sat back thinking of my mother, small, sharp-witted, acerbic, and my father, tall, wise, the patriarch to whom all our relatives and friends came for advice. Theirs was the immigration experience of the first generation, sweating their way up the ladder from poverty to the middle class so that their children would get the education they never had. Perhaps their passion for education was why I felt so much empathy for our young people in the camp who were determined to go to school. My parents had given me the chance for education; but they had never come to terms with how I used it. Their highest ideal for me was to be a secretary or a schoolteacher. For them I was the maverick in the nest who caused them both pride and apprehension. A teenager in Germany, a young woman in her twenties flying across the Arctic—they were in constant fear that I might be killed and they would lose me forever. They were warm and loving, they had molded me, but found it hard to understand me. In their Old World yearnings, I was a stranger who had invented myself.

Now, for the first time, I was doing something they could understand. I was helping Jews. Maybe somehow I could even help rescue the relatives in Wolyn—if they were still alive.

Ickes studied the photographs I had taken on the ship. He kept shaking his head. "Look at those children! What those people must have gone through!

"Let me read one of these case histories," he said.

He picked the first one in the pile. It was marked

SCHLEUME FRISCHWASSER

The horrors of the concentration camp at Dachau are briefly described here. This story must be kept confidential. Mr. Frischwasser begged me not to reveal it, for fear that the Nazis would harm his wife and daughter, who are still in an Austrian concentration camp.

Statement of Schleume Frischwasser:

"I am 55 years old. I was a textile merchant in Vienna. On May 27, 1938, I was captured in my business and taken prisoner. I had to close my business; they took the key and sent me to Dachau. The trip was terrible. My wife and daughter are in the concentration camp in Theresienstadt under Hitler. I am afraid that they will be harmed.

"I was in Dachau, then in Buchenwald, about 11 months in both. As I left the camp, they said, 'If you say anything about what happened to you here, we will harm your wife and daughter.' So please, please don't say that I was there.

"They beat us with sticks as soon as they threw us in the trucks. In the concentration camps they made us stand for hours looking into light. They then made us stand and keep twisting our heads in both directions. They made us beat each other on the toes and kick each other. Men and women were hanged constantly. The worst thing came when one of them escaped. Then all of us had to stand out in the open until he was caught. About 20 percent of the camp died during one such period. Others contracted pneumonia and TB.

"The Nazis had their jokes, they put all the doctors to work cleaning out latrines. They called them Division 4711, the name of a German eau de cologne. Other times they would ask for all the chemists and then would put them to work in latrines.

"Please don't tell this; my wife and daughter will be harmed."

Ickes wiped his glasses.

"Of course we won't publish this," he finally said. "That man has suffered enough without endangering his wife and his daughter—if they're still alive. Is this one the most dramatic?" He placed his hand on the stack of case histories.

"They're all dramatic, Mr. Secretary. They're all people still in pain."

"I can almost hear them talking to you." He drew another history from the pile, shaking his head as he read, occasionally muttering, "My God."

I sat silently, remembering our talks on the ship: *You are living witnesses. You are the ones Hitler tried to kill. . . . You have a mission . . . to tell America and the world what's happening right now.* Now, I thought, Ickes will have documentary evidence when he speaks to the President and the Cabinet.

The phone rang; Ickes pressed a button. "I want no interruptions," he told his operator. He hunched his shoulders over his desk and continued reading.

He's a fighter, I thought. He's been fighting all along. Maybe now he'll fight harder—against the isolationists in Congress, against the State Department, against men like Breckinridge Long. But not only the isolationists are guilty. We are all guilty. Why didn't we scream? Why didn't we march on the White House?

Ickes lifted his massive head. Once again he wiped his glasses. Then he put the case histories into a bulging briefcase. "I'm going to finish reading the rest at home tonight. I want Jane to read them, too."

He snapped the briefcase closed. "Now what are the problems you want to discuss with me?"

CHAPTER EIGHTEEN

At last, on a day when the sun turned the camp into a haven of warm light filtering through the trees, and diffident cool winds presaged the autumn, the quarantine was lifted.

It was September 1, 1944. Ickes had asked me to go back to the camp to help with the open house.

The whole town of Oswego, 22,000 strong, was invited. People who had stood outside the fence for nearly a month making new friends now swarmed inside. Zlatko Hirschler's sister, Vera, came up from Crossville, Tennessee, and threw her arms around her brother and his wife, laughing and weeping. Zlatko still wore his only pants from the ship; they had a hole in each knee.

Joseph Flink, dressed in his American Army uniform, searched for his parents. He found them standing in front of their barrack, unable to move toward him, so great was their joy.

Ralph Faust, the principal of the high school, came toward me, clearing his throat. "I'm a little shaken. I just saw an elderly woman kneel down and kiss the ground."

All morning and through the afternoon, thousands, surrounded by the press, milled through the camp. Florence Bates and all the members of the town's Advisory Committee led throngs of friendly and a few unfriendly townpeople into the barracks. The sparse GI furnishings, the communal toilets and showers (now neatly curtained) scotched the stories of lavish living at taxpayers' expense.

The bathtub rumor died with the open house.

And Oswego opened its schools.

Ralph Faust interrupted his vacation to meet with the camp's young people.

"I'm twenty," Steffi Steinberg said worriedly. Steffi spoke English well, with a German inflection. "Can I still go to high school? I'm afraid I'm too old. It's six years since—"

"Of course you can come."

Steffi registered with nearly forty others, whose ages ranged from sixteen to twenty. Faust himself selected the classes they would enter, depending on how much schooling and how much English they had had. A day before school opened, he took a group on a tour of his high school, proud of the handsome four-story brick building that spanned a whole block on Mohawk and West First. In the basement carpentry shops, he kept hearing *"Magnifique! Magnifique!"* In all of his years as an educator, he had never known such enthusiasm.

So important was this next day, when the gates swung open, that most of the camp, parents, single men and women, mothers with babies, stood at the fence waving goodbye to 193 children and teenagers.

For the children themselves, it was a day never to be seen again; for some a day of joyous anticipation, for others of painful loneliness and even fear.

Tamar Hendel and her cousin Giselle, both nine, squeezed each other's hands tightly as they walked two short blocks to P.S. 2, a little American schoolhouse on Mitchell Street. The principal, Susan Donovan, greeted them solemnly and asked a little girl to escort them to the third-grade classroom. Tamar looked around the classroom, observing everything, the curious chairs attached to wooden desks, the big blackboard, the American children staring at her, the lady teacher behind a big desk calling names from a book. She was elated; there were so many things she would tell her parents back in the camp. Giselle sat beside her, lonely and miserable. The language was mysterious, the classroom was strange, the children seemed cold. She had no parents to confide in.

Branko Hochwald sat toward the back of the room. In the month of quarantine he had acquired a few words of English, but none of the words helped him or his good friend Ivo Hirschler as the teacher began the morning lesson.

Farther downtown, twenty-four youngsters lined up on a vast green lawn and then marched into the Fitzhugh Park School, a brand new three-story junior high school on East Tenth Street.

Henny Notowicz, fourteen, witty, with the gallows humor of a survivor, entered her class humming an English song under her breath. She had learned it in one of the camp classes in the accent of the volunteer refugee teacher:

> I valk to de vindow
> Und I valk to de door,
> Behind me is de vindow
> Und before me is de door.

> Above is de ceiling
> Und below is de floor,
> I valk to de vindow,
> Fon de vindow to de door.

Irene Danon, in the row behind Henny, felt that her world was being turned upside down. With ink-black eyes, she was bright, bubbly, effusive in camp; but now she was frightened. Schools had bad memories. She had been expelled from her first school in Belgrade when all the Jews were expelled. Her parents had innocently enrolled her in a private school, not aware it was a school for juvenile delinquents; but soon even that school was barred to Jews. With her parents and her little brother, she began to run, hiding in sewers, living furtively on a false passport as a Russian Orthodox Serbian. Her picturesque Serbian name, Ljiljana, so fit her joy and effervescence that even in the camp she was Ljiljana. But there was no joy this first day. She had dressed in her best clothes, a pair of slacks. The teacher motioned to her angrily. "You go right back to the camp and change to a skirt." She thought she heard the teacher mutter, "Damn refugees."

"I don't believe this," Sonia Sommerburg whispered to herself. "A classroom! The eighth grade. I never thought I would ever in my life sit in a school. I never thought I would even be alive at fifteen."

She had told me much about herself. Her first memory, as a child of four in Hamburg, was the day Hitler came to power. Her father, Rudolf, who was not Jewish, was an anti-Nazi political writer who had been jailed several times trying to prevent the rise of Nazism. Her mother, Miriam, who was Jewish, was already becoming well known as an artist. With four small children, the family fled to the Italian Riviera. Sitting in the classroom now, watching the teacher draw rounded vowels, *e* and *a*, on the blackboard, Sonia thought of her father. He had been unhappy in Italy. German was his language, not Italian. He decided to return to Germany and granted Miriam the divorce she wanted. The family never heard from him again. Miriam hid their Jewishness from her children until they discovered it themselves when they were arrested by the Italian Fascists. They were sent to a small mountain village, where they had to report to the police every day. Miriam later explained that she had hoped she could save their lives by denying their heritage.

For Sylvan Boni, it was a day of sheer adventure. How proud Papa would have been, he thought, if he knew I was now in junior high. Papa had saved the family's life and the lives of one hundred other Jews fleeing Bulgaria. He had bought a boat with his last money, and hired a captain for the four-hour voyage from Albania to Italy. They took no food and little water. Nazis came aboard while they were still in harbor; they hid below the deck, silencing the children. As soon as the Nazis left, the captain, the only seaman aboard, weighed anchor, got drunk, and was never seen again. No one knew how to sail the vessel. They drifted for days; the ship sprang a leak; they were half in the water when British soldiers sighted them and towed them to Brindisi. Papa died of a heart attack soon after the rescue.

In the high school, Ralph Faust waited at the entrance to greet the young people who had crossed the bridge over the Oswego River.

"We're going to have an assembly this morning," Faust explained as he led them into the building. "Wait here, we'll be calling you in a little while."

In his office, he sent for the president of the Student Council. "This is a unique experiment in American history. I would like you to give the welcoming address."

"I won't do it."

"Why not?"

"I don't think they should be in our school, or even in our town. The whole community should have been asked if we wanted refugees in Oswego."

"You may leave now. I'll welcome them myself."

The assembly began. The American students, already seated, stared at the unprecedented spectacle of foreigners walking down their aisle in strange clothes, tall and short, fat and scrawny, acne-faced and clear-skinned, plain-looking and handsome, some shy, some apprehensive, some filled with hope.

Among them was Paul Arnstein, slender, medium height,

bright-eyed, as curious about the Americans as they were about him. Paul could hardly wait for the classes to begin. In Zagreb, his mother, a realist, had forced them to flee with the clothes on their backs. "Nobody will harm us," his father had insisted naïvely even after most of the town's 25,000 Jews had already been murdered or had disappeared. "Everybody knows us; they come to buy their clothes in my shop."

The two Levitch brothers, Eddie and Leon, were already distinguished in the camp. During the quarantine, their father, a pharmacist who wrote poetry, had pushed his last five dollars through the fence and asked a stranger to buy him a clipper, a straight razor and a shaving brush. He practiced his new art on Eddie, who then gave haircuts to the teenagers in the shower rooms, which now doubled as "Levitch's Local Barber Shop." Leon, a talented pianist at seventeen, accompanied most of the singers in the camp and formed the Youth Choir, for which he arranged the music for the children and young people. They gave several concerts.

In Yugoslavia, their father had taught his two sons, his little daughter, Manon, and his lovely wife, Fortunée, how to hang themselves if the Nazis caught them.

Rosa Moschev, portly and soft-spoken, came next. Her mother too had saved their lives. Daughter of a Yugoslav banker and married to a Bulgarian, Bella had sewn cloth over her gold napoleons and worn them as buttons on her dress. From Bulgaria, Rosa and her parents fled in a covered wagon driven by oxen to Albania, where, with her gold napoleons, Bella bought a sailboat and crowded seventy people on the deck. It took them six hazardous days in the Adriatic to reach Italy.

Adam Munz, searching the auditorium for his Ping-Pong friend, Jim, the big ace, followed with some thirty others, among them Lilly and Edith Bronner, two handsome Hungarian girls who had danced the Hungarian czardas in the camp's first festivities. They had been expelled from their native Hungary when Hitler invaded Poland. Their father, born in Poland, had never been allowed to become a Hungarian citizen, and their mother had lost her Hungarian citizenship when she married him; as stateless Poles, they were thrown into jail in Hungary, then transferred to a concentration camp; after a year, they were told they would be released only if they left Hungary immediately. The family fled to Yugoslavia, already crowded with refugees from Poland. Soon the Germans invaded Yugoslavia; they were forced almost overnight to wear yellow armbands with the word JUDE and work as slave laborers for the Nazi Army, cleaning latrines, washing soldiers' laundry, mopping the floors of the barracks. They decided to make their way to the Italian-occupied Dalmatians, but, just as their train neared Split, Yugoslav fascists examined their papers and found they were false. The Bronners were pulled off the train and handed to the stationmaster, who promised to have them jailed. It was Christmas Eve. The stationmaster, an Italian, brought them a tray of cookies. Their mother, strong until now, fainted. The stationmaster, who hated the fascists, helped them escape.

Three young women walking together saw Ralph Faust smiling at them. In the weeks before school began, Steffi Steinberg, Lea Hanf and Edith Weiss, inseparable friends who spoke English, had become Faust's indispensable aides. Behind them came Rolf Manfred Kuznitzki. An only child from a small town in East Prussia, Rolf had learned to speak and even write English with style. But Ivo Lederer, who followed him, boasted that the first English word he had learned on the ship was "fuckin.' " "I kept hearing the sailors up on the bridge shouting, 'Those fuckin' refugees,' " he had told me. "I thought it was a wonderful word."

Then it seemed that the whole auditorium turned to gape. Edith Semjen was strolling down the aisle nonchalantly, her blond hair gleaming. In two days Faust would catch her smoking a cigarette in the corridor and, calling her "the Blond Bombshell," would ask her to leave. This would not trouble Edith. She had signed up for high school only to get out of the camp. She would find other ways to get out; she had not been with the partisans for nothing. In fact, she had already found a way out. Joe Smart's son, Stanley, had fallen in love with her and even proposed marriage. She told him she would think about it. Meanwhile, like many others, they had broken the quarantine: Stanley hid her under a blanket in the back of his father's car, drove easily past the guard at the gate, and took her out jitterbugging and to the movies.

Last in line was Kostia Zabotin, tall, round-faced, with awesome green eyes. Kostia's father, a gifted painter and a nobleman, had caught Eisenstaedt's eye for his *Life* portraits. Baron Vladimir von Zabotin was Russian Orthodox; Kostia's mother, a landscape painter, was Jewish from Germany; Kostia himself had been born in Karlsruhe. In Italy they had been imprisoned in three different jails until they were reunited in the Ferramonte concentration camp.

Faust watched them solemnly as they took their seats. Then he asked everyone to rise. The refugee students stood at attention while the Americans pledged allegiance to the flag and sang "The Star Spangled Banner."

Thus, in all the schools of Oswego, the first day began. Of all the schools, the high school was to be the most pivotal in the lives of these young people who brought with them a commitment, an eagerness for knowledge, that was to penetrate the town.

Within weeks, Frieda Schuelke, the American-history teacher, came into the camp with members of her honor society to describe the clubs the refugee students could join. In the recreation hall, she realized that not only her students but hundreds of adults were crowding in to hear her. She spoke to the parents in German. "Your young people have shown us they are thrilled to go back to school. They read voraciously, with a dictionary always beside them. I find them delightful, and their hunger for education heartwarming. We are all benefiting from their presence in our classes. I think the whole community will benefit from your presence in Oswego."

The shop teacher, Thomas Crabtree, piled a group of young men in his car and drove them to Syracuse. It was illegal; no one was supposed to travel outside Oswego, but Crabtree wanted his students to see American industry at work. He took them into industrial plants and showed them such mind-boggling mechanical equipment that several decided that very day they would become engineers.

In the Fitzhugh Park Junior High, thirteen-year-old Joseph Langnas was elected president of Class 7B1. "In Austria," his beaming mother boasted, "Joseph could not even go to school, and here he's president of his class."

The students joined the after-school clubs, played baseball and football, basketball and softball, and spent their nights doing homework. But when one of Ernest Spitzer's high school classmates complained that Ernest studied too hard and played too little, he told him, "In prison camp, I was too hungry to study."

And standing outside the high school, an American senior watched the refugee students head for the Gothic-style public library. "At first a lot of us laughed at them for being grinds," he told me. "It made you feel small, but then you felt, if they can do it, when they came here knowing so little English, we can do it, too. I guess I'll be taking myself over to the library."

Lord, what is man that Thou art mindful of him?

The voices of the congregants reading the ancient words filled the synagogues.

It was Yom Kippur, the Day of Atonement, the holiest of all the Jewish holidays.

Man is like a breath,
His days are as a passing shadow.
In the morning he flourishes and springs up afresh,
By evening he is cut down and he withers.

Outside the sun shone on the camp and the barges and ships sailing on Lake Ontario, while in the barrack synagogue near the lake we sat singing, fasting, reading the prayers, soul-searching, asking forgiveness for sins we had committed "publicly or in private, through haughtiness of heart, by word of mouth, by the violence of hand, for showing disrespect to parents and teachers . . . For all of these, O God of forgiveness, forgive us, spare us, let us atone."

This was their first Yom Kippur in a free land.

In Hitler's Europe, Yom Kippur was a day of heightened terror. It was a favorite Nazi technique to choose Jewish holidays for their worst sweeping "actions," when the SS rounded up scores of Jews, herded them onto fields and cemeteries and riverbanks, made them strip naked, and shot them.

The Ark of the Torah was opened. Rabbi Tzechoval and the other men drew their prayer shawls over their heads like ancient Jews praying in the desert. We stood facing the Ark, singing the solemn words:

"On Rosh Hashana it is written and on Yom Kippur it is sealed, who shall live and who shall die . . .

"Who shall perish by water and who by fire, who by the sword and who by hunger, who by earthquake and who by plague . . ."

Some sobbed as they sang:

"Who shall be cast down and who shall be exalted."

The weeping ended. We found refuge in the affirmation: "But Repentance, Prayer and Charity avert the evil decree."

The day was long, but almost no one left the synagogue. In the afternoon we read the stories of the martyrs in the Middle Ages taunted by kings to convert. They had been tortured and burned, yet they had kept their faith, dying with the songs we were singing now on their lips.

All through the day we repeated the words:

Remember us to life, O King, who delightest in life,
Seal our fate in the Book of Life for Thy sake, O living God.

Now, through the windows, we could see the sun setting over Lake Ontario. The first stars appeared in the sky as we recited the welcome *Ne'ilah*—the closing at eventide.

The ram's horn was sounded.

The eerie desert notes filled the night air. The congregation rose, smiling, men shook hands, women kissed their children.

Joyously we walked to the mess halls and broke our fast.

Two days later, Eleanor Roosevelt arrived with her good friend Elinor, the wife of Henry Morgenthau, Jr.

"The First Lady of America." Dr. Otto Lederer stared unbelievingly. "The First Lady of America and she comes without police guards, soldiers, or ladies-in-waiting. Who would believe this in Europe?"

Shaking hands, smiling, Mrs. Roosevelt walked among the people, acknowledging their love. They presented flowers, embroidery, drawings, pieces of sculpture, encircling her as if she were someone they had always known. And as she walked she asked questions—about life in the camp, about self-government, about the schools, about the reactions of the townsfolk.

Joe Smart was prepared. He led her toward Barrack 154 and, still on the street, introduced Dušanka Grin, the twenty-six-year-old wife of a Yugoslav physician. "It would be an honor," Dušanka said, "to have you visit my apartment."

With artful simplicity Mrs. Roosevelt said, "I wonder if I might first visit that barrack across the street."

"I hope the bed is made," one of the council members muttered in German.

Mrs. Roosevelt knocked on the door. A young woman, nursing her baby, opened the door. The room was bare but spotless. The army cot with its khaki blanket was neatly made. A sprig of flowers on the wooden table was the only decoration.

The President's wife apologized for coming unannounced, admired the baby in his mother's arms, and then asked the young woman how she felt coming now to America.

"Happy. Very happy. Just to stop running. To rest. And now—to meet you. I—I don't know what to say."

The President's wife put her arm around the shoulders of the young woman. No words were spoken, but a bond seemed to form between the tall, graying, motherly American and the no-longer-frightened refugee.

In her syndicated column, "My Day," on September 20 Mrs. Roosevelt described Dušanka's apartment.

Although clothes have to be hung on hooks in the wall, she had covered them with a piece of unbleached muslin, and up above had painted and cut out figures of animals, stars and angels, which were placed all over the plain surface to become a decorative wall covering. The effort put into it speaks volumes for what these people have undergone, and for the character that has brought them through.

Walking again through the camp, she asked Dr. Juda Levi, head of the camp council, what the most serious problem was.

He pointed. "The fence."

"All camps . . ." she started to say, then stopped.

"We see Nazi prisoners of war outside our fence," Dr. Levi said. "True, they have soldiers guarding them. But they are outside, and we are inside." He continued, "Even our children have a card and a number, and they must show it or shout their number to the guard when they go to school and when they come back."

"Dear Mrs. Roosevelt," Magrita Ehrenstamm, a motherly fifty-eight-year-old woman from Frankfurt, asked, "what will happen to us when the war is over? Will we be sent back to Europe? I have no home to go back to. The Gestapo took everything. My daughter is here, and she wants me to live with her in New York. My son Hans is a sergeant in the U.S. Army in Europe. I want to be here when he comes home."

Mrs. Roosevelt shook her head. "I don't know," she said with an honesty no one could doubt. She walked for a while in silence. Then, learning that a large white wooden building was the hospital, she climbed the steps to visit the sick. Five refugee doctors and the Oswego chief of staff halted their work to introduce her to their patients.

She stopped at David Levy's bedside. Dark-haired David, twenty-two, was truly a survivor. His entire family had been killed in Yugoslavia. He had one goal now—to get a university education. When Mrs. Roosevelt asked him how he liked America, he wasted no time. "I love America, and I love the camp. But I want to go to college."

Mrs. Roosevelt turned to Joe Smart. "I believe I was told all the young people are in school?"

Joe tried to explain that the State Teachers College was prepared to take them in. "But unfortunately the semester started before we could finish the arrangements. Rules, regulations, the problem of who would pay for the buses—all the other schools are within walking distance; we were stymied."

"For the sake of these young people," she said pointedly, "I hope you will find a way. If you need my help, please write me."

"We're doing our best," Joe tried to assure her, "to get them into the spring semester."

David put his hand out to Mrs. Roosevelt's. "I have the feeling your coming here today was *beshert*—like the hand of God."

While the two visitors joined the refugees for a lunch of soup, salad, pie and coffee, the camp's actors and singers rehearsed for a special afternoon performance in their honor.

Hundreds followed the women into the auditorium. The house lights dimmed. The spotlight lit up the stage. The people's eyes were fixed on the tall woman listening intently to the chorus, the skits, the soloists. "An opera singer from Yugoslavia sang for us," she described Mirković in her column, "and I have rarely enjoyed anything more."

The lights went on. She climbed the stairs to the stage, looked at the people whose bursts of applause sent ripples of love toward her. Somehow they seemed to know that she had been fighting for them for years, fighting against the restrictionists and the quotas, fighting to open the doors.

"My visit to this shelter has been one of the most wonderful days I have ever spent." She paused for a moment. "I know how the fence troubles you. I know the restrictions are plentiful. But at least the menace of death is no longer ever present."

The people murmured, "Yes, yes." She seemed so truly to understand them.

Gracious as always, she thanked the staff and the citizens of Oswego. "Oswego is a community that is cooperating with the government and is doing a wonderful job. Both the shelter and the city, I believe, can profit by their contacts. This haven has shown me that if the *human side*"—she stressed the words—"of a government undertaking is understood, complete cooperation is possible."

The human side was what she personified, and even those who did not understand her words understood her meaning.

In a few weeks her husband would be running for his fourth term as President. But while his strong image filled the hall—he was the Great Father who had gathered up these men and women and children—her presence spoke not of politics but of understanding and love.

She ended her column that night: "Somehow you feel that if there is any compensation for suffering, it must someday bring them something beautiful in return for all the horrors they have lived through."

The crowd thronged around her as she entered her limousine. She seemed to them to represent all that was idealistic, unselfish, compassionate in America.

CHAPTER NINETEEN

After a month back in Washington, I was asked by Ickes to return to the camp. He wanted a progress report, and I welcomed the assignment.

Minutes after I entered the camp gate, I was simultaneously hugged and kissed and assaulted with complaints.

Rabbi Tzechoval's wife, Mindla, pulled me to the side as we walked toward my office in the jail. "Dear, beloved Miss Ruth," she said in Yiddish, "it is terrible for the women."

"What is terrible?" I asked the thirty-year-old *rebbetzin,* a peppery little woman who wore a flowered scarf over her head. As an orthodox woman, she had shaved her head on her wedding day to make her unattractive to any man except her husband. On holidays and Shabbat she wore a brunette wig.

"What is terrible?" she repeated my question indignantly. "The women can't sleep with their husbands."

"Why can't they?"

She stared at me with consternation. "Because we have no *mikvah*." This was the ritual pool in which women cleansed and purified themselves before they had sex with their husbands.

"What did you do for a *mikvah* when you were running?" I asked.

"We used the rivers. The lakes."

I waved my hand toward Lake Ontario. "You have a lake right here."

"This lake—" her voice was shrill—"this lake is freezing. We would freeze to death."

I tried to be sympathetic. I knew how important the *mikvah* was to orthodox Jewish women. The *rebbetzin* would have to understand. "I can go to the government of the United States," I told her, "and explain why we should have black bread, and why we need additional funds for winter clothes. But how can I go to the government and ask for a *mikvah?*"

She looked at me slyly. "Because we'll get sick if we don't sleep with our husbands. And they'll get sick, too. I won't give up. I'll get my *mikvah.*"

At lunchtime, Joe brought me up to date.

Lydia Franco from Libya had given birth to a girl, and Washington was in another legal hassle. No one could decide whether little Miriam Mary was an American citizen. The lawyers in Interior argued that any child born on American soil was a citizen. The lawyers in WRB argued that Fort Ontario was different. They asked Justice to determine the issue. But thus far no decision had been made. Little Miriam Mary, I thought ruefully, is probably the first child in history born in America but still in limbo.

"The Army Intelligence," Joe continued, "came back to recheck some thirty of our people. The Army wants more detailed information about their homelands—countries we have to liberate. One of our refugees, they told me, is the legal heir presumptive to the throne of Lithuania. So among us"—his light eyes crinkled—"we may have a king. Imagine a king living in this emergency shelter!"

The next days raced by as people invited me into their homes to sip tea, to chat, to show me their children's report cards, to let me see how they had turned their barrack apartments, with a few handmade doilies and tablecloths, into little replicas of their homes in Europe.

David Levy, recovered from his bout of illness in the hospital, burst into my office. "Tell Mrs. Roosevelt she did it. She did it. We're going to college in the spring semester." Once again the government had bent its rules for education. The students would be allowed to leave the camp each day and travel by bus to the college campus; the private agencies would foot the bill.

Meanwhile several small private and religious agencies had begun to help individuals in the camp. Their intentions were good, but chaos threatened until three national agencies agreed to form the ''Coordinating Committee of Fort Ontario.'' The three— HIAS (the Hebrew Immigrant Aid Society), the National Council of Jewish Women, and the National Refugee Service (NRS), which was funded by the United Jewish Appeal—were soon joined by a host of other Jewish, Christian and secular agencies: representatives of the three communities close to Oswego— Rochester, Buffalo and Syracuse—ORT (the Organization for Rehabilitation through Training), Hadassah, the National Jewish Welfare Board, the Jewish Labor Committee, Agudath Israel, the American Friends Service Committee, the Catholic Welfare Committee, the Unitarian Service Committee and the American Committee for Christian Refugees.

The agencies were genuinely eager to make life in the camp bearable and to prepare the people for life after Oswego. They agreed to fill the refugees' educational, recreational, rehabilitation and religious needs, thus lifting the burden from the government and the taxpayers; the government supplied the basics—food, shelter, clothing and medical care. The government took the position that its responsibility was to maintain the people in the state in which they had arrived—like freight in transit.

Joe Smart informed the Coordinating Committee that many of the people complained of foot trouble. Bernie Dubin of the NRS sent Dr. Harold Lefkoe of Philadelphia to the camp with Louis Yellin, a Philadelphia dealer in orthopedic appliances. Some two hundred people turned up to be examined by Dr. Lefkoe. At the end of the day, he told Dubin, he was ''bleary-eyed,'' while Yellin dreamed all night he was casting arch supports.

Malnutrition in Europe, running, climbing mountains with torn shoes or no shoes at all, had weakened the refugees' feet. Hundreds now wore arch supports and orthopedic shoes, courtesy of the NRS. Many, whose teeth had deteriorated in the years of flight, were also outfitted with false teeth.

The Coordinating Committee assigned each agency the kind of service it performed on the American scene. The NRS assumed major responsibility for most of the programs. ORT and the NRS furnished the educational and vocational services. B'nai B'rith provided the furniture and equipment for the synagogues, the Service Club and several smaller clubrooms. The clubs were a defense against loneliness; one even called itself the Club of the

Lonesomes. It was a kind of Harvard Club for people over fifty, organized by Magrita Ehrenstamm and run by a corps of volunteer "welfare workers."

I attended one of the Wednesday-afternoon meetings in the Service Club. Outside the door hung a sign: "CLUB OF THE LONESOMES. Ladies of an Uncertain Age Have the Use of a Reduction of 50 percent." There was nothing to reduce; everything was free. Middle-aged and elderly men and women sat in the deep soft chairs donated by B'nai B'rith, drank coffee, ate cake, and listened to songs composed by one of their members and sung by another. Some shut their eyes during the lilting music, as if they were dreaming of a romantic past lost to them forever.

"But we must learn English," the adults clamored. A few classes in English were still given by refugee volunteers; but the classes were sporadic, and the people talked in a circus of languages.

They surrounded me. "Remember how you taught us English on the ship? Why can't we have regular classes here?"

The Coordinating Committee in Oswego delayed a decision; professional teachers, books and supplies would require a budget of thousands of dollars. Joe Smart asked me to call Ickes to intervene.

I decided to tackle the problem myself.

I made a quick trip to New York to meet with Ephraim Gomberg and Bernard Dubin of the National Refugee Service, and with the chairman of its board, Joseph Chamberlain, professor of law at Columbia University, whose long white hair and fine-boned face made him look like a minister ready to do battle for his flock. I knew they were friends the moment I entered their office, in a nondescript building at the foot of Manhattan. It took only minutes to convince them.

"I'm one hundred percent behind you," Chamberlain said.

Dubin telephoned the National Council of Jewish Women. It was agreed that both organizations would underwrite all the cost.

I returned immediately to tell Joe and the jubilant people. Within days teachers were hired, and soon there were twenty-nine classes with five hundred adults enthusiastically "breaking their teeth," mixing their *v*'s and *w*'s, bravely trying to fathom the mystery of why they should not pronounce words like *though*, *thought*, *through* and *tough* the same way.

From nine in the morning to nine at night, the camp seemed like a giant school for adults. ORT set up classes where the people worked in mechanics and in carpentry, learned jewelrymaking, painted, sculpted, sewed and learned the art of beauty culture. Edith Semjen sauntered into the beauty-culture class one morning and, at twenty-one, found herself. "She has golden hands," the women told each other as they made appointments weeks in advance for her to style their hair.

The agencies would help solve some of the smaller problems. The big policy decisions still had to be made in Washington.

"But it's so cruel," Magrita Ehrenstamm protested at my desk. From the first days on the ship, she had asked if she could leave to live with her daughter in New York. The answer came now. It was No.

"They've examined us up and down." She was desolate. "Can't you do anything to help us?"

I shook my head sadly. Even Ickes could do nothing. The decision had been made by the War Refugee Board. No visits outside the camp. No one could leave even overnight; they could, however, go into Oswego for six hours, with a pass.

But they were survivors. And the humor that had sustained Jews through centuries of persecution became part of the business of surviving in the camp.

"Let's sing our national anthem for Ruth," Otto Presser announced at the opening of the evening's entertainment in my honor. I stood up, expecting "The Star Spangled Banner," then sat down swiftly. They were singing "Don't Fence Me In."

Survivors, they even breached the fence. You needed a pass to go out, but if you crawled under the fence no one knew if you hitchhiked down to New York, as Adam Munz and David Hendel did frequently, exploring the wonders of New York and sleeping in Central Park. Only their friends knew of their escapades. There were no bed checks, no sergeants counting heads.

Ickes will be pleased, I thought, when I report to him that the refugee terror in people's eyes had almost disappeared and nearly everyone had gained weight. "Look at me," Mirković said, strutting a little, "I've put on nearly sixty pounds. A singer needs weight for his breath."

Whether it was the food after long starvation, the suddenly cold nights, or the sense of having found refuge at last, the life juices that had begun to return on the ship now flowed so freely that a dozen women walked around the parade ground with burgeoning bellies. Manya came to tell me that she was expecting a baby, and, like most pregnant women, she looked radiant.

Each day the hole under the fence grew larger, until it became a two-way street. Boys slithered through to make dates with

Oswego girls. Bobby-soxers from junior and senior high, in short skirts and saddle shoes, crawled through the hole, struck up friendships with the boys, walked with them down near the lake, and found empty barracks near the little post cemetery where they shared Dixie Cups and Eskimo Pies and, the boys assured me later, kissed harmlessly.

The girls in the camp were caught between the old morality of Europe and the free ways of this brave new American world. Zealous adults and ingrained mores inhibited them. Still, they had their own romances. Fredi Baum had eyes only for Jennie Baruch; Elfie Strauber was in love with David Hendel; Renée Reisner and Alex Margulis were inseparable, as were Vesna Culić and Rajko Margulis. Kostia Zabotin fell in love with an American girl; Henny Notowicz had a crush on Rolf Kuznitzki, who was infatuated with Edith Bronner; several girls pined for Adam Munz's affection, and Edith Semjen had become temporarily engaged to Stanley Smart.

On a brilliant autumn morning, Joe drove me out of the camp. The countryside was ablaze with golden birch and flaming scarlet maple and oak trees. New York State had never looked more beautiful.

We were on our way to visit some of the apple and pear orchards being harvested, and to see some of our men at work.

The work policy had been fixed. The refugees would maintain the camp themselves, with as few outside employees as possible. They would all earn the same wage, $18 a month, whether they were doctors, chefs, house leaders or maintenance men. Any unable to work would receive $8.50 a month, $7 if they were between the ages of twelve and seventeen, $4.50 if they were under twelve.

No one was to work outside the camp. But the farmers in the area were desperate. "We have to have manpower to harvest our crops," they pleaded with Washington. "The Army has taken most of our workers."

Pehle at the War Refugee Board relented, "for this harvest only." Fifty men immediately signed up.

Joe and I visited a large orchard where a taciturn farmer led us to a sorry sight. "See that," he said as though his anger was burned out. Most of his pear crop lay rotting on the ground. For him the decision from Washington had come too late.

Toward the end of the day we drove to the Birdseye cold-storage plant. I stopped in dismay at the entrance. A handful of refugees were stacking crates of apples, heavily outnumbered by a contingent of Nazi POWs. Suddenly I was back on our ship looking out at the shipload of POWs. The cold-storage plant seemed transformed into a warehouse theater of hunters and hunted, of Nazis and refugees.

I heard the foreman explaining to Joe Smart, "We pay the government fifty cents an hour for the POWs. The government gives them eighty cents a day, and the Treasury Department pockets the rest."

Eighty cents a day. "And the refugees?" I asked the foreman.

"We pay them the regular wage—fifty cents an hour."

Joe interrupted. "The men decided to put twenty percent into a fund to be used by the whole camp. Besides, in a few weeks they'll be back in the camp, getting eighteen dollars a month."

I did some swift arithmetic on a pad. Eighteen dollars a month for five and a half days a week came to just about eighty cents a day. Apparently that was the government wage for refugees *and* POWs.

They were two sides of the same coin, and the coin was war. A hundred thousand POWs . . . one thousand refugees.

On the whole, Ickes was pleased with the progress report.

"I had a call from Dillon Myer," he said. "He asked me if I'd release you. He says Joe Smart would like you to stay up there all the time."

"And?"

"I told him I thought you could do them more good going back and forth. He also tells me the refugees all love you."

"Maybe," I said slowly, "maybe people love you when they know how you feel about them."

"You never said it in your report, but I caught it between the lines—you really do love them."

"They're part of my life."

The news from Europe was bad. On Saturday, December 16, Hitler launched the Battle of the Bulge and threw back the 8th Corps of the U.S. First Army.

Depressed, anxious, the people read newspaper stories of the appalling weather which grounded the Allied air forces. The Germans pushed forward on the ground, their panzers unaffected by the blinding snowstorms. Eight thousand Americans were dead, 47,000 wounded and 21,000 missing.

Just before Christmas, Joe Smart telephoned me in Washington.

"We're going to be on national radio. The National Broadcasting Company is going to do a Christmas broadcast right from here. We're still big news, I guess."

December 23, I turned down an invitation to a pre-Christmas party in town. I wanted to be alone in my apartment listening to the broadcast.

Dorothy Thompson, who had decried Nazism long before most of her fellow journalists took Hitler seriously, opened the broadcast. "In Oswego, New York, tonight," she began quietly, "around a thousand people are singing Christmas carols and rejoicing over the greatest boon that could possibly have befallen them. That boon is that they are in the United States, and that to save their lives the United States has actually waived the usual visas. Legally, it is dubious whether they are here at all."

Her voice darkened. "A thousand people are very few in a world in which millions are dying and concentration camps are teeming with the politically and racially persecuted. . . . What is one, or what are a thousand, amongst the millions? . . . The whole fate of mankind is contained in a single person, and in a single person is the whole fate of mankind. . . . Therefore . . . it is to the credit of the United States that it tried to save some human beings, and that it has saved a thousand of them."

She was paraphrasing the Talmudic phrase my father had taught me as a little girl. *He who saves a single life, it is as if he had saved the world.*

The broadcast switched to Oswego. The camp choir sang "Silent Night," then Joe introduced several of the Christian refugees. Fifteen-year-old Visko Marinković talked of the terror on the island of Vis, where his father was a farmer and a fisherman, and where he had seen twenty of their neighbors killed. "Now we go to school in Oswego, and fear has passed."

The program ended as Margaret Weinstein told the audience, "I am a Christian married to a Jew, and in Vienna we were both thrown into prison. Now we want only freedom and security and the right to live as human beings, not as hunted animals. I wish for you in America and for all of us in the camp peace."

Then, on December 28, tragedy struck.

Karoline Bleier, a frail thirty-two-year-old Yugoslav woman, tormented herself with guilt. A married woman with two children, she had fallen passionately in love with Geza Bleier some years earlier. She divorced her husband and was forced to give up custody of her children in order to marry Geza. She had given birth to two more children, Ronald, now an apple-cheeked two-year-old, and nine months ago little George. But she grieved for the two children she had left behind. "Why did I abandon them?" she kept flagellating herself. "If they are dead, I am to blame. I killed them."

During the winter, first Ronnie then Georgie contracted whooping cough. Karoline spent sleepless nights, exhausted and despondent. Geza tried to comfort her. "There's a movie in camp tonight. You go. I'll watch the children."

Karoline protested. She was in no mood for a movie, but Geza prevailed and Karoline left the barrack. The camp, engulfed in snow, was once again whipped by a blizzard. Neighbors began returning from the movie; Geza heard their steps. "Where's Karoline?" he asked them. No one had seen her.

Hours passed and Karoline did not appear. Geza alerted the camp police. They set out to search, digging through snow drifts ten feet high.

"Maybe she went walking and lost her way," some of the score of people who had joined the search spurred each other on. The wind howled off the lake. The waves broke in huge whitecaps, angry as an ocean. The holiday spirit only exacerbated the anxiety for Karoline.

The searchers bent their bodies against the wind, which was blowing now at fifty miles an hour. Karoline could easily have been blinded by the snow, a victim, not of her own demons, but of the vicious winter that had turned the camp, so idyllic in the summer, into a bleak prison.

Through the night Geza begged them not to give up. "If we don't find her soon, she'll die of exposure." They continued searching until they too felt stiff and frozen.

Early the next morning they found Karoline on the banks of the barge canal. An autopsy revealed she had swallowed one hundred tablets of aspirin.

CHAPTER TWENTY

Karoline's death shattered the holiday spirit.

Geza was numb with pain. A band of sorrowing women led by Magrita Ehrenstamm brought him food, bathed and fed little Ronald and George, and in the end, seeing Geza incoherent with grief, scarcely able to rise from his stool of mourning, placed the two little boys with a family who could care for them.

Men, sorely needed to maintain the camp, complained of strange pains in the chest, headaches, backaches, swollen legs. The doctors were the arbiters of the work force. Each day they filled out a batch of slips "Unable to work." The deterioration threatened to tear the camp apart.

Dr. Ernst Wolff brought me a manuscript which he had titled "Storm in the Shelter." Suave, crinkly-eyed, with a light mustache, Dr. Wolff was the author of sixty novels that had sold three million copies. He had even worked in Hollywood in the twenties as a screenwriter before returning to his native Vienna.

"I've been up all night writing this for you. Please read it now." He settled himself into a chair, watching me through large troubled eyes while I read.

Night. I am lying in bed, and outside the storm is howling—no, it isn't howling; it's racing—at forty-three miles an hour. It pipes in a hellish concert through all the seams in my lightly built quarters. I thank the Lord for the noble American nation and its wonderful President. Yes, I thank them with all my being—*but*. It is a "but" even after I am offered humanity, radio, underwear, clothes, shoes, food, quarters for living and recreation and so forth. Despite all this, "but"? Yes, *But*. Because none offers me that for which my heart is languishing and to the sanctuary of which every last creature on God's earth is entitled: FREEDOM! . . .

I am told we refugees are prisoners (we were told we would be guests—what irony!) because we have not status under the law: So we exist in a legal vacuum, under a sentence more cruel than that of a common criminal—the sentence of uncertainty . . . For what have we cried blood from our eyes and mankind beaten its breast in lamentation over us? That we should be prisoners in the Land of Promise? For what freedom is America fighting a war abroad only to lose it in shame in Fort Ontario?

I will not be supported any further: I will be a free man again.

January continued bleak and cold. Fifty inches of snow fell in less than a month, freezing so high that the elderly could not leave their barracks even for food, and the sick were marooned.

Fewer visitors came. One or two newspapers occasionally carried stories of the haven on Lake Ontario.

On January 17, news came that Russia's Marshal Georgi Zhukov had entered Warsaw. The Allies were advancing on all fronts in Europe. Hope grew that the war would be over soon. That the killing would end. They would know whether their families had survived.

But the misery in the camp fed upon itself. "I fear," Joe Smart wrote, "it is becoming impossible to maintain the people in health and safety without actual peril to life."

A psychologist, Dr. Curt Bondy, sent to the camp as a consultant by WRA, recommended "giving the residents permission to make visits of, say, up to thirty days duration with their relatives and friends." Such "sponsored leave," he hoped, would "diminish some of the stress in the shelter."

On January 31, 1945, a number of private agencies, led by Professor Chamberlain, issued a statement strongly urging sponsored leave. They would assume all financial responsibility, promising that "none of these individuals would become a public charge."

Ickes approved the idea and wrote to General William O'Dwyer, who had just been appointed executive director of the War Refugee Board (John Pehle had returned to Treasury), urging that the refugees be granted sponsored leave until the United States decided what it wanted to do with them.

A copy of the letter went to Attorney General Francis Biddle; Justice would have to approve any change in the status of the people.

"On a number of occasions," Biddle answered, he had "assured members of Congress that the admission of these refugees did not give them any right to be at liberty here or to remain permanently in the United States, and that they would be de-

tained in a refugee settlement until they could be safely returned
to their homelands.''

Biddle was not to be moved by Ickes's arguments, nor was
President Roosevelt, who had informed Biddle earlier that he
''wholly agreed that the people should *not* be permitted even to
apply for immigration to the United States. They should in fact
be returned to Europe as soon as a favorable opportunity arose.''

Ickes showed me the correspondence. I read it, appalled.
Roosevelt, in his original cable, had announced that the people
would go back; I had been sure it was largely to placate Congress.
But this confirmation to Biddle was even sharper than his message to Congress. Anyone, anywhere outside America, could
apply for immigration, but not the Oswego refugees. It was as if
they were being punished for having been invited to the United
States.

In February, the daytime gates were flung open for a handful
of fortunate young people. They were to enter the Oswego State
Teachers College.

Traveling in a bus provided by the Coordinating Committee,
they drove to the outskirts of town and pulled up in front of a
handsome brick structure with white steps, white columns and a
covered walkway. On the lawn was a bronze statue of a bearded
educator, Edward Austin Sheldon, who had founded the college
as the Oswego Normal and Training School in 1861. Sitting in a
bronze chair, he smiled at a young lad looking up at him. The
pedestal said simply, ''The Children's Friend.''

Among those winding their way around the statue into the
portico were Mira Lederer, who wanted to be a writer; Jetta
Hendel, who dreamed of becoming an architect; David Levy,
who had evoked Mrs. Roosevelt's aid; Vadim Mikhailoff, who,
with his parents, was one of the leading actors of the Russian
Orthodox group; Samuilo Romano; Tina Koerner; Walter Maurer,
the brother of International Harry; and Rajko and Alex Margulis.

Some twenty younger children also descended from the bus.
They had been transferred from P.S. 2, the little schoolhouse
near the camp, to the far-better-equipped Model School of the
Teachers College, where skilled teachers and young teachers-in-
training would soon be teaching them to speak English almost
without accent.

For these young people, Oswego meant the opening of doors
to a new life. But for too many of the adults it had become a
galling and demoralizing experience.

*   *   *

A temporary thaw began to melt the snow. All winter, ledges of ice had built up around the piles of coal stacked in the open, near the main entrance of the camp. Now the ice began to defrost. On the morning of February 19 the coal crew arrived to shovel the coal, fling it onto a truck and deliver it to the camp's furnaces.

"I'll start shoveling today," Arpad Buchler offered. A quiet man in his early forties, Arpad worked cheerfully at any task he was given. On Shabbat, people noticed the joy with which he shepherded his young wife, Renée, their four little children, all under ten, and his widowed mother, Emilia, to the orthodox synagogue.

"Arpad, it's not your turn today," his friend Silvio Finci protested, not too vehemently.

"That's all right. I'll shovel today and you can wait at the truck."

Arpad dug into the coal closest to the ground, humming happily. Suddenly the top ledge of ice, melting in the sun, broke loose with a barrage of coal and crashed over him. The work crew rushed to pull him loose, pushing the coal with their shovels, their hands, their bodies. When they reached Arpad, he was dead.

First Karoline's suicide, now Arpad's death.

The demoralization grew worse. The doctors diagnosed 110 people as victims of neurosis.

Searching for some way to stem the disintegration, the War Relocation Authority and the Coordinating Committee asked Dr. Rudolf Dreikurs, a Chicago psychiatrist, to visit the camp.

It was late March when Ickes called me to his office. "This Dr. Dreikurs will probably need your help. I'd like you to go up there immediately."

The next night was the beginning of the Passover, the most joyous family celebration of all the Jewish festivals.

At the gate Abe Furmanski greeted me. "I know you've come with a proclamation from the President—that we're all free."

I stopped in my tracks. "Where did you hear this?" Was it possible that Roosevelt had changed his mind while I was on the night train?

"Everybody has been talking about it. For weeks people have been rushing around Oswego buying suitcases. They bought every trunk in the stores. When the trunks ran out they bought foot lockers. Some even dropped their subscriptions to newspapers."

I checked the rumor with Joe Smart. "I'm not sure how it

started," he said. "Apparently somebody in New York saw somebody else who knew that Professor Chamberlain had gone down to Washington to talk with O'Dwyer. They figured that was the only thing Chamberlain could have talked about."

I spent the day trying to quench the rumor. It had seemed so logical that they would be released on the very holiday celebrating the Exodus from Egypt to the Promised Land. Of course a loving President and a caring government would set them free for the Passover.

The snow had melted, the barren trees were sprouting buds, and the wind off the lake seemed gentle. But even the end of the long winter failed to raise their spirits as they forced themselves to accept the depressing truth. The Yugoslavs were especially agitated. The Yugoslav consul in New York must also have heard the rumor; he had sent a notice warning the Yugoslavs that if they did not go back as soon as the camp was dissolved they would lose their citizenship.

But in the orthodox mess hall, known as Kitchen 93, there was only joy.

For weeks before the holiday, Kitchen 93 had been in a turmoil of excitement. Every corner of the mess hall was swept to make certain there was no "leaven" left; crumbs were packed together and burned. The old dishes were now all stored away; the Coordinating Committee had purchased brand-new dishes for the Passover week.

As evening fell in the camp, I entered the dining hall. It had been transformed into a living tableau. Rabbi Tzechoval, in a long white robe and a white skullcap, reclined on white pillows and a couch at the head of the table. Thus "freemen" had reclined in ancient times, no longer slaves unto Pharaoh. Joe Smart sat in a seat of honor next to the rabbi.

The rabbi beckoned to me. "How do your children look to you?"

I looked around at the people, the holiday lights casting a warm glow on their rounded faces. "You're all grown," I said. Even the rabbi's face, once pale and painfully thin, was now pink and plump.

The seder began, as it had for millennia, with the rabbi explaining it once again to all of us and especially to Joe. "Everything tonight," he said while Joe listened entranced, "is about freedom. Even the matzoh means freedom, because it means that the Jews escaping from the tyranny of Egypt had no time to bake bread."

"Look around you," Abe Furmanski, sitting next to me, said.

"For some of us, it's the first Passover in six or seven years. We didn't dare have seders in concentration camps, or when we hid out as Catholics in Italy. Last year I made my first seder—I couldn't wait anymore. We were in Rome under false papers. We put the children to sleep so there would be no sounds. We waited until one in the morning, we locked the doors and held the seder in whispers."

Now, instead of whispers, there was a commotion. The rabbi rose from his couch and nodded to the men, who surrounded Joe, lifted him out of his chair and carried him to the center of the floor. Then, locking hands, they formed a circle around him, dancing, singing with ecstasy, leaping faster and faster until they could no longer catch their breath.

At last the rabbi returned to his couch; Joe, beaming, took his seat, and the story of the Exodus continued far into the night.

"I want to talk to you later at great length," Dr. Dreikurs told me the next morning. "I will want whatever insights you can give me."

He was of medium height, with a friendly unthreatening smile and a German accent. He had made a reputation as a leading Adlerian psychiatrist who believed in solving problems through group activities.

"I see this whole camp as a Greek tragedy with all the dynamic forces interacting. I see all the players, the government in Washington, the staff here, the outside groups and the refugees; and I see the intentions of each group colliding with the intentions of the others."

We were in a hospital room where he was to interview and diagnose some of the 110 people with neurotic symptoms, and some of the staff. I promised to spend more time with him, and left him to begin his work.

Saturday afternoon he invited the entire American staff to meet him in Joe's office.

"I can't imagine anybody living here as a refugee, or working here on the staff, remaining sane," he began.

We looked at each other uneasily. Was he telling us that even the staff was neurotic, that working here made "normal" people abnormal and mentally healthy people insane?

"The antagonisms," he went on, "the mutual distrust, the human relations of people living close together, create a vicious cycle, in which all of you are caught. The malaise in this camp is paranoia. The closer people live to each other, the more paranoiac their attitudes become.'' He looked at the staff. ''Do you have questions?''

''It's the work problem,'' one of the staff members raised his hand. ''Especially in sanitation and feeding. We have some who are willing to work, and they're good. In fact, they overwork. But then we have nonworkers, and the workers complain we do nothing against them. They say we should bring sanctions.''

Dreikurs nodded. ''Even among the nonworkers, you have two kinds of people: those who say, 'How can you ask us to work? We are guests of the United States,' and there are those who get sick with stomach ailments and so forth. The doctors don't find any stomach ailments, but the people really feel pain. It's a psychiatric pain, and it must definitely be treated. In fact, we have to do education with both kinds of nonworkers. And we have to treat the malaise among you, the staff and the refugees.''

In the evening, notices were sent to all the barracks. Everyone was invited to a Sunday-morning lecture by Dr. Dreikurs entitled ''Common Solution of Common Problems,'' in the post theater.

On the stage, talking to a packed house the next morning, Dr. Dreikurs established his connection with the refugees. ''I too am a refugee from Vienna. We all have problems of insecurity. We all feel ourselves uprooted; but I tell you, the average American feels just as insecure as you. Your problems, whether you are having difficulties in your marriage, problems with your children, are typically human problems. But in camps, there is one problem—may I say it very strongly without insulting you—a great number of people feel morally responsible to be unhappy. I confess I would feel the same if I were in a camp.''

A few heads nodded in agreement.

''You believe you are unhappy because of the terror you lived through, because you are forced to live here, because you have no future. All of you have the same troubles, yet some of you are courageous while others break down and suffer more. Yes?''

The word ''Yes'' rose and fell in different corners of the theater.

''The cause of this, for those who suffer, is the feeling of insecurity. Whether we are big or small, fat or thin, we are all here because we have no social status. Yet it is the petty things that disturb us, not the big ones.''

''Yes, yes,'' people shouted again.

''We have to work for a solution. If you think of yourself alone, you can't work for a solution. The camp is full of pain and suffering. But as long as you must be here, do you want to make it better or worse? Do you want to be more wretched, so that more people will break down, or, when the camp finally closes, do you want to go out healthy? I am looking for peace workers who will help me to help you. Who will be a peace worker? Raise your hand.''

Hands went up across the theater.

"Will I find more peace workers among the men or the women?''

The men shouted, "Men.''

The women shouted, "Women.''

Dr. Dreikurs smiled. The people smiled, too, as they walked out of the theater.

After eleven days of interviews, Dr. Dreikurs returned to Chicago and wrote a report recommending more group activities. He singled out Magrita Ehrenstamm and her fellow workers in the Club of the Lonesomes and suggested that similar clubs be organized not only for the refugees but also for the staff. His hope, he wrote, was to help the staff help the refugees and "make their good intentions, courage, determination and perseverance more effective.''

Dreikurs's visit had helped.

But the fear that time was running out filled the camp with bitterness. The people knew that there were jobs in America, that there was desperate need for their skills in Oswego. Even the townspeople were angry. "It's an outrage,'' Edmund Waterbury, the publisher of the *Oswego Palladium-Times* told me, "that they aren't permitted to help solve the difficult work problems created by the manpower shortage and that they are treated worse than German or Italian prisoners of war. We pamper the Nazi prisoners while these innocent people whom the Nazis tried to kill are treated as though they were Nazis. I just don't get it.''

"Work and freedom" became the dream and the obsession. To work outside the camp. To be free.

Artur Hirt, the Polish judge, said ironically, "I am a judge, so I shovel coal in America.''

Israel Willner, the cook in the kosher kitchen, read the advertisements offering chefs five hundred dollars a month.

"The years are flowing by. I am losing my youth. I want to go out and work and make something of myself. I have a visa to the United States in my pocket, and now I am wasting my life.''

In the hospital, Dr. Eugene Svecenski talked bitterly as he took me on his rounds. "I'm forty-seven. When I signed up to come to America, I said, 'If I'm lucky, Europe will never see me again.' Who knows now? Will I ever be able to resume my work and make a living?"

Back in Washington, I wrote up the report of my visit for Ickes, calling it "Eight Months Later."

For most of the refugees, I wrote,

> the camp has meant new life. The little Europe which we had on the ship, the Balkanization of the camp in the first months, are disappearing. The melting pot is boiling again, and democratization has set in. But a camp is a camp is a camp, and even with the best will in the world, people deteriorate in camp life.

Only a major decision could halt the spread of hysteria and depression. I recommended that we try to close the camp as soon as possible. It was true the refugees had signed a release in Italy that they would go back at the end of the war. But at that time no one really knew the people; there were even fears there might be spies among them. We knew them well enough now to be sure that they were not spies.

I ended the report:

> We should permit those who are eligible for entry to the United States to cross the border into Canada and re-enter the United States under regular quotas on an individual basis. It is time we showed that this administration has a policy of decency, humanity, and conscience, and the guts to carry that policy through.

"Quite a picture you drew," Ickes said solemnly. "I agree with you. I would like to see the camp closed as soon as possible. But my hands are tied. We've got to get the War Refugee Board and the rest of the government to see it. Meanwhile, until we do close the camp, we have to try to get sponsored leave."

He put his hand over his chin as if he were mulling over the words.

"It would be a crime to send them back. A crime if a country of one hundred thirty seven million could not absorb one thousand refugees."

On April 12 the camp went into mourning.

A full-page obituary in the *Ontario Chronicle,* the weekly

newspaper the refugees wrote themselves, mourned the death of the President.

In the synagogue, the congregants stood reciting the Kaddish, the prayer for the dead. Then, led by the rabbis, they walked across the camp and entered the old fort. They raised the American flag; the orchestra played "The Star Spangled Banner," and Mirković, his face stricken with grief, sang Sibelius' "Prayer of Peace."

In the mournful silence, the people listened as Fredi Baum delivered the eulogy.

"He was a great fearless leader of warm qualities, upon whom the whole world focused its attention, to lead it out of barbarism to the light of liberty, freedom and happiness. Though we are not citizens of this country, though most of us have become stateless, we understand perhaps better than any others what this death means to the entire world."

Sobs shook the people. They were in America because of this American President. They were banded together in sorrow. Their father, their savior, their protector, was dead.

What now lay ahead?

CHAPTER TWENTY-ONE

The victories in Europe pulled the camp temporarily out of its depression. The people followed each campaign as if they were on the battlefield; many knew every inch of territory regained.

Saturday, April 21, Marshal Zhukov, "the general who never lost a battle," entered the outskirts of Berlin. Manya, carrying Diane, the baby she had just given birth to, called me in Washington. "Ruthie, do you believe it? It's the city where I was born."

In Italy, the Allied armies captured Bologna. General Mark Clark issued his order of the day: "We now stand inside the gateway to the Po Plain, poised to destroy the Germans who continue to enslave and exploit Northern Italy."

In the camp, the people rejoiced for the peasants and the

villagers who had risked their lives for them, given them shelter, shared their food.

A week later they rejoiced even more. Italian partisans captured Mussolini and his mistress, Clara Petacci, in their hideout near Lake Como. They met a dreadful death. They were shot, their bodies thrown into a van and taken to Milan, where they were exhibited to the world hanging by their heels from the girders of a filling station.

And two days after that, on April 30, word came: Hitler and Eva Braun committed suicide in the Führerbunker in Berlin.

The cry that went up in the camp carried over the fence into the streets of Oswego.

In the camp, three of Joe Smart's advisers knocked on his door at night. "We must speak to you in strictest confidence."

Dr. Otto Lederer, Dr. Arthur Ernst, the editor-in-chief of the *Ontario Chronicle,* and Dr. Edmund Landau, associate editor, entered his living room. Dr. Lederer spoke first. "We have just received reliable information. We are all to be sent back to Europe. The date has been set. June thirtieth—it's less than two months away. The War Department has already committed a ship."

"I've heard nothing of this," Joe said. "But your information is often much better than mine. What is your source?"

"It's a man with good connections in Washington," Dr. Ernst said. Joe sat back, stunned.

"You have been working very hard for us, Mr. Smart," Dr. Landau spoke next. "But we think this problem is so big, and the crisis is so urgent, only an outside organization can influence the Administration. Especially President Truman."

Joe mulled over the idea. "An outside organization with big names like Mrs. Roosevelt."

"That's right, Mr. Smart," said Dr. Lederer, "we need powerful voices to reach the new President."

"Let me sleep on this," Joe said.

The next morning Joe called his three advisers to his office. "I've made my decision. I want to promote your idea, but I cannot do it as shelter director. I am going to resign."

"You would give up your job?" Dr. Lederer asked. "We didn't expect that. Your livelihood—your family—"

"I am prepared. In my opinion, I am the logical person to take on this job."

Joe released the announcement to the press. A few days later he walked into my office in Washington. "Go ahead, Ruth. Let me have it." He looked like a little boy expecting a whipping.

I had no intention of tongue-lashing him. "What really lay behind your resignation?"

"The conviction that this was the only way to get things done. I'm going to New York, open an office and set up a new committee to try to mobilize public opinion."

Joe had hardly walked out the door when my secretary brought in copies of the *New York Daily News* and the *Jewish Morning Journal*. The story that the camp was to be closed June 30 was front page. The source was General O'Dwyer himself, the new executive director of the War Refugee Board.

I telephoned O'Dwyer's office, only to be told he was in California making a speech. His assistant, Florence Hodel, came to the phone. I could hear her gasp as I told her of the newspaper accounts that O'Dwyer planned to shut down the camp.

"How did that rumor get started?" she asked.

"Is it a rumor?"

"It may become fact."

"When was it decided? We were never told."

"We're planning to wind up our work June thirtieth. That's when WRB will be dissolved. The board may therefore take the position to send them back on the thirtieth."

If the rumor was indeed fact, I was prepared to fight. "I would like to know what General O'Dwyer is really planning."

She answered swiftly. "I'm in no position, and General O'Dwyer is not, either, to make a disposition of these people. We can only make recommendations to the board. General O'Dwyer feels the refugees are in jail here. But it is something he inherited. He was not director when this whole thing started."

At four-thirty she telephoned again. "I've just spoken to General O'Dwyer in California. He is furious. He wants you to know that he never said he was shutting down the camp."

But in the camp the people talked of little else.

In the *Ontario Chronicle*, Dr. Landau described the bewilderment of the people:

> Could it be really the intention to send a resident who unfortunately was born in Germany or Austria, back to the countries of Buchenwald, Auschwitz or Dachau? Could a salvation action of a people who have suffered so much, have sense when the saved people will be sent back to Poland, where, as everyone knows, the political situation is more than confused? General D. Eisenhower has recently given the

184 / *Ruth Gruber*

order that no Polish citizen who is now liberated from German camps can be forced to return to Poland against his own free will. For many of us a return to "their homelands in Europe" signifies no more or less than a death warrant.

On May 7, 1945, Germany surrendered unconditionally. The shooting and the dying in Europe was over. The death camps would be opened—Dachau, Buchenwald, Theresienstadt, Auschwitz and scores of others whose names we were yet to learn.

The people congregated on the parade ground, hugging one another, laughing, weeping, repeating the unbelievable words, "The war in Europe is over." Some joined hands and danced in circles; some sat in the synagogues and churches praying; some stayed in their barracks alone with their hopes and their grief.

A week later I was called back to New York. My father lay in bed, stricken, his arms and legs paralyzed by a stroke, but fully aware. His eyes misted as he saw me. "It's good you came."

Early in the evening, the whole family sat at his bedside. His face seemed to brighten like a candle before it flickers out. Then my brother Harry, a physician, rose, looked at his face, and wept.

"Papa is dead."

CHAPTER TWENTY-TWO

I was at my desk on a quiet Saturday morning in Washington, catching up with mail from the refugees and from would-be homesteaders in Alaska, when the phone rang.

"I want to raise an issue with you." Florence Hodel, O'Dwyer's assistant, spoke diffidently. "Would Interior like to take full responsibility for the camp when the War Refugee Board goes out of existence next month?"

I said nothing. It was almost too good to believe—Ickes and WRA in full charge, making the decisions, their hands untied.

"What are the other possibilities?" I asked.

"The State Department."

"State!" I tried to keep my voice calm. To put the fate of

the refugees back in the hands of Breckinridge Long was unthinkable.

"We've also considered the Bureau of Immigration—"

"In the Justice Department." It was just as unthinkable.

"We would rather have you take it over in Interior. What do you think?"

"I would welcome it. I'll talk to some of our people and call you back."

"We can do a good job," Abe Fortas, our Undersecretary, agreed. "But don't forget, State and Justice must still make the final decision on the legal status of the refugees."

Ickes had no hesitation. "We'll take it. Just let them make a formal offer."

Meanwhile, word raced through the camp that they were soon to be deported.

Caught in the growing panic, twenty-seven of Oswego's leading citizens, led by the mayor, sent a memorial to President Truman and to Congress on May 21, pleading that the refugees be allowed to stay. The memorial cheered the people, but in the White House and in Congress it was one more piece of paper in the burgeoning file folders marked "Oswego."

The panic spread. The private agencies were charged by angry columnists with timidity and inaction.

Professor Joseph Chamberlain, the widely respected chairman of the National Refugee Service, came to Washington. His face was drawn; he seemed years older than at our first meeting. "I'm terribly worried. What was started in this country last August when you brought the people to America was the beginning of a much bigger refugee movement. Oswego has become the center, the world showpiece of refugees. Thousands of refugees, here and abroad, are looking to see what's happening at the camp in Oswego. I tell you, the United States cannot afford to take the lead in sending displaced persons back to countries where they would starve."

"We've got Ickes on our side, fighting it everywhere, in the Cabinet, up on the Hill—"

"If Ickes can get State and Justice to postpone decisions about the final disposition for six months," he said, "we can work on 'sponsored leave.' We can resettle these families quietly all over the country and place the orphaned children in foster homes."

But with the war in Europe over, State and Justice were in no mood to postpone a decision for six months, and now we were faced with a new dilemma.

From Miriam Wydra, whose family came from Germany, I learned that her boss, Congressman Samuel Dickstein of New York, was planning to investigate the camp. Dickstein was chairman of the House Committee on Immigration and Naturalization. "You better come up on the Hill," she said, "and see the Congressman."

"This whole matter is getting out of hand," Dickstein, short, nattily dressed, told me. "Congress has got to look into it. After all, we're responsible for immigration. We write the law. I've decided to take my subcommittee up to the camp and determine what should be done with the people."

The next day Dickstein announced his decision to the press, promising "open hearings" in Oswego and New York.

Bernie Dubin, the financial officer at the NRS, called me in alarm. "Can't you stop Dickstein? Congressional committees are dangerous; what recourse will we have if they vote to shut the camp down and send the people back?"

"You can't stop a congressman from holding hearings. The only thing we can do is present our case so forcefully, and so humanly, that the committee will vote in our favor."

Ickes agreed there was reason for alarm. "You never know what these congressional committees can come up with. You could get a subcommittee of isolationists who would like to see America shut its doors altogether. The best way to handle them is public opinion. Go up to New York right away," Ickes ordered. "See if you can get some of your friends on the newspapers and the weeklies to write editorials. Then get the private agencies to send a group of their top people down here to see Morgenthau and O'Dwyer. Tell them I'll be glad to see them, too."

At three o'clock on a warm June day we trooped like a little army into the office of the Secretary of the Treasury. I introduced the people to Morgenthau: the three representatives of the National Refugee Service, Professor Chamberlain, Mr. Dubin and Mr. Zatkin; Miss Jones of the American Friends Service Committee; Mr. Bisgeyer of B'nai B'rith; Mr. Goldman of the Jewish Labor Committee; and Mr. Cohen of the American Jewish Committee. I knew how carefully the agencies had selected them for this critical day.

Morgenthau sat behind a huge desk, a tall, intellectual-looking figure with a balding head, a strong prominent nose and pince-nez. The office was austere, the desk bare save for a silver ashtray with the engraved letters "FDR to HM Jr. Xmas 1939."

Behind him on a table were photographs of his family. John Pehle, the former director of the War Refugee Board, sat on the windowsill.

Chamberlain presented the argument for allowing the Oswego refugees to stay. His voice was strong, his language precise; he spoke like a lawyer committed to the law but with a deep sense of justice and humanitarianism.

Morgenthau pulled the pince-nez off his nose, held it for a few moments between his thumb and forefinger, replaced it, and finally spoke. "You're asking that we change the instructions issued by the President. We wrote those instructions here. We can't go back on them now. We've got to keep faith with Roosevelt." He readjusted his glasses. "I can't go back on my promise to the dead President; I couldn't sleep with my conscience."

The air was heavy. I was prepared for such words from State and Justice. But Morgenthau was the man who had brought the cables to the President. He had exposed the State Department's machinations. He and his men, Pehle, DuBois and others, had created the War Refugee Board. They had done a magnificent job, they had saved thousands of lives in Hungary alone. They had circumvented the State Department's rigid stranglehold on immigration and created this haven at Oswego.

I heard his words with despair. *I could not sleep with my conscience.*

"Mr. Secretary," I said, "I have the feeling that if the President were alive, he would be the first to change his own memos. He would see how inhumane it is to keep people—" I stopped. I saw him glance briefly at Pehle, who nodded but remained silent.

"The only way to do it," Morgenthau said with finality, "is through Congress."

"But we're worried about Congress," Chamberlain countered. "A number of people, Ickes for instance, whom we saw this morning, say the Hill is hostile to more immigration, particularly of Jews."

Morgenthau hardly heard him. "I wouldn't take any second-hand opinion. I'd go right to see the Speaker of the House, Sam Rayburn, and the President of the Senate, Ken McKellar. We are very lucky in having two such men. I would ask them how many votes they could promise on this issue."

Chamberlain looked stricken. "We feel, Mr. Secretary, we mustn't let Congress touch this issue. They might upset the whole immigration apple cart. This problem has worldwide refu-

gee implications. We don't want to do anything that will undermine the possibility of getting a new law through Congress.
We're trying to legitimize the status of some ten or twenty
thousand people who are now in the country illegally or on
temporary visas."

"Well, that's an entirely different problem." Morgenthau bit
his lower lip. "You come to me on one problem, Oswego; my
heart goes out to it. When Mrs. Morgenthau came back from the
camp after a visit with Mrs. Roosevelt, she kept me awake
prodding me with the camp. I couldn't sleep. Now you come to
me on this problem; I give you a solution; I tell you what to do;
then you bring in all these other things. That's not what you
came to me for; that's another whole story entirely."

I could not help feel we had placed him in an embarrassing
position. Disappointed and discouraged, we left.

In the outer office we found General O'Dwyer. Still working
in Washington, O'Dwyer was already campaigning for the office
of mayor of New York. He shook our hands, smiled broadly and
told us eagerly, "I've seen people in the White House, I've seen
people in Justice; I'm going to see the Secretary now and, if
necessary, I'll go to see Truman. I'm carrying in my hand, right
here, recommendations to get the people out of the camp
immediately. All of you go to my office. I'll be there soon and
tell you the whole story."

His office in the basement of the Treasury was filled with
visitors and aides. His desk, like Morgenthau's, was bare, save
for an assortment of cigars and a large ashtray. He could have
closed shop in minutes and left Washington for good, I thought.

We sat waiting impatiently. Half an hour. An hour. At last he
strode in, puffing a long cigar. He sat behind his empty desk
talking about Oswego.

"Those poor sons-of-guns up there, they've been through hell
and high water, they've been driven all around the world, and
we keep them up there in a prison. I'm against picking them up
from one incarceration and dumping them over in Europe into
another incarceration. Those poor people should be allowed to
look out of the bars at the blue sky and smell the good fresh
air."

Goldman of the Jewish Labor Committee, sitting at my right,
whispered, "Have you decided whom you're going to vote for
yet? He's running for mayor right here."

"It tears my heart," O'Dwyer went on, "when I think of
those poor sons-of-guns who suffered so much already, and the
whole government of the great United States, the President and

all the people can't do a thing for them. How can I sleep with my conscience if we don't do something for them now?

"Gentlemen," he said, "I am glad you came to Washington today. I am going to do something for you. I am going to read you this report with the recommendations I'll be making to the War Refugee Board. It's strictly confidential; you must make no notes; it mustn't go outside this room. But I want you to know what my thinking is."

The recommendations were the very ones we wanted to hear—freedom, sponsored leave, the right to stay in America.

"I'm getting out of the picture soon," he said. "But this thing lies close to my heart. Even as a defeated candidate for mayor of New York I'll come back and fight."

I was prepared to give him my vote right there.

In the power plays of Washington, good news and bad, life-and-death decisions, arrive on intergovernmental memos.

The memo arrived at Ickes's desk. The War Refugee Board was pleased to transfer its powers and responsibility to the War Relocation Authority on the thirtieth of June.

Ickes asked me to draft a letter immediately to President Truman requesting permission to close the camp in thirty days and grant the refugees sponsored leave.

He sent the letter. But before the President could act, Congressman Dickstein announced that on Monday, June 25, Subcommittee VI of the House Committee on Immigration and Naturalization would begin its investigation at the camp itself.

Ickes was a past master at congressional investigations. He gave me new orders. "Check into the backgrounds of the six congressmen on the committee. Then escort them to the train going up to the camp. That way you'll get a chance to know them personally. And, of course, I want you up in Oswego during the investigation. My instincts tell me they'll be calling you to testify."

His instincts, as usual, were sound. A few days before the hearings were to start, Miriam Wydra, the first woman appointed chief clerk to the House Committee on Immigration and Naturalization, asked me to come to her home, where she told me, "Dickstein wants you as a witness. But you can be much more. If you see that the hearings are taking a wrong turn, feel free to tell him what you think. But don't misunderstand. If Dickstein doesn't agree with you, he'll say so. I just want you to know that he has a lot of confidence in you, and that he's a decent man who listens to reason."

CHAPTER TWENTY-THREE

Grand Central Station seemed empty and cavernous as I waited for the six congressmen on a quiet Sunday morning. In Washington Ed Marks and I had tried to anticipate the pitfalls. Ed was chief of the War Refugee Division of WRA, and one of Dillon Myer's ablest assistants.

We had spent hours choosing the refugees we hoped would most impress the six men of Subcommittee VI. Of the six congressmen, the two most likely to be hostile were Lowell Stockman of Oregon and Clark Fisher of Texas. Their records on immigration were little different from the State Department's; the quotas, for them, were chiseled in stone.

The six men sauntered into the huge terminal. Dickstein greeted me jovially and introduced me. Stockman was a giant out of Grimm's fairy tales. Everything about him seemed larger than life—his huge hand that engulfed mine, his enormous feet, his body that seemed to grow as I looked up at it, his strong rugged chin, his long eyes. He was like a tree out of his own Northwest. He had been a rancher in Oregon. Dwarfed by him, Fisher was medium-sized, with regular features and a slow Texas drawl. He had been a district attorney before coming to Washington, and he too owned a cattle ranch.

We headed straight for the dining car for breakfast. "Come join us." Stockman pulled a chair for me next to the window. "Fisher and I can use some female companionship."

The landscape rushed beside us. It seemed to me the wheels were grinding the words "Stockman and Fisher." The names were synonymous with danger. I tried to get some inkling of how they felt; but they were in no mood to discuss the inquiry. They were two ranchers vying with each other to tell me cowboy stories.

They were still trading yarns when the train pulled into Syracuse. Limousines were lined up to drive us directly to the camp.

Summer had restored the beauty of the camp. The people

crowded around us. "Our liberators have come," someone shouted as we climbed out of the cars.

Manya rushed forward to show me little Diane. International Harry, a precocious one-year-old, raced near the cars, followed by Olga, out of breath from chasing him. Ed Marks, who had gone up earlier, came forward with Malcolm Pitts, the acting director, to welcome the congressmen.

"We'd like to see some of the camp," Dickstein said. There had been processions before, but never one like this, with Dickstein commanding his troops, followed by hundreds of refugees, who had never seemed more full of hope. Apparently no one had told them of the dangers of a congressional hearing.

It was a carefully calculated tour to show them the Americanization of Fort Ontario: the classrooms where the people had studied English and learned the Bill of Rights; the exhibition hall with works of art that had recently won prizes in a museum in Syracuse—oil paintings by Vladimir von Zabotin, terra-cotta sculpture and watercolors by Miriam Sommerburg. The artists' works had gone to Syracuse, but not the artists. Syracuse was out of bounds.

Early Monday morning, the huge gymnasium filled up with Washington brass, members of the staff, refugees who were to testify and rows of journalists and photographers. Once again, Oswego was front-page news.

At the stroke of ten-thirty, the congressmen took their seats at a long table. Dickstein, sitting in the center with the committee counsel, Thomas M. Cooley II, at his side, opened the hearings formally: "By a mandate of the Congress of the United States, the Committee on Immigration and Naturalization is authorized to make an overall study . . . to determine just what should be done with regard to the number of people in this camp, from the standpoint of some humane justice for them."

Ed Marks, as the first witness, gave the history of the project, the activities in the camp, and the restrictions on freedom which gave the people an "indeterminate kind of sentence."

General O'Dwyer was next. He had promised us he would fight, and he fought with passion. "To send stateless people who have no homelands back to a destroyed Europe," he said, would "in my opinion not be in accordance with the late President's commitment and our government's political and humanitarian policies."

Whatever his political motives, whether or not he had his eye fixed on the Jewish, Catholic, Greek Orthodox, Polish, Yugoslav or any other ethnic vote in New York City, not only failed to trouble me, I was delighted. The reporters were scribbling furiously in their notebooks.

Now, subtly, Congressman Fisher began his attack.

MR. FISHER: General, just to get the record straight, do you understand these people, who were brought here under the conditions that have been described, understood when they came here that they were going to be taken back as soon as the war was over?

GENERAL O'DWYER: I would say they were told that. I would agree they were told that, but I do say that this committee should keep in mind the mental condition of the people at the time they were told that, running through trouble, from pillar to post, harried, and coming to America was something to them at that time, and they took their chances on what would happen to them after that.

MR. FISHER (in disbelief): You understand that these people feel they were brought here under false pretenses, do you?

GENERAL O'DWYER: No; not at all. I don't believe that was anything like that, but I do say that we won't run into people like this again in our lifetime. You have them in a very confused mental state, and they were going to America. I think any of them would have signed any piece of paper you handed to them at that time. And they were going to America, that was the only place in the world, having been harassed the way they had, everyone wanted to go. The same thing happened to me thirty-five years ago, and I know how it is.

Fisher now pressed O'Dwyer. "Wasn't the Department of Justice under obligation to keep faith with the President's directive?"

O'Dwyer agreed; that had been his position earlier. But this committee, appointed by Congress, could end that obligation.

Fisher turned belligerent. "We certainly aren't called upon to amend the immigration laws, to make any special exceptions."

"All that is needed," O'Dwyer said calmly, "is just a matter of interpretation."

But as Fisher prodded him O'Dwyer became more impassioned. "I am afraid I don't make my point to you, Mr. Fisher. You at the present time have millions over in Europe, millions of displaced persons where a resettlement program for each one of them will have to be made by the United Nations. . . . What are you going to do with the handful we took? Are you going to say to them, 'The war is over; go back'? If you do, you are going to tell every neutral, 'This is the way to handle it.' "

He recommended two actions. First, that the refugees leave the camp now; the private agencies were prepared to assume complete financial and personal responsibility for them. Second, that Congress make no decision about their final status until the United Nations Relief and Rehabilitation Administration (UNRRA) had worked out a policy for the millions of displaced persons left homeless by the war. His ploy was brilliant: to show that the camp at Oswego was a displaced-persons camp on American soil, and that the thousand refugees were part of the whole displaced-persons tragedy.

But Fisher seemed unmoved. And it was hard to tell how Stockman reacted; he had been silent, allowing Fisher to carry the ball for the isolationists.

The morning session ended.

We lunched in the camp hospital and then strolled through the grounds. The congressmen chatted informally with the people who thronged around us, asking me to interpret for those whose English was still limited. Unaware of the morning debate, the refugees continued to beam at their "liberators."

The session reconvened at two. Bugles sounded. The Fort Ontario Boy Scouts and Cub Scouts, in full khaki uniform, marched down the gymnasium, with standard bearers carrying huge American flags. Like soldiers parading before a chief of state, their young faces were solemn.

Photographers rushed forward, flashbulbs popping, capturing the excitement in the hall. Together the Scouts recited the Boy Scout oath in English: "I will do my best to do my duty to God and my country." Our strategy was to make the congressmen see how in this one year the children had become one hundred percent Americans.

Dickstein questioned several of the boys like a grandfather showing off his progeny. "You have no home at all? Would you like to stay in this country? Do you believe in our form of government? Would you be ready to defend it if the country wanted you? With a gun?"

Sylvan Boni, though a little frightened, responded to Dickstein's questions with a resounding "*Yes!*"

I was the last witness for the afternoon session. Determined to win over Fisher and Stockman, I told them of the days and nights on the ship hearing the people's stories; of the scene at the Statue of Liberty with the refugees in their terrible rags; and some of the case histories. Tom Cooley, the committee's counsel, informed the subcommittee that the case histories would become Exhibit 19.

Fisher and Stockman listened, but said nothing, while Geroge P. Miller of California and Cooley asked questions about the Army's screening in Europe and health examinations.

"They had very careful medical screening by army doctors," I assured them, and related how the GIs had even helped deliver International Harry.

"Thank you very much," Dickstein said. "You have done a splendid job. We will adjourn until ten-thirty tomorrow morning."

Back in my hotel room, I opened the window to look down at the Oswego River sparkling in the late afternoon sun. It was nearly a year since I had first seen this river. It seemed to me I was generations older, sadder and, I hoped, wiser. I had tried my best at the hearings. But had I really reached Fisher and Stockman? Had I helped these two ranchers from the West, with vast lands around them, understand what it meant for a refugee to be in America, fenced in; what it meant to children who had been hungry and frightened to wear Boy Scout uniforms, to go to school and bring the Bill of Rights home to their parents?

History had come to this small American town on a river and a lake; and from its schools and movies, from its library and shops and corner drugstores, the refugees had absorbed the spirit of democracy.

The congressmen would have to see it.

I knocked on Naomi Jolles' door in the Pontiac Hotel. She was typing her first story for the *New York Post*. Ted Thackrey, the editor of the *Post*, had sent Naomi, a bright, sophisticated reporter, to cover the hearings, at my request. Naomi had written an article about the refugee children attending Oswego's schools, called "The Fourth R," for *The Women's Home Companion;* the fourth *R* stood for refugees. I told her of my fears that Fisher and Stockman were still hostile. "We've got to work on these two congressmen," I said. "Will you help?"

Naomi shut her portable typewriter. "I'll take Fisher; you get Stockman."

In the hotel dining room, Naomi took a seat beside Fisher; I sat next to Stockman. The two men seemed delighted to have companions. We ate well but hurriedly; we were due back at the camp for a cabaret show.

In the post theater, the six congressmen joined in the National Anthem, applauded the dances and skits, and rose with Dickstein as Mirković sang, "Eli, Eli, my God, my God, why hast Thou forsaken me?"

As we filed out of the theater, Stockman took my arm. "It was really impressive. But after all of that, Fisher and I need a drink. How about you and Naomi joining us?"

We drove to a popular watering place called the White Horse Inn, dark and deserted except for the four of us. Stockman dropped some nickels into the jukebox, and we began to dance. Naomi and Fisher made a handsome couple, but I scarcely came up to Stockman's solar plexus. Like many large men, he was surprisingly graceful and light, while I felt awkward and clumsy. In a mottled wall mirror I caught a glimpse of us and giggled. Fortunately Stockman was telling me a joke.

It was almost midnight when we returned to the hotel, shook hands with the two congressmen in the lobby and thanked them for a lovely evening. Naomi and I agreed that dancing in the White Horse Inn might turn out to be as helpful as the testimony in reaching Fisher and Stockman.

The hearings resumed the next morning as Dr. Ralph Waldo Swetman, the tall bespectacled president of the State Teachers College, talked enthusiastically of the students' eagerness and their determination to do good work. He singled out Alex Margulis. "We had a special assembly at the time of the VE-Day celebration, and Alexander Margulis gave a talk. There were four hundred students in the assembly, and you could hear a pin drop, he spoke with such force and fire."

I could hear Alex's voice. "It is a rainy day, cold and miserable," Alex had begun his speech. "For four years from 1941 to 1945, I kept thinking how glorious it would be on this day; we would dance in the streets. Yet now this day has come and there is no elation. There is just profound regret that so many of the people we loved are not sharing this day. We feel almost guilty that we have survived while so many who are more worthy have not. To them, we can make only one pledge: We will try to prevent this from ever happening again."

The whole gym, even the congressmen, applauded when Ralph Faust announced that in his high school, "just today, I notified eight Fort Ontario students that they are eligible to join the National Honor society."

Edmund Waterbury, the publisher of the *Oswego Palladium-Times,* risked the wrath of his townspeople. "There is more talent in this group than there is in all of Oswego together, and I am not discrediting my own hometown, but when you get painting, sculpturing, music, acting, dancing and playwrighting, they would do credit to a city of five hundred thousand population.''

Now some of the refugees themselves testified with stories of murder and their own escapes.

Young Alex Margulis presented a letter to the committee from the dean of the Harvard Medical School; he had been accepted in the first-year class, and his brother Rajko, because of his outstanding grades in Yugoslavia, was admitted as a junior, an unprecedented event in Harvard's history, he was told. Would they be allowed to leave the camp in the fall to go to Harvard? It seemed inconceivable that two brilliant young medical students might be barred from Harvard because they had entered America outside the quota.

''Would you be willing to protect our country in case of war?'' Dickstein asked Alex.

''Yes.''

''Would you be ready to join the Army now?''

''Yes.''

''Any other questions, gentlemen?'' Dickstein asked. Since there were no other questions, Dickstein thanked the witnesses and the citizens of Oswego, ''so kind and humane,'' who had ''displayed real Americanism, and I surely want to thank the press.''

The congressmen departed.

Back at the hotel, the reporters told me they had polled the congressmen; five were now prepared to vote to keep the refugees in America. Stockman had been converted. Only Fisher remained unconvinced. He told them he wanted to put the problem into the hands of the Attorney General.

Monday morning in Washington, I went up the Hill to see Dickstein. He was triumphant. ''The subcommittee has just voted unanimously to allow the refugees to remain.''

So Fisher too had been converted!

''Tomorrow morning,'' Dickstein said, ''I'm reporting to the entire Committee on Immigration and Naturalization. I want you there.''

The full House committee assembled around a large table, and Dickstein, its chairman, summarized the testimony in the camp. Many of the full committee, we knew, were isolationists, who were aided now by Robert Alexander, one of Breckinridge Long's men in the Visa Division of the State Department. Alexander kept moving around the table, whispering, handing out notes, as the isolationists began probing, jabbing, questioning Dickstein.

Dickstein became a boxer. He danced around their thrusts, protecting his face with his gloves, never allowing a fatal punch.

When the restrictionists realized they could not knock him out—get him at least to postpone the vote he sought—they tried a familiar technique. "Why don't you have the subcommittee take a few more days and write us a resolution?"

"Okay." Dickstein was affable. "But if you do that, you spoil a perfectly good speech for me tomorrow in New York."

That was the language congressmen understood; it was a gentleman's agreement, you didn't spoil a colleague's chance to make a speech.

The subcommittee left the meeting room for privacy to draw up a resolution based on the hearings. I remained in the large room as the full committee waited. Alexander moved around the table until he reached Ed Gossett of Texas, a strong isolationist, and showed him a slip of paper. Gossett looked pleased.

"I'd like to suggest to the subcommittee," Gossett said, "that they put this phrase into their resolution: 'No groups should be brought into the United States under these conditions in the future.' " It was as if Roosevelt had done something sly and unclean in inviting the refugees to America.

A messenger took the noxious phrase to the subcommittee, who felt they had no recourse but to accept it. They returned to the committee room.

Dickstein read the resolution urging the government of the United States to allow the refugees at Fort Ontario to leave the camp.

A motion was made to accept the resolution as read.

I felt a wave of gratitude. Fisher himself seconded the motion.

The resolution was passed unanimously.

Exhilaration filled the camp. The "liberators" had voted to liberate the people.

The fence would come down. The people would enter America.

The exhilaration lasted just three days.

The isolationists on the full committee lobbied hard. The resolution they had passed was easily tabled. Sponsored leave was not even to be considered! Immigration laws were not to be tampered with!

On Friday, July 6, 1945, the House Immigration and Naturalization Committee voted that not Congress but the Departments of State and Justice "should ascertain the practicability of returning the refugees to their homelands." If that were found to be not practicable, the Attorney General should declare them "illegally present in the country" and "undertake deportation proceedings."

The refugees were in even graver danger of being shipped back to Europe.

CHAPTER TWENTY-FOUR

Edith Semjen and Mirković were pacing the parade ground.

"When we first came," Edith said, puffing her cigarette nervously, "I was sure I would go back the minute the war was over. But now I've learned that everything we had was destroyed; everybody, our relatives, our friends, everybody is dead. There's nothing to go back to."

They were discussing the notice that had just come from UNRRA; the *Gripsholm* was sailing to Europe in August, and there was space for a number of Yugoslavs who might want to be repatriated.

Mirković put his arm through Edith's. "After that whole business with the congressmen, with our hopes going up and down like an escalator, it looks to me as if they really intend to send us back. But it's still a gamble whether we stay or not. I'm taking the gamble. Europe to me is a nightmare."

Dr. Rafailo Margulis had learned he was dying of cancer; he wanted to die in Yugoslavia, and he wanted his wife and his two sons with him. He told Rajko and Alex, "You must leave with me. They'll never let you out of this camp to go to Harvard. The camp will never be closed by September, and you'll be stuck here behind the fence."

The two young men tried to reason with him. He knew what Harvard meant to them. Maybe they would all be released before the fall term started; if not, surely some provision would be found so they could attend the most prestigious medical school in America.

Dr. Margulis insisted they sign on to the *Gripsholm* and go with him. They obeyed.

Of the 368 Yugoslavs now in the camp, fifty-three registered for the voyage. Parties and tearful farewells were given to the much-loved Mathilda Nitsch, to Dušanka Grin who had shown her apartment to Eleanor Roosevelt, and to relatives and friends who were to sail on the twenty-eighth of August from. New York. Thirteen Yugoslavs had sailed on the first voyage of the *Gripsholm* in May; two others had left, one for Uruguay, one bound for Czechoslovakia; and Elsa Neumann, who had taken such delight in her "villa by the sea," had rejoined her children in South Africa. Of the original 982, only sixty-nine in all had opted to leave the camp.

The rest waited, in anguish and despair and hope.

Letters went back and forth from Interior to State and Justice. Conferences were held. And, maddeningly, nothing was done.

But inside the camp, all was not bleak.

The little *rebbetzin*, Mindla Tzechoval, greeted me slyly on one of my visits. "I have a big surprise for you." She led me to one of the barracks.

There was the *mikvah*, the ceremonial pool.

"How did you get it built?" I asked.

She put her hands together as in prayer, lifted her face to the sky and said, "*Riboyne Shel Olem*, O Master of the World, You heard our plea, and we thank You."

She had persuaded one of the ultra-orthodox agencies to pay for building the *mikvah*.

Maria Montiljo, whose little daughter Elia had died on the ship, gave birth to another daughter on the sixth of May. She named her baby Rosica.

Kostia Zabotin entered the American Legion public-speaking contest in the high school. Kostia spoke on the American Constitution, and won first prize. The American Legion was not about to give him the award; he was not a citizen. But Ralph Faust "raised hell," he told me in describing the incident. Kostia walked away with the award.

And on graduation day, families and friends applauded loudly as Anita Baruch, Alfons Finci, Lea Hanf, Gordana Milinović, Steffi Steinberg and Edith Weiss, dressed in long white robes and white mortarboards, marched down the auditorium. Smiling and grateful, they shook hands with Ralph Faust, who had made all this possible. They walked off the platform with diplomas, full-fledged graduates of the Oswego High School.

July Fourth. Dillon Myer chose Independence Day to make a welcome announcement. The hated "leave policy" was to be relaxed. The town of Oswego would no longer be the outermost frontier. The people could travel twenty miles in any direction, provided they returned at night. But Syracuse, thirty-five miles away, was still forbidden territory.

And the cruel separation of wives and husbands who had rediscovered each other when we arrived was ended. Conjugal visits were allowed. American wives or husbands could spend a night at the camp, or a night in the Pontiac Hotel. Even visiting children were allowed to sleep over.

Then, early in the summer, Esther Morrison with eleven other members of a Quaker-sponsored team arrived and turned Fort Ontario, for the children at least, into an American summer camp.

The Quakers taught the young people Indian crafts; they led them on hikes and arranged picnics and scavenger hunts; they built puppets and presented "Snow White and the Seven Dwarfs" with costumes, a miniature stage and music; and in the cool of the evenings they sat in the bleachers and taught children from eighteen lands folk songs about the home where the buffalo roam and the deer and the antelope play.

Thursday nights, Esther taught the adults American square dancing, and bachelors and married men fell in love with her. She was tall, with brown eyes and a lilting Mississippi accent; she could have been a Southern belle with nothing but beaux on her mind. Instead, she had a master's degree in social work and had spent four of the war years in group work at a YWCA in Beaumont, Texas. She had applied to the Philadelphia Quakers for summer work, though she was no Quaker herself, and had been recruited for the summer work camp in Fort Ontario.

It was what she did for the pre-teenage girls that was to endear her to them forever. She had only to enter a room, and seven- and eight- and nine-year-old girls felt safe and happy. She led children whose earliest memories were of flight and hunger and fear into the security of American life.

In an era of accepted sex discrimination, she was told, when she helped organize the first Girl Scout troop, that there was no money for uniforms. The Boy Scouts, early in the camp's life, had all been given uniforms. Esther was solution-oriented. She brought the girls into her apartment and taught them how to bake cookies. She took small groups into the camp kitchens, where they collected fat. They sold the cookies in town, and sold the fat to rendering-plants for soap. With the money they earned, she bought them Girl Scout scarves and pins, which they wore as proudly as if they had khaki uniforms.

One day she asked them, "Who has family in Europe?"

Hands flew up around the room. "I have straws here," she said. "Every one draw a straw. Whoever gets the winning straw will get a package which we will send to her family abroad."

Nine-year-old Esther Danon screamed with delight. She had won. Esther Morrison and the girls bought a silk blouse in town, packed it and sent it to Esther Danon's sister, who was with the partisans in Yugoslavia. Little Esther had learned that her seventeen-year-old sister had been wounded in the fighting and was destitute. The blouse became a symbol among the partisans; whoever had a birthday wore the blouse from Fort Ontario, America.

The Quakers, who lived together in one of the officers' red brick buildings overlooking the parade ground, asked me to spend several evenings describing the experiences on the ship and the backgrounds of the people. For they, like almost all of us whose lives had touched the refugees, had become part of the extended family, caught up, they wrote in their "Oswego Log," "in the camp's total heartbreak."

"We are not deceived into thinking that our contribution can make any appreciable lessening of the camp's total heartbreak," they wrote, "but we like to think that we are here as a symbol of many Americans who carry in their hearts a concern for all displaced persons."

Oswego had a thousand displaced persons. But now there were half a million displaced persons in Europe, aftermath of the war. President Truman sent Earl G. Harrison to investigate the DP camps in Germany.

Harrison, a recognized expert on refugees, and dean of law at the University of Pennsylvania, had already expressed his views on Oswego in a letter to the Attorney General: "The worst thing that could happen right now would be to require that all of the people at Oswego be moved immediately, somewhere—anywhere just so long as it is outside of the United States."

In Germany, Harrison was devastated. He saw survivors of the Inferno living in a new inferno of chaos and suffering, squeezed into tents or horse stalls or former Nazi death camps, twenty and thirty in a room. "We appear to be treating Jews as the Nazis treated them except we do not exterminate them," Harrison wrote.

Men and women who needed each other, who needed to prove themselves alive, strung blankets around their beds to make love.

He saw few children, none between the ages of one and five. Hitler had murdered more than one million children.

He saw few elderly people; they too had been exterminated. Only the strongest had survived, most of them young people in their late teens, twenties and thirties.

He had gone to Germany expecting to recommend that the refugees be repatriated to their former homes. He discovered that at first many of the Jews had believed as he did: They wanted to be repatriated. They had gone back to their homelands, only to find their families dead, their homes plundered, and the smell of blood in the streets. Their neighbors, staring at them as if they were ghosts, found time-honored ways of driving them out.

Anti-Semitism, Harrison discovered, had not died with Hitler's suicide in the Berlin bunker. Polish Jews, especially, were fleeing in terror to Germany—the deathland—into the DP camps, because the Americans were there, and the Americans, they were sure, would help them.

Harrison returned to the United States and reported to Truman. The solution, he told the President, was not repatriation but resettlement. Some of the people wanted resettlement in America; some in Canada, Australia, South Africa; but most wanted Palestine, the homeland that had been promised them by the League of Nations in 1922.

Truman, shocked by Harrison's report, turned to Britain's newly elected Prime Minister, Clement Attlee, and asked him to allow 100,000 Jewish refugees to enter Palestine. Attlee dared not refuse point-blank. England, financially and physically battered, was too dependent upon the United States to anger Truman. Attlee suggested the appointment of a new commission; it was the eighteenth commission to study the problem of Palestine.

In Oswego, the refugees read the newspaper accounts of this new "Anglo-American Committee of Inquiry on Palestine" with excitement and hope. Oswego was a DP camp in America. Harrison had recommended resettlement in Palestine. They too sought resettlement—in America.

The President was asking Britain to open the doors of Palestine to 100,000. But for the one thousand in Oswego, the doors of America were still not open.

Weeks were passing, then months, while State, Justice and Interior fought over them. Joe Smart's committee had one hundred prominent leaders, including Eleanor Roosevelt and Robert

A. Taft, the powerful Senator from Ohio, all trying to win support to keep the refugees in America.

The dread of spending another fierce winter imprisoned by mountains of snow threw the camp into gloom. Late in November, Ickes sent me back to try to bolster morale.

Just past midnight my train pulled into Syracuse. Clyde H. Powers, who had become the camp director during the summer, drove me to Oswego.

"You'll find a lot of changes," he warned me.

His warning hardly prepared me for the changes I found the next morning. Some of the men had aged badly; their eyes were watery, their faces sagged, even their skin looked weary. Some of the women, heavier than ever, looked nervous and confused.

The wind howled off Lake Ontario, whistling through the naked branches of trees. The parade ground was frozen and deserted.

At lunch Artur Hirt sank into a chair beside me. "The first days when we came, America worried about us. But now nobody worries. We're forgotten."

"Not true," I protested. "You don't know how hard we're fighting for you."

"That's you. And your department. But what about the other government agencies?"

"The fight isn't over. We have the American press with us almost one hundred percent. Only one or two columnists like Westbrook Pegler are trying to stir up sentiment to send you back." I showed him some of the articles and editorials I had brought with me.

"Then *you* must do something. You know I was a judge. Juridically the paper we signed in Italy, that we would go back at the end of the war, doesn't hold. The Poland I would have to go back to is no longer Poland. My part of it is Russia. I don't want to go to Russia. I hate the Communists. I hate Stalin. Where should I go? I warn you, we can't hold out much longer."

Hirt was cocky and fighting mad, but others walked with their heads stooped, as if their lives were anchored by memories of terror and flight.

In the evening, the artists gave a special performance so that the people could welcome me back—and hear if I had any news to report.

The performance began patriotically as always with the National Anthem, followed by the camp's own anthem, "Don't Fence Me In."

Then Otto Presser, looking like a saddened Eddie Cantor,

made a little speech. "Our Mother Ruth is really like Moses. He led the Jews through the wilderness for forty years. But he couldn't see the Promised Land. Our Mother Ruth led us to Oswego—and sometimes it seems we have been here thirty if not forty years. But that's where her role changes. She goes back and forth, but her *children* can't see the Promised Land."

It's true, I thought dismally, but not funny.

Charles Abeles played a tuneful song he had composed for me. Leon Levitch arranged a haunting piano solo. There were new comic skits. The Russians put on an amusing circus act. But I was too distressed by the changes in their faces to laugh, and the laughter around me seemed bitter.

Presser now called on me to speak.

I walked slowly to the stage and looked out. They were all there—Fredi and Jennie, Adam Munz and David Hendel, Edith Bronner and Edith Semjen, Olga Maurer, Furmanski, Hans Goldberger of the *Pentcho*, Ernst Wolff, Steffi, Jetta, Zdenka. I saw them in the bright theater lights, row upon row.

Some smiled up at me encouragingly. Others sat cold. I too was the enemy.

I began in a low voice. "I wished I might have good news for you. We had all expected that there would be a final decision by now. But unfortunately the wheels of government move slowly."

Silence.

"This is how a democracy works. With checks and balances, so that decisions take longer. If this were a dictatorship, we would have had an answer right away. I say, 'Thank God it is not a dictatorship!' If it were, none of us would be here tonight. There would never have been a haven in Oswego."

Applause started slowly, then faded.

"Some of you tell me that you think you are forgotten. That is not true! Every day conferences are taking place, government officials are meeting, letters are being written from one branch of the government to another. Your cause is being defended with all the eloquence and passion which your friends can command."

Magrita Ehrenstamm smiled encouragingly.

"You have an important mission. You are the first DPs who were brought to this country. You are the vanguard. What the government decides should be done for you may influence what the world will do for hundreds of thousands of DPs. Your struggle is their struggle, your agony their agony. Like you, they want the right to live in a land they dream of, with decency and dignity, without hunger and without fear."

Ernst Wolff in the second row threw me a kiss.

"We must not give up hope."

The applause began.

I went on. "My philosophy is that wherever there is a door, it can be opened. There are still a few doors."

"Bravo," someone shouted.

"Let me assure you that every one of us who loves you and has faith in you is working tirelessly, day and night, to do two things: to shut the camp down so that you can work, move around and live as free human beings again; and to get you into the country legally under the quota."

Applause burst through the hall. Swelling. In waves.

I put my hand up for silence. I felt tears in my eyes. "That first day, at the Statue of Liberty, you told me the air of America smells like free air. Believe me, we want you to breathe it."

I walked off the stage.

CHAPTER TWENTY-FIVE

The war in Europe was over; the war in the Far East was over; but the war in Washington between the bureaucracies was at fever pitch.

On December 5, 1945, Justice and State, fighting to send the people back to Europe, prepared a letter to be signed by Ickes, Attorney General Tom C. Clark and Secretary of State James F. Byrnes. The letter was to be sent to the chairmen of both the House and Senate Committees on Immigration and Naturalization and recommended that the refugees leave the United States.

Ickes objected to the draft letter and refused to sign it. Instead he asked me to draft a letter to Undersecretary of State Dean Acheson, explaining our position. Secretary of State James Byrnes was out of town.

On December 12, Acheson took action. He dictated a telegram to New York inviting the private agencies to send a delegation to his office on Friday, the fourteenth, at 2:30 P.M. I was to accompany them.

Every hour counted now; I was certain this would be the decisive meeting. I prepared documents to show Acheson who the people were. I talked with Chamberlain in New York; the agencies were working ceaselessly, collecting letters of support. William Green, the president of the American Federation of Labor, wrote a strong plea that the refugees be allowed to stay. Other labor leaders had feared that they might take jobs away from Americans. Green's letter, we hoped, would pull the plug on that argument.

Early Friday afternoon, the delegates, in heavy overcoats, thick gloves and winter hats, arrived in my office. Led again by Joe Chamberlain, they included Clarence Pickett, the executive secretary of the American Friends, who had sent the Quaker team to the camp; Judge Nathan Perlman of the American Jewish Congress; Isaiah Minkoff, director of the National Jewish Community Relations Advisory Committee (NACRAC); and Bruce Mohler of the National Catholic Welfare Conference, who had come as the personal representative of Archbishop Spellman of New York. The Archbishop wanted Acheson to know he was deeply concerned for the future of the Catholics in the camp.

In freezing cold, we walked from Interior to State and waited for Acheson in a large reception room.

Exactly at two-thirty, his secretary appeared. "The meeting has been postponed until five-thirty."

We decided to stay where we were. In Washington, the treadmill of government grinds to an early halt. By four, most of the State Department staff had put on their hats and winter coats and headed for home or dates or a friendly bar. We were alone, growing more apprehensive as the hours dragged by.

In low voices, we tried to analyze the three-hour delay. Perhaps Acheson had slipped out a back door to see the President.

The refugee problem had become a world crisis. The Anglo-American Committee of Inquiry on Palestine was meeting this very day in Washington, taking testimony. Earl Harrison had described the chaos in the DP camps. Witnesses were repeating Truman's request that Britain act magnanimously, that she open the doors of Palestine to 100,000 DPs. And here we were, four men and a woman, watching the clock, waiting for Acheson, hoping desperately that our government too would act magnanimously and open America to one thousand DPs.

Acheson himself was an enigma. Ickes had told me that he regarded him as a good friend, but that Acheson was opposed to a homeland for Jews in Palestine. Whether this would influence his thinking about a homeland for the Oswego refugees in America we could not judge.

At five-thirty, a massive wooden door swung open, and Acheson emerged from his private office.

He shook our hands. "I'm sorry to have kept you waiting. I have nothing to report to you right now. I'm going to see the President tomorrow and I'll get back to you."

Chamberlain had carefully drawn up a strong legal document; he handed it to Acheson, and we left.

Dusk had already darkened the ice-cold streets. The men looked somber as they said goodbye to me and took the train back to Philadelphia and New York.

I taxied home to my apartment.

There were still doors to be opened, I had promised the refugees in November. The White House door was the last.

Saturday morning, December 22. I worked at my office desk, then turned on the radio for news.

The announcement came quietly: "President Truman will make a major statement from the White House this evening on immigration and refugees."

I tossed papers into desk drawers, pulled on my coat, and walked through the great bronze doors of Interior. The snow-covered streets were crowded with Christmas shoppers; jolly Santa Clauses with fake beards were ringing Salvation Army bells; church bells chimed Christmas carols.

All afternoon my phone kept ringing.

"Ruthie, what does it mean?" Manya called from the camp.

"I don't know."

"You don't know! Then what should we think?"

"Stay close to the radio. I'll phone you after his talk."

In the evening, I moved the radio next to an armchair, not to miss a single word. The music stopped. The Midwestern voice, honest, unadorned, came through the box.

"The war has brought in its wake an appalling dislocation of populations in Europe . . . The immensity of the problem of displaced persons and refugees is almost beyond comprehension."

I nodded, as if I were watching him at his desk in the Oval Office. I knew how he hated reading speeches, how he read them into a recording machine, listening to himself, repeating words over and over to get the right emphasis. The emphasis now was fine.

"A number of countries in Europe, including Switzerland, Sweden, France and England, are working toward its solution. The United States shares the responsibility to relieve the suffering.

"To the extent that our present immigration laws permit . . ."

Could I be hearing right? He was making no recommendations to change the immigration laws.

". . . everything possible should be done at once to facilitate the entrance of some of these displaced persons and refugees into the United States."

Maybe he planned to circumvent the immigration laws, as Roosevelt had done.

"Most of these persons are natives of Central and Eastern Europe and the Balkans." Just like Oswego, I thought. "The immigration quotas for all these countries for one year total approximately thirty-nine thousand, two thirds of which are allotted to Germany. Under the law, in any single month, the number of visas issued cannot exceed ten percent of the annual quota. This means that from now on only about thirty-nine hundred visas can be issued each month to persons who are natives of these countries."

So, 3,900 refugees would enter the United States each month—under the law. The quotas would not be changed!

The words I was waiting for came in the middle of his talk: "There is one particular matter involving a relatively small number of aliens." He recounted President Roosevelt's decision to bring one thousand refugees to America and his message to Congress "that these persons would be returned to their homelands after the war."

"However," he said, his voice buoyant, "surveys have revealed that most of the people would be admissible under the immigration laws."

His words came into the apartment like shafts of light.

"In the circumstances it would be inhumane and wasteful to require these people to go all the way back to Europe merely for the purpose of applying there for immigration visas and returning to the United States.

"Many of them have close relatives, including sons and daughters, who are citizens of the United States, and who have served and are serving honorably in the armed forces of our country.

"I am therefore directing the Secretary of State and the Attorney General to adjust the immigration status of the members of this group who may wish to stay here, in strict accordance with existing laws and regulations."

"We're staying," Manya wept into the telephone. "The camp has gone wild. Everyone kissing and laughing and crying. Are you there? Do you hear me?"

I heard, but my voice was blurred with tears.

*　　*　　*

Sunday morning's newspapers headlined the story.

"TRUMAN ACTS TO AID ENTRY OF REFUGEES," the *Washington Times-Herald* ran a banner headline.

"TRUMAN REFUGEE PROPOSAL WINS SUPPORT ON 'HILL.' "

Representative E. H. Hedrick (D.) of West Virginia, a member of Dickstein's House Immigration Committee, saw no objection "as long as the quotas are not increased."

Lowell Stockman, the giant rancher from Oregon, told the press he doubted there would be much criticism, since the current quotas were not affected. But he personally believed, he said, that the quotas should be cut in half.

Representative Rankin (D.) of Mississippi said there was still "a good deal of cloakroom sentiment for shutting off immigration for a while." He favored stopping all immigration "till we get our own house in order." But as long as the President did not envisage increasing the quotas, Rankin said, "nothing can be done about it."

"We won," Ickes said Monday morning, exultant. "It was a rough battle with State and Justice and some of those congressmen. But well worth it. You'd better go back to the camp and help the people get ready to leave and prepare for a new life."

At the camp, Adam Munz pumped my hand. "Do you know what it means to wake up in the morning and say, 'I'm free'?"

Once again the camp was inundated with journalists, government officials and representatives of the private welfare agencies.

The refugees staged a gala Sylvesterabend, to be the happiest New Year's Eve of their lives.

Otto Presser thanked President Truman "for the gift of freedom." Then, rolling his eyes like Eddie Cantor, he said, "I've been in camps for five and a half years and I don't know what it will be like to sit alone on a toilet seat."

The camp staged an operetta written by Miriam Sommerburg, with music by Charles Abeles, called "The Golden Cage." It was the saga of Oswego, with Manya and Mirković in the lead roles. Well-dressed women stood outside a fence listening to poorly clad refugees singing:

> "We are in a cage without reason,
> We are in a cage, golden cage;
> We're missing nothing but our freedom."

Mirković sang:

"I feel myself a monkey
In the zoological garden;
Are we to be on display?
There's nothing missing but the warden!"

The operetta ended in a grand finale. The cast, arms intertwined, laughing, dancing, thanked Roosevelt, "who sent an angel to the world to free us from this farce."

At the stroke of midnight we stood up in the post theater, cheering, blowing horns, kissing each other.

Nineteen forty-six! The first year of freedom. The running was over; the Golden Cage had swung open; they were free.

In the cold starlit night we left the theater and dispersed to the Service Club, where tables fringed the walls, laden with food and soft drinks. All of us, refugees, reporters, government officials joined hands, dancing the hora until the room began to spin.

"Silence!" Presser shouted.

The huge Service Club grew still.

"You all know I have been looking for a girl of seventy-five to marry. I have found my girl. She's not seventy-five. Now, in front of all of you, I want to say, I have proposed marriage and she has accepted."

"Who?" we asked each other.

Presser came across the room and led me to the center of the crowded hall.

In a mock ceremony, one of the men placed a prayer shawl around my shoulders, held his hand over my head and married me to the camp comedian. While the audience cheered and applauded, Presser led me in a wild Viennese waltz around the hall.

New Year's Day broke over the camp, cold and clear and free.

Speed was important.

The Oswego refugees would be the first to enter the United States under Truman's directive for 3,900 DPs a month. They had to be processed by immigration inspectors, border patrolmen, officials of State, Immigration and the Public Health Service. Seventy communities from New York to California offered to resettle them, find them housing, help them get jobs and place their children in schools.

Packing the pictures in her little apartment, Magrita Ehrenstamm told me, "My daughter has already leased an apartment for me in New York. I still can't believe this—that I'll have a kitchen of my own and," she said slowly, "privacy."

To enter the United States legally, they had to leave it. On January 17, 1946, the first three busloads, carrying ninety-five refugees, left the camp at six in the morning. They drove across western New York State to Buffalo, where the community invited them to a roast-beef lunch in Temple Beth El. Then the buses traveled to Niagara Falls and crossed the Rainbow Bridge to the town of Niagara Falls in Ontario, Canada. There they were greeted by George Graves, the American consul, who gave each refugee the longed-for visa embellished with a red seal and a ribbon.

They drove back across the Rainbow Bridge and at last entered America.

Some traveled in chartered buses directly from the Canadian border to the office of the National Refugee Service in New York, where relatives waited for them. One of the first off the bus was Dr. Hugo Graner, almost smothered by his two children, while his wife, Elsa, waited to embrace him, her eyes filled with tears.

Ivo Lederer, his parents and his sister Mira were welcomed by Mr. Lederer's brother, Leo Lenski, who had come to take them to his apartment on West Seventy-seventh Street.

Talking to the press, fourteen-year-old Ivo summed up what he and most of the refugees were feeling. "It was worth everything, just to be here."

Husbands embraced wives, fathers hugged their children, sisters, brothers, cousins, aunts talked and laughed and wept with joy and relief.

Magrita Ehrenstamm, holding her new grandchild tightly, went directly to the apartment her daughter had furnished for her, "with privacy." Henny Notowicz Haas heard her Uncle Aaron in Brooklyn order his daughter, "Move over. Your cousin is sleeping with you."

Immediately after President Truman's Christmas present allowing them to enter America, they had sat in the camp with social workers from the War Relocation Authority and the private Jewish and Christian agencies, learning about towns in America where they might begin their new lives.

Most of them yearned for New York, the fabled city whose skyline they had glimpsed from the deck of the *Henry Gibbins*. But they were gently dissuaded by the social workers, who had swiftly canvassed and received commitments from communities across the country, prepared to take in families, help them find homes, jobs, and schools and give them interest-free loans.

Some who had come from Eastern Europe's small towns and villages preferred settling in small towns. They cherished the quiet beat and rhythm of a town where they would soon know their neighbors.

Rena Romano Block's father, Alberto Romano, selected Baltimore because he wanted to be near the sea. The last syllable of the name "Baltimore" means ocean in Yugoslavian. Fortunately, he discovered, Baltimore was on Chesapeake Bay.

In the next days, the people dispersed by train to the towns and cities they had selected across America.

Irene Danon, her parents and her two younger brothers were warmly welcomed by the Cleveland Jewish community. Her father worked in a zipper factory, her mother in a sewing shop, while Irene and her brother Ića, stuffed envelopes. But after a few years they moved to New York and found an apartment at Forty-second Street and Ninth Avenue. "I loved New York," Irene told me. "I opened my window and I could hear Italian, Spanish, Jewish. I loved everything about being alive in that wonderful town."

Others too found their way back to New York. One day in the subway, I met one of Mirković's best friends. "Jellinek," I exclaimed "what are you doing in New York? I thought you settled in Pittsburgh?"

"I couldn't stand the provinces," he said.

Of the families destined for New York, most arrived in Grand Central Station, where they were met by Hebrew Immigrant Aid Society and NRS social workers and escorted to dormitories in the HIAS shelter on Lafayette Street, the former Astor Library. It is now Joseph Papp's famous Public Theatre.

Postwar housing in New York was tight, but there were empty cold-water flats on the Lower East Side, tenements that had housed the tempest-tossed from Europe for over a hundred years.

And so they began their new lives.

PART FOUR
After They Crossed the Rainbow Bridge

CHAPTER TWENTY-SIX

Thirty-five years later, some fifty of us, with spouses and children, returned to Oswego to dedicate a monument at the camp.

"Everything I have today I owe to this place." Irene Danon, the vivacious Ljiljana, who had flown in from Los Angeles, flung her arms out. "I love it. It's my America."

The reunion had been set up by the Syracuse Council of Pioneer Women/Na'amat, an organization of American volunteers who help provide education and social services in Israel. The most famous of the Pioneer Women was Golda Meir, Prime Minister of Israel.

Jetta Hendel Gordon had come from New York; her cousin, Tamar Hendel Fishman, from Washington, D.C. Their arms around each other's waists, unable to talk, they retraced familiar paths.

Through Ray Harding (Branko Hochwald), one of the former Cub Scouts who had stolen the show in Congressman Dickstein's hearings, and now a leader of the Liberal Party in New York State, Governor Hugh L. Carey had proclaimed this "Oswego Refugee Commemoration Day."

Walter Greenberg, the former captain of the young Cub Scouts, cased the grounds with his crew of cameramen and sound engineers. David Hendell, formerly Hendel, graying but scarcely changed since the days he had slipped mischievously under the fence and hitchhiked to New York, shot his own movie film.

"Geri!" Edith Semjen Starkman shouted to a woman walking toward her. Geraldine Desens, the Oswego waitress who had disguised herself as a refugee the first day, wrapped her arms around Edith in a bear hug.

"See, Murray," Edith Bronner Klein showed an empty site to her husband, the president and owner of Zabar's, one of New York's most famous gourmet shops. "This is where the street of the barracks was, and about here, this was where our barrack was."

Ralph Faust, white-haired but ramrod-straight, was pummeled

and hugged by former students who had never forgotten what they owed him and the high school. Oswego schoolteachers, Boy Scout leaders, old girlfriends searched for the refugees whose pictures they had kept all these years.

It was late October, the color of the trees was muted, the day flooded with sunshine.

Fred Baum and his wife, Jenny, joined my husband and me as we strolled across the parade ground, greeted townspeople from Oswego and Syracuse, and discovered we were heading, as always, toward the blue-green, endless waters of Lake Ontario.

"Doesn't the camp seem smaller to you?" Fred asked.

"Don't all things from the past seem smaller?" I answered his question with another question.

But the camp *was* smaller.

The white wooden barracks had all been torn down. Only a few of the handsome red brick Georgian buildings with white colonnades still stood: the guardhouse with the jail that had been my office, the post theater, a few warehouses and the recreation hall where Mirković and Manya and Presser and scores of others had entertained us. Part of the chainlink fence that had meant prison to some and security to others still stood.

After the last of the refugees left in buses on February 6, 1946, the camp had become a temporary housing project for veterans of the war and their families. Then, in 1951, it was decided that Fort Ontario should be turned into a New York State historical museum and park. Its multilayered history from the French and Indian War to World War II was to come to life again with blown-up photographs, letters and waxwork models of the soldiers who had been stationed here for nearly two hundred years.

The restoration began in interim steps as seven buildings inside the old fort, a spruced-up cannon and the massive five-pointed ramparts were refurbished to look like a camp in Civil War days. Of the eighty-acre camp we knew, thirty-six acres were given to the museum; the rest was parceled out to the city of Oswego for parks and streets and highways.

Early in the spring of 1981 the Pioneer Women had learned that the restoration was nearly completed. But thus far no markers had been planned to show that Fort Ontario had been a haven for refugees too.

In Syracuse, speaking at a dinner, I was approached by two leaders of the Pioneer Women, Celia Meren and Belle Shiro. "Would it be appropriate for our organization to erect a marker for the refugees?" they asked.

I reacted instantly. Of course it would be appropriate to link this haven in Oswego with Israel, which had become the haven for over a million refugees. I offered to do everything I could to help.

The idea took fire. Within six months enough money had been raised from the community and the refugees themselves to buy a magnificent granite boulder.

Now, on the twenty-fifth of October, 1981, with an autumn wind blowing off the lake, the ceremony began. The townspeople crowded around us as we walked toward the boulder, on a slight promontory overlooking Lake Ontario. The color guard of Jewish War Veterans, men in their sixties and seventies, members of Onondaga County Post 131, marched with the flags of the United States and Israel. Their World War II rifles sparkled in the sunlight.

The wind grew fierce, flapping the flags as we sang "The Star Spangled Banner." Memories of that first Sunday in the camp when the refugees had listened to the anthem solemnly, unable to grasp its words, flooded over me. Now it was their anthem, and they sang it with passion.

Two rabbis from Syracuse recited the prayers; then I stepped forward, raised the white cloth, and read the words chiseled into the stone:

FROM 1944–1946 FORT ONTARIO
SERVED AS A HAVEN FOR
982 SURVIVORS OF THE
EUROPEAN HOLOCAUST

The air was still, filled only with the sound of the waves of Lake Ontario beating against the embankment. The Jewish War Veterans stood at attention. Then they cocked their rifles, and fired three volleys into the sky.

The wind fought us. Some ran, some lowered their heads and walked, others drove across the empty grounds toward the ramparts of the old fort. Shivering, we entered one of the renovated buildings, where chairs had been set up in an auditorium. Celia Meren, who had worked ceaselessly to make the day memorable, introduced the speakers: the beloved Ralph Faust; Jack Cohen of Rochester, who had collected every newspaper article on the camp; Francis T. Riley, one of the former history teachers; young Barry Silverberg, director of the Syracuse Jewish Federation, so fascinated by the Oswego story, though it had all happened before he was born, that he had given the Pioneer Women free range of his offices and help from his staff; and Charles Mitchell, the regional manager of the Central New York State Park and Recreation Commission, in overall charge of the museum and park.

Belle Shiro, president of one of the local chapters of the Pioneer Women, rose to make a welcome announcement. The money raised for the monument had been so generous that an "Oswego Refugee Perpetual Scholarship" would be given each year to a worthy student in Israel for higher education. One more link with Israel, and how fitting that it should be in education.

Mine was to be the keynote address; I made it brief. The contagious joy of the refugees, meeting again after thirty-five years, was more eloquent than words.

In a Syracuse café at brunch, Alice Pearlman, president of the Syracuse Council of Pioneer Women/Na'amat, introduced a small panel of speakers—a survivor of the concentration camps, a woman politician, religious leaders and, finally, Adam Munz, who was to talk on behalf of the refugees.

Adam used his prerogative as a psychologist to discuss a psychologcal phenomenon where "reality is unacceptable and fantasy takes the place of reality." He turned to me. "Dear Ruth, you tenaciously insist on the reality that you came to us in the Bay of Naples through very conventional means, when all of us from the shelter know that you came down from the heavens on wings."

Somehow Adam and a score of others had convinced themselves that I had landed on the *Henry Gibbins* in a plane, "dressed in white—just like an angel." Laughingly, I tried to tell them that a plane landing on that overcrowded deck would have sunk the ship. It was useless. One of them insisted he watched me in the sky through binoculars.

"The fantasy is more powerful than the reality," Adam insisted. "For us, that is as it shall always be!"

He then described what coming to America had meant for him. "I arrived here some thirty-seven years ago, starved for freedom and human warmth, embittered at the human race for allowing and participating in the carnage that was the Holocaust. But then I left through the gates of the shelter on the way to that round trip to Canada, and on that cold January morning became convinced that the world was not all bad and the human spirit at times prevails."

Adam's was to have been the last speech. But Mrs. Pearlman

rose with another announcement. "Dr. David Hendell has asked to be allowed to say something."

David made his way around the overcrowded tables to the microphone. "We want to make a presentation to the person who brought us to America and who became part of us." He opened a bag, drew out a large plaque mounted with a scroll in brass and read:

TO
RUTH GRUBER
HUMANITARIAN
For your friendship, love and dedication
to the refugees from Nazi oppression,
and for your determined support in our efforts
to join the mainstream of American life.
YOU HAVE FOREVER BECOME A PART OF US
THE OSWEGO REFUGEES
1944–1946
Presented October 25, 1981

David kissed me. Unashamed, I wiped my eyes, said a few words of gratitude, and then, still shaken, joined my friends, for we had begun the joyous task of catching up with one another's lives.

The reunion in the camp should have been the beginning of an epilogue—a testimonial, capturing, like photos in an album, the passages of life and the disruptions of death. Instead, it became the beginning of an unexpected and new chapter in the Oswego story. Soon after that reunion, I began to crisscross the country to search for more of the survivors of the one thousand.

My starting point was the Association of Yugoslav Jews in the U.S., with a clubhouse on West Ninety-ninth Street in New York City and an up-to-date directory. I had first learned of the association in 1962, when I was invited to speak in honor of the eighteenth anniversary of their arrival in Oswego. It was a significant year. "Eighteen" in Hebrew is *Chai*, which means life.

Fred Baum, living in Hillsdale, New Jersey, was a walking directory, as was Zlatko Hirschler in San Francisco. Several, like Steffi Steinberg Winters, rediscovered me through my books and wrote letters reestablishing our friendship. Others, like Liesl Neumann in Kansas City and Fortunée Levitch in San Francisco, came to talks I gave in their cities. Sharon Lowenstein, writing her Ph.D. thesis on the Oswego experience, shared her list of the refugees she had found. One person led to another.

There was no order in the way I found them, nor is there any particular order in the way I have written capsules of what happened to them after they crossed the Rainbow Bridge from Canada. For this is a random sampling. But, like a pollster's survey, it can be seen as a profile of what happened to most of the people whom President Roosevelt invited to a safe haven in America.

ADAM MUNZ and his family were settled in a five-flight walk-up railroad flat in New York City. Adam, a graduate of Hunter College, with a Ph.D. in psychology, is director of psychological services at St. Luke's Hospital as well as associate professor of medical psychology at Columbia University and consultant to their mental health clinic. Married to Dr. Letty Pogul, a child psychologist, and the father of a teenage daughter, Adam runs his department, sees patients, teaches at Columbia and in the summer escapes to Maine, where he works as a miniaturist in watercolors. One of his delicately limned landscapes recently won first prize in a national contest.

Success has not brought Adam optimism. "I thought after our release," he told me at a quiet family dinner in his home, "that Fort Ontario was at least an attempt by this country to right the grievous pains of the war, to do something in the years of the Holocaust.

"I thought, too, that history would forbid the repetition of the kind of abominations Germany had perpetrated on the world. I was naïve. Where are we really headed, when hooligans in Europe take to the streets shouting 'Death to the Jews,' when countries plot only how to destroy Israel, and speeches poisoned with hate come out of the United Nations? 'It can't happen here' has become a meaningless phrase, because if it happens anywhere it happens here."

LEO MIRKOVIĆ enrolled in a cantorial school and was hired as the cantor of the Washington, D.C., Hebrew Congregation. Attendance grew so rapidly that services were held in Constitution Hall until the congregation built another synagogue. President Truman came to the ceremony as the cornerstone was laid for the new temple, and Mirković sang the hymns.

In 1954 Mirković became the cantor of the Brotherhood Synagogue on West Thirteenth Street in New York City. Like the chapel in the camp, the building served as a church on Sunday and a synagogue on Friday night and Saturday.

For more than a quarter of a century Mirković was the Brotherhood Synagogue's much-loved cantor. He then retired to Miami Beach, where he lives now, unmarried, content, still surrounded by caring women from the camp. They meet nearly every afternoon on benches overlooking the Atlantic Ocean, as they once met each day for tea in the camp.

Just around the corner from Mirković, also in retirement, live the Reverend HAYIM HAZAN, the rabbi who held services in the camp chapel, and his wife, RIKA. The Hazans and their young sons, JOSEF, ten, and JACK, born in the shelter, were settled in Cincinnati, where Hazan worked as a *shochet*, a uniquely Jewish profession, authorized to slaughter animals according to kosher ritual. JACK is now a dentist in Tampa, and JOSEF is a photographer in Los Angeles.

MANYA BREUER settled in Los Angeles with ERNST and little DIANE, dreaming of becoming a singer. With no formal education and no money, she borrowed opera records from the public library, studied the parts and soon won the role of Flora in *La Traviata* with the Santa Monica Civic Opera Company. She also sang with the American Opera Company, the Los Angeles Opera Company and the Beverly Hills Symphony.

"When I sing," she told me, "I stop crying."

She gave birth to two more children, then her marriage to Ernst broke up, and in 1965 they were divorced. She took a variety of jobs, as a manicurist, a singer, a model, and was especially happy working in art galleries.

Miraculously her whole family survived, Papa in Italy, Willie in an Italian orphanage, Sigi in Auschwitz, and Mama, who had made her way to Israel. Manya is nourished by the love of her three children, Diane, an airline stewardess, Marsha, a hair designer in Eugene, Oregon, who organized a group of "Children of Survivors of the Holocaust," and Gregory, a commuter airline pilot and air controller.

In the late 1970s Manya was invited to address the Los Angeles Press Club on behalf of the Vietnamese people floundering in the South China Sea. She addressed the press: "My name is Manya Breuer, former refugee from Germany. Ladies and gentlemen, while we are here safe and free, out there, clinging to their lives in the water, are human beings nobody wants. No country will take them in. They are forgotten and drowning like animals. They are women, men and children. They are us. We must help them.

"I know what it is to be a boat person. I have been a refugee myself. It was in Antwerp Harbor in 1939, that I stood helplessly watching a ship of refugees that no country took in. They were returned to Germany to certain death. We must not let it happen again. *Ever!*"

Manya has finally come to peace with her life. "I look upon my being saved and coming to America as the biggest miracle of my life," she said. We were sitting in her flower-filled apartment in Culver City. "I've learned how to cope with my pain; for the first time I've learned how to face life without screaming, 'Why me? What have I done to deserve all this?' "

INTERNATIONAL HARRY (Harry Maurer) became neither the brigadier general the GIs who helped deliver him had predicted nor the doctor his mother had forecast at his circumcision. His first ambition was to be a philosopher. He majored in philosophy at New York's City College, from which he graduated in 1966. Laughing, with the same feisty humor that had helped his father and mother survive, he told me, "I was going to be a big philosopher, like Socrates, but no one bothered to hire me. In the newspapers, I saw that the highest-paid jobs were in computer science. So that's what I became." He grew more serious. "I went to work for NASA [the National Aeronautics and Space Administration] as a scientific computer analyst. Then I worked as a civilian for the Air Force in California, and now I'm an EDP [electronic-data-processing] manager in Ontario, Canada—a long way from philosophy."

Harry is married to Dianne, who was born in Canada, and they have two children, Kathy, ten, and Aaron, eight. His brother WALTER, also married with two children, designs fur coats in New York. Their father, LEON, died in 1982; OLGA, their mother, still feisty, is alive and well in Queens.

ALEX (AĆA) and RALPH (RAJKO) MARGULIS discovered on their return to Yugoslavia that they had made a terrible mistake by going back.

"We were horrified by what had happened to the country," Alex told me in a restaurant in San Francisco's Chinatown. "My father, even though he was dying of cancer, used whatever influence he had to get us readmitted to the United States. The only way we could reenter was on student visas, and he succeeded in getting them for us."

Harvard Medical School honored their acceptance, and the two young men married the young women they had courted in the camp. Ralph married VESNA CULIĆ, has two children and is now a gynecologist in Royal Oak, Michigan. Alex married RENÉE REISNER, who died of systemic lupus in 1979.

"As I look back," Alex said, "I think Oswego was one of my most wonderful experiences. Of course, people at various ages respond differently. In the camp the older people were disappointed and resented being cooped up. The young people were happy. They felt it was an island of plenty."

Alex, a world-famous radiologist, is chief of the Radiology Department of the University of California Medical Center. His department helped develop the CAT scanner, the popular name for the computerized-axial-tomography machine, with General Electric. He is now working on another revolutionary technique, called nuclear magnetic resonance (NMR), for diagnosing cancer, heart attacks and strokes by producing pictures with magnets without "invading" the body and subjecting it to dyes or X rays.

KOSTIA ZABOTIN, the first-prize winner of the American Legion speech contest, settled in New York with his father, the Russian Orthodox former BARON VLADIMIR VON ZABOTIN, one of the camp's best protrait painters, and his mother, ADELHEID, a landscape painter. Adelheid died of cancer soon afterward.

Like most of the camp's young people, Kostia took any job, however menial, during the day and went to school—Brooklyn College—at night. He found a job with Air France and has been with them ever since. He is now their customer service manager at Kennedy Airport, is married to Anita, a travel agent, and is the father of an eighteen-year-old multilingual son, Mischa.

The walls of their apartment in Manhattan are hung with Adelheid's and Vladimir's paintings. On the dining-room walls are Vladimir's portraits of some of Oswego's loveliest young women.

Kostia's best friend, VADIM MIKHAILOFF, another of the Russian Orthodox group and one of the camp's talented young actors, enlisted in the Air Force, fought in Korea, and is now a retired Air Force captain.

FRED BAUM (no longer Fredi) settled in New York with his parents and was immediately hired by United Nations Relief and Rehabilitation Association to work with DPs in Germany. His refugee experience, his administrative skills and his fluency in languages were so invaluable that he was made a team director, overseeing nurses and welfare workers in seven DP camps in Hanover. Then, with the simulated rank of a lieutenant colonel, he was made assistant regional director for UNRRA in all of Schleswig-Holstein.

After a year he returned to America and found a job with the Atlas Trading Corporation, importing shoes from the Far East and exporting leather and shoe supplies from America to markets around the world. Today he is the president of Atlas and the owner of a chain of retail stores called Shoe Experience.

Fred's fiancée, JENNY BARUCH, her sister, ANITA BARUCH LOEB, and their parents moved to Los Angeles, where Jenny and Fred were married under a *chupa* in 1949.

In New York, Jenny gave birth to a daughter, Leslie, now in the business world, and a son, Ronald, who met a tragic death at twenty-one while mountain-climbing in the Yosemites.

EDITH SEMJEN, the "Blond Bombshell," whose "golden hands" had become famous in the camp, went to work immediately in New York as a hairdresser. She and her mother, ELIZABETH, shared a tiny flat. After a few years Edith married Bernard Starkman, a certified public accountant, a quiet workaholic totally unlike most of her previous suitors.

Not Edith but Bernard described her phenomenal success. "First she bought a decrepit fifty-year-old beauty salon up a flight of stairs on a side street. In less than three years, she had five employees and the walls were too small to hold her customers. So she bought the Flair Beauty Salon on Broadway and West Eighty-first Street—another failing business. It grew until she had eighteen employees; it was the most successful beauty salon on the Upper West Side."

Edith's only training had been in the ORT class in the camp, yet she was so inventive, Bernard told me, "that some of the best beauty salons in New York kept asking her to join them." After twenty-eight years of running her own business, Edith decided the pressures were too great. She closed the shop and donated all the equipment and supplies to New York City as training material for the prison on Riker's Island.

"I wanted to repay some of the things done for me," Edith says. "I figured if we could train some men and women in the prison to become hairdressers, they would have something so they too could begin a new life."

Edith still works as a hairdresser in a salon off Broadway, with a retinue of delighted followers of whom I am one.

*　　*　　*

JETTA HENDEL and her sister GISELLE, whose parents had smuggled them out of Yugoslavia but failed to save their own lives, moved into an apartment in Manhattan with their aunt and uncle, HANA and ISAAC HENDEL, and their cousins, DAVID and TAMAR.

During the day Jetta worked as a secretary, and evenings she attended Hunter College. In 1949 she married Dr. Myron Gordon, a clinical psychologist in private practice and a professor at Queens College. She continued her graduate studies at the East Central European Institute of Columbia University until she bore two daughters.

A summer spent on a Pacific island in Micronesia with Myron and the two girls led Jetta to immerse herself in the study of the South Pacific. Recognizing her interest, the Pan-Pacific and South East Asia Women's Association, an international nongovernmental organization, asked her to serve as their United Nations representative, a position she held for ten years.

Following in both Jetta's and Myron's footsteps, their daughter Tamar is working toward a Ph.D. in anthropology at Berkeley, doing field work in Tonga in the South Pacific. Her sister, Eve, plans to enter a Ph.D. program in clinical psychology.

GISELLE, Jetta's sister, received her Ph.D. in 1969 from Columbia University, where she worked in anthropology under Margaret Mead. Married to Zoltan Sebestyen, a refugee who had escaped from Hungary during the uprising, she is now associate professor of anthropology at the State University of New York in New Paltz, where she teaches cultural anthropology and is doing research in medical anthropology.

Their cousin DAVID HENDELL (he added a second *l* to the family name) attended City College in New York at night while he worked with his cousin HERMAN KREMER (now an engineer in Montreal) delivering advertising copy to the *Newark Star-Ledger* in New Jersey. David received a B.S. in biology and chemistry and entered the Army expecting to be sent to Korea. Instead, as a chemistry major, he was sent to the Dugway Proving Grounds for Chemical Warfare in Utah. Mustered out of the Army in 1955, he entered the Columbia University School of Dentistry, where he is now a professor. Today, at fifty-four, he is one of the country's leading practitioners of the art of bonding, a simplified technique for reshaping teeth, and is called upon constantly to lecture and teach.

Early in the fifties, David married ELFIE STRAUBER, a member of the dance group in the camp, now a social worker in New York. In 1958, their daughter, Deborah, was born, and then their son, Reuben. Their marriage ended in divorce. A few years later he married a tall blond Hungarian, Agnes, a fashion coordinator.

David is fair, with even features, light-blue eyes and a mischievous grin. "That period of our life in Oswego," he said when we talked one afternoon in my apartment, "was paradise. It was a peaceful, protected, sheltered life. It was like a dream life. There was no pressure on us. We had stability and security. Our parents were also relaxed, taking a deep breath. Oswego gave us a chance to adjust to American life. Some, it's true, complained that there was an illegitimacy about us. But, I tell you, we felt good."

David's sister TAMAR, who fell in love with her elementary school and her teachers in Oswego, became a public-school teacher in New York.

In 1958 she married a young Brooklyn intern, Dr. Jacob Robert Fishman, and moved to the Washington area. Jacob did his residency in psychiatry at the National Institute of Mental Health, while Tamar taught, worked for a master's degree in art therapy at George Washington University and took time out to have four children. She now works as an art therapist associated with her husband's psychiatric practice.

Her enthusiasm has never flagged. "The whole Oswego experience for me was so positive," she told me one day in Washington, "that the very way I live now, the kind of home I live in with my husband and my children, the quiet street, the one-family homes, could have been transplanted from Oswego. This land that had always absorbed immigrants absorbed us completely."

Soon after the camp closed, David Hendell's aunt, BERTHA KREMER, a young energetic widow with two sons, married SIGMUND ALSTER, handsome, with a shock of white hair, a leader of the Austrian group in the advisory council and one of the popular actors in the camp's theatricals. Settling in New York, Sigmund held a variety of jobs totally unrelated to the theater, while Bertha became a samplemaker in the garment center. The two boys worked part time and went to school.

A few years later, Sigmund died of cancer. Bertha then married Harry Meyer, who owned a small dry-cleaning store with a French name slightly misspelled, "Bonne Cleaners." Bertha entered the business and, with her usual energy, expanded it to two more shops, one in the Empire State Building and one on East Thirty-fourth Street, now run by her younger son, William, who had been a tool- and die-maker. Herman is a civil engineer in Montreal and a gentleman farmer in Montgomery, Vermont. Both Herman and William are married, and each has two children in college. Bertha has now retired to Florida and makes frequent visits to New York, still lively and energetic.

The BRONNER family, whose daughters had danced the Hungarian czardas in the camp, moved into a fifth-floor cold-water flat on the Lower East Side of Manhattan. "It was so cold," EDITH told me, "we wouldn't get out of bed until my mother turned up the kerosene heater. Yet we didn't mind. In Oswego I had terrible nightmares: I used to wake up in the morning and not believe I was in America. Now, even in the cold flat, it was good to wake up after a nightmare and know that the fear was behind you."

Edith worked in a factory and finished high school at night. Then she became a key puncher working an IBM machine for a drug company. In 1950, Murray Klein, whom she was to marry a few years later, came to the United States. Born in Russia, he had been sent during the war to a labor camp in Siberia. His first New York job was in a supermarket on Broadway owned by the Zabar family; he worked as a delivery boy. Today he is president and one of the owners of Zabar's, the popular gourmet emporium on the Upper West Side. Their daughter, Deborah, has a master's degree in hospital administration and is married to Dr. Jonathan Himmelfarb. Their son, Roger, is finishing high school.

Edith's sister LILLY BRONNER GLASS is married to a supervisor in the Post Office and has two married sons, Steve, a teacher, and Gary, a certified public accountant. Her brother JACK BRONNER, one of the Bar Mitzvah boys in the camp, joined the Army at seventeen and fought in both the Korean and Vietnam wars. He became a career noncommissioned officer in the Army, and worked as an administrator in the Walter Reed Hospital. He now works for NASA in Washington.

RAYMOND B. HARDING changed his name while he was still a teenager, when his parents became citizens. "My parents were repulsed by everything Germanic," he told me. "They hated our name, Hochwald, and they asked me for suggestions for an American name. There was a radio serial that I listened to with rapture, called *David Harding, Counterspy;* I suggested the name Harding and took the name Ray from a favorite cousin." Branko Hochwald became Raymond B. Harding. The *B* was his tie to his childhood—little Branko, one of the Cub Scouts who marched before Congressman Dickstein.

"My father had been a successful businessman in Yugoslavia," Ray reminisced in his law office in New York. "He was wiped out completely by the Nazis. I try to tell my sons that my parents, like all the others who were in Oswego, never stood on pride. They went to work in a little restaurant on the Upper West Side called Neugröschels. Then my mother took a job with an insurance company and worked there twenty-one years; my father was a banquet waiter at the Commodore Hotel."

Ray too worked while he was at school, driving cabs and waiting tables. He was graduated from City College, joined the Army and became a second lieutenant. In 1961 he received his law degree from the New York University School of Law. He and his Austrian-born wife, Elisabeth, have two sons, Robert, a graduate of Brooklyn Law School, and Russell, a student at Clark University.

For five years, from 1975 to 1980, Ray was special assistant to New York Governor Hugh L. Carey, and then he became a partner in a large law firm. In 1958 he joined the Liberal Party and today is one of its leaders, the potential heir to the late Alex Rose, a powerful kingmaker in New York politics.

Ray's closest friend was JOHN HUNTER, formerly Ivo Hirschler, whose father, JULIUS HIRSCHLER, was photographed by Eisenstaedt for the famous issue of *Life* magazine. John entered the computer world after finishing at City College and taking a master's degree in business administration at Columbia in 1960. He went to work immediately as a management trainee for the Radio Corporation of America, and realized he had a special aptitude for marketing and finance.

"I think the groundwork for my career was laid at the model elementary school of the Oswego State Teachers College," he told me. "The teachers gave several of us from the camp special problems in math, different textbooks, because they found us so advanced. I've often speculated on the various elements that cause people to have a burning drive and ambition and need to succeed. The experience in Oswego was certainly one of those elements."

Distinguished-looking, with a large mustache, lively twinkling eyes and dark hair laced with gray, John in 1970 founded Delta Resources, a computer firm, which today has 250 employees and revenues of $40 million a year.

"Columbia University often invites me back to address their

students working for an M.B.A. I tell them I really believe that our society is open to any level of achievement if one has the willingness and the commitment and the need to achieve. I always had that need, and I attribute it to a basic sense of insecurity, the desire to have the financial security that I didn't have in my childhood. I was displaced; I was a refugee.

"Why did I change my name?" he repeated my question in his office on the Avenue of the Americas. "It was a desire to assimilate into the business world I was entering. I made the change when I was hired by RCA in 1960. Big firms like IBM and RCA had few Jews working for them at that time, especially in the higher levels of management. I took the name Hunter from Hunter Mountain in New York, where I worked in the summer as a waiter in the Star Hotel when I was an undergraduate."

John, who never married, says, "I tell the women in my life, 'There are many men who have mountains named after them. But when will they meet a man named after a mountain?' "

"This Best of All Possible Worlds," MIRIAM SOMMERBURG, the sculptress who wrote the book and lyrics for the camp operetta, "The Golden Cage," described her life in a biographical sketch for England's Intercontinental Biographical Association. After leaving Oswego, she wrote, "I was lucky to be able to find a sixth-floor walk-up slum apartment. We had arrived in the New World almost 'in-the-nude.' We had no money, no clothing, property, reputation or artworks. All that was lost and gone." Miriam had lost all her sculptures, mosaics and paintings in flight. "Our rented railroad apartment, however, had six windows overlooking a wide, horizontal range of vision, a fascinating view of the East River."

She described waking up to watch the sun rising over New York's bridges, and being spellbound at sunset as the sun lit up the "intricate colossal structures." "For twenty-five years I then delightedly absorbed, sketched, painted, transformed and imparted into various art forms this truly inspiring scenery . . . I exhibited over about half the world. Slowly I carved and rebuilt my life's lost work and reputation."

The Metropolitan Museum of Art bought some of her work for its permanent collection, as did other museums. She won twenty-one awards, including three first prizes, and held nine one-woman shows.

Her oldest son, Sascha, had joined the Jewish Brigade while they were in Italy, fought in Israel's War of Independence, married Rachel, a refugee survivor from Rumania, and had a daughter.

Of Miriam's four younger children who attended the Oswego schools, DIMITRI is a carpenter, SONIA is an art director for a New York publishing house, PETER is an architectural engineer in Atlanta, and GIOCONDA (who was born in Italy) is a systems analyst and a dancer who has immersed herself in Isadora Duncan's style and philosophy of life.

In her last years, Miriam worked in a studio apartment in the Westbeth artists' complex in New York's Greenwich Village. In her soaring expressionistic wood sculptures, which filled her studio to the ceiling, she "sought to convey and communicate This Best of all Possible Worlds' forever-surviving wonder—its sound of prophecy," she wrote.

At the age of eighty, Miriam died in her studio. Her body was cremated; at her request, her ashes were strewn over Lake Tiberias in Israel.

"Cleveland was good to us," said PAUL ARNSTEIN, now a veterinarian doctor and a researcher in Berkeley, California, remembering the first days out of the camp. "The Jewish Family Service took us in, got us an apartment, and gave us interest-free loans which we, like all the others, were happy to repay. Then they found jobs right away for my father and me. My father, who had been so sure in Zagreb that the Croatians wouldn't touch us because his store with five tailors and ten clerks was so well-known, went to work as a clerk in a textile factory; I loaded sweaters onto trucks." Two years after they left Oswego, Paul's father died of a massive stroke.

A few years later, Paul was admitted to the Veterinary School of Ohio State University, and after graduating he entered the U.S. Public Health Service. Now veterinary director in public health, Paul is known for his research and his papers on rabies control, on psittacosis—an infectious disease of birds transmissible to humans—and now on cancer. He has been using a strain of mice that do not reject human cancerous tissue. "This way we can graft human cancer tissue on animals," he explained "and study the changes human cells go through from normal to cancerous."

Still modest and hard-working, Paul is married to an American-born librarian, Helen, and has three children. David, twenty-five, completing studies for a doctorate in mathematics, works for General Dynamics; Judy, twenty-two, has just received a B.S. in business administration; and Michael, twenty, now enrolled at the University of California at Davis, plans to become an aeronautical engineer.

"I feel," Paul says, "that this must never be forgotten—that one small group of people in the world who were supposed to have been exterminated survived and came to America."

Helen agreed. "The danger is that what was so monstrous happened, and it could happen again. Only the next time they will be more efficient."

Paul's brother, WALTER, a computer designer, is married, has a young daughter and works for a subsidiary of Xerox. Their sister EVA ARNSTEIN BOGAR owns an art gallery in Indianapolis and is married to the chairman of the Department of Economics at the Indiana Univeristy.

IRENE DANON (Ljiljana) is a real-estate tycoon in Los Angeles. Widowed, she raised her three little girls by taking in sewing. Then she became interested in real estate, studied and became a real-estate broker.

"The camp for me was a marvelous experience," she says. "I was not able to finish school then, so now I never stop taking courses. I live in a beautiful home near Century City. In the morning I make coffee, go to my patio by the Jacuzzi, surrounded by my orchids. I feel the sun on my face and hands, and I just pray and give thanks for being alive. I am so patriotic that when I hear anybody say anything against America, I want to stand up and scratch their eyes out. Where else can a little refugee girl end up in a beautiful home, own apartment houses, drive a big car and keep going to school? It's only in America."

In Tom Crabtree's high-school shop class, PAUL BOKROS vowed to become an engineer.

But it took time. The Bokros family settled in Philadelphia, and Paul had to work while he attended the Technical Institute at Temple University. His father was seventy; his mother, thirteen years younger than her husband, worked in a sweatshop doing piecework. After four years she died of leukemia.

The Korean War broke out, and Paul enlisted in the Air Force. He became an electronics instructor, and as a sergeant taught electronics to airmen. While in the service, he married Greta, who had come from Norway. At war's end, he entered La Salle University in Philadelphia and received a B.S. in physics.

"After we got out of the camp, I spent my entire life teaching and working in industry," Paul recounted in his ranch-style home in San Diego, "always doing defense and space-related work in electronics. For a number of years I worked in missile and space exploratory programs. Now I work for a branch of General Dynamics." Paul is engineering director in charge of the design and development of the computer equipment used to maintain the F-16 aircraft.

"What am I happiest about? That I had the opportunity to live my life as a free man, as an American, as a husband and father. That my children, Debbie and Allan, grew up in a free society where, unlike me, they had to learn about real fear through books. When I landed in New York on our way to Oswego, I had one dime in my pocket, and I did not speak English. In these years I have helped in the defense of my country and, in a small way, in the conquest of space. In spite of all the problems which we have today, I have seen the world change for the better. What else could I wish for?"

In the Philadelphia area, Paul's sister, NELLY BOKROS THAL-HEIMER, reminisced of the Bokros family's arrival in the City of Brotherly Love. "The social workers from the Jewish Family Service here were wonderful to us. It was wartime and there were no apartments available when we came, so we temporarily lived at the Philmont Country Club for six weeks. Can you imagine what it meant to live in a country club after what we had gone through? We were among those who had been taken from Bari to Naples in a cattle car. We lay the length of the car with our heads against the wall; one group lay one way, one group the other, with our feet touching. Then came the voyage and the air raid! When we finally arrived in Oswego, things settled down. The camp itself was a secure time. There was a feeling of togetherness, of camaraderie, of belonging."

It took Nelly one semester in Philadelphia to get her high-school diploma while she worked part time in a bakery. Then it took her six and a half years, attending Temple University at night, to get her bachelor's degree. Two years later, she married Hans Thalheimer, also a refugee, who runs a successful metal business selling brass, bronze and nickel alloys. They have three sons: Philip, twenty-five, a psychiatric aide at a hospital near Phila-delphia; David, twenty-three, who writes; and Jeffrey, twenty-one, a student at the University of Pennsylvania.

After the boys were grown, Nelly returned to school; she and her son David attended the University of Pennsylvania, graduat-ing on the same day in June of 1981. David received a bachelor's degree in economics and Nelly a master's degree in social gerontology. She now works as a geriatric social worker for the Philadelphia Corporation for Aging.

The youngest of the three Bokros children, MIRA BOKROS HALPERN, at ten, had been a lively member of Esther Morrison's Girl Scout group. Instead of going to college at night, Mira went to work for the Internal Revenue Service, climbing the bureaucratic ladder from typist-clerk to auditor. She continued to work after she married Myron Halpern, a New Yorker who had a Ph.D. in anatomy and physiology, and who now teaches in their home state of New Jersey at Camden County College.

"I was very traditional then," Mira says, "so when I got pregnant, I gave up my job." They have two sons, David, twenty, and Donald, nineteen, both students at Indiana University.

A few years ago Mira decided, "I'm no longer traditional, now I'm a nonmilitant feminist," and went back to school. "I was forty-three when I received a B.A. in finance from Glassboro State College in New Jersey. Now I work as procurement agent, a funny title," she laughs, "for the Defense Industrial Supply Center of the U.S. Department of Defense."

In high school, ROLF MANFRED KUZNITZKI wrote a composition for Gladys Baker's English class called "The Flower and I," a metaphor for refugees longing for a home, so powerful that Congressman Dickstein made it part of *The Congressional Record*.

Rolf, who later dropped the name Kuznitzki and became Rolf Manfred, studied engineering and became one of the fathers of both the Polaris missile and the Minuteman missile. As project manager and director of research for Aerojet in Sacramento, Rolf's work led to the planning of the MX missile. Then the curve of his life changed. He turned his back on instruments of death and looked to energy, searching for nonnuclear alternatives for oil.

Earlier, living in Ohio, he married, fathered a daughter and two sons and was divorced. He now lives in Belmont, California, married to Helena, a Swedish woman who works as a travel agent.

As an official of EPRI, the Electric Power Research Institute, which represents most of the electric utility companies in America, Rolf travels around the country and the world promoting coal-water slurry as a fuel which will replace oil in electric utility industries.

Visiting me recently while in New York with his youngest son on a whirlwind tour of major utilities, Rolf looked back philosophically. "The greatest influence in my life was my English teacher in high school, Gladys Baker, who has since died. But all the teachers, including the principal, Ralph Faust, were caring people who allowed us to integrate at our own pace. They didn't force anything down our throats. They didn't say, 'You're a bunch of refugees, learn this, learn that.' They taught us about America. I'm an American, and I still get goose pimples when I see the American flag."

HENNY NOTOWICZ HAAS, who had blithely entered her first classroom humming, "I valk to de vindow, I valk to de door," was nineteen when she married a young New York accountant, Harold Haas, who is now vice-president, treasurer and chief financial officer of the giant Music Corporation of America. They have two daughters, Gilda, an urban planner, and Linda, an artist and photographer. After twenty-nine years of marriage, they were divorced.

Henny, a skilled Braillist certified by the Library of Congress, worked for twelve years at the Braille Institute and ran a craft department. Today she lives in Beverly Hills, buys paintings and prints in countries like Mexico and Italy and sells to galleries.

Recently, reminiscing about the *Henry Gibbins* at lunch in Los Angeles, Henny burst into laughter. "But I always thought the name of our ship was *Secret*. That's what you taught us. Remember? 'The name of the ship is Secret, and we came from the North Pole.' "

ANNY PICK, the star of countless musical-comedy skits with Otto Presser, knew the trials and trauma of a single parent raising two small children. Her husband had been killed before Anny came to the United States. Both her children now have Ph.D.s; PETER works in art history in San Francisco; GERALDINE CASSENS, born in the camp, teaches at Harvard Medical School, where she is assistant professor of psychology, and is the mother of two children.

Anny works in a gift-and-card shop in Hallandale, Florida, to keep busy and to try to forget the past. Her employers say, "Anny could sell ice to an Eskimo."

The "Weinstein orphans," who had discovered their mother was alive in Switzerland, had to wait another three years before she was given a visa and could join them in New York. "It was very hard for my mother," Miriam told me, "without my father.

But it was rough for all of us. My mother took care of the smaller children, while we older ones went right to work.''

Miriam, now married, is the mother of two sons and a daughter, and grandmother of four.

Across the years, several of the high-school students continued their friendship with Ralph Faust, the principal, but his most loyal correspondent is STEFFI STEINBERG WINTERS, who writes him warm, newsy handwritten letters.

"Oswego," Steffi says, "prepared me completely for life."

Highly organized, multilingual and thorough, Steffi had no trouble finding work in an office in New York. GERTRUD, her widowed mother, was delighted to get a job in a doll factory through RUZA LEDERER.

Steffi is married to Samuel A. Winters, an exporter of scrap metal and, like Steffi, a Berliner, who came to America in 1938. Their son Ronald works in a bank, and Alan, their second son, is a student at the Wharton Business School in Philadelphia.

The search for more survivors became a kind of joyous pilgrimage, with luncheons and dinners and home-baked pies in each other's homes. Fred Baum held a reunion around his swimming pool in his home in New Jersey. Zlatko Hirschler organized several dessert-rich evenings in his apartment in San Francisco. Across America, friends opened their homes for more reunions.

In Baltimore, Esther Danon Kaidanow corraled a whole group who sat around a dining-room table reminiscing and laughing far into the night. Proudly, Esther gave me one of her prize possessions, a photograph of the Baltimore-Oswego group with General David Elazar, Israel's former Chief of Staff. Elazar, born in Yugoslavia, a friend of the Danons, was one of the heroes of the Six-Day War in June 1967.

A number of reunions of the people who lived in Greater New York, New Jersey and Philadelphia took place in my apartment in New York City. As immigrants had done in America for hundreds of years, they had settled in little clusters, finding security and companionship in their closeness.

Some of Oswego alumnae had remained friends through the years, but others were meeting for the first time since the camp had closed. On a Sunday afternoon, some twenty-five people came to my apartment. ABE FORMAN, formerly Abe Furmanski, who had been with the underground in France, is now a coins-and-medals dealer. BELLINA BONI came up from Philadelphia, escorted by one of her three sons, RAYMOND, an engineer who lives in Queens. REGINA GAL came from the Bronx, small, fast-moving, with an endless store of anecdotes. "I sent my children to a religious school here," she said, "even though I lost my faith in Europe when I saw what they did to children and old people."

BELLA MOSCHEV, who had bought a boat with the gold napoleons she had sewn as buttons on her dress, came with her husband, ALBERT, the treasurer of the Association of Yugoslav Jews in the U.S., their daughter, ROSA LEVY, and her husband, Marcel.

Many settled on Manhattan's Upper West Side, where MAURICE KAMHI, known affectionately as Puba, lives. Puba, a twelve-year-old in the camp, dark and ruggedly handsome, produces television programs for New York City's Human Resources Administration. His daughter, Katherine Kamhi, is one of the young stars of the soap opera *All My Children*, playing the role of a college student who falls in love with her music teacher. His mother, EMICA AGRIMI, works as a hair-dresser—the skill she learned in the camp—at a fashionable New York hotel.

A young teenager who wept as she drove away from the fence on the last day, LIESL BADER FRIEDMANN is now an occupational therapist, working with the well-known Dr. Howard Rusk at the Institute of Rehabilitation Medicine in New York. She is married to Dr. Lawrence Friedmann, physiatrist, professor of rehabilitation medicine at the State University of New York at Stony Brook and chairman of the Department of Physical Medicine and Rehabilitation at Nassau County Medical Center.

Liesl's parents, KARL and MAGDALENE BADER, who were among the Austrian leaders in the camp, worked hard after they settled in New York and now live in Kissena, a senior-citizen housing project organized by Selfhelp Community Services, a refugee organization. At eighty-two, Karl is still a leader; in a lecture on the Holocaust in 1979, Gabriele D. Schiff, Selfhelp's deputy director, who had been a social worker in the camp, singled Karl out: "My personal pride and joy is the engineer who became the creator of the garden in Kissena II and is one of my old Oswego clients."

On a quiet, tree-lined street of Forest Hills in Queens, HELEN and MANE HARDING, the parents of Ray, the Liberal Party's leader, live next door to IRMA GRUNBERG LIPTCHER. Irma had come to Oswego with her late husband and her eleven-year-old son, WALTER GREENBERG, who had been the captain of the Cub

Scout troop. Walter, now a documentary-film maker, lives in Monsey, New York, is married to Celia, born in Cuba of Polish parents who fled in the thirties, and is the father of two daughters and a son.

Like many children of the Holocaust, Walter had been unable, in all these years, to talk of his own experiences. He lectured about art in the concentration camps, especially about the artists in Theresienstadt, but he completely blocked off his own feelings about "the terrible years of world amnesia" when, as a child, he had lived through several concentration camps, a jail and finally hid in the mountains before he came aboard our ship and entered the camp at Oswego.

"Those eighteen months of confinement in the camp," he told me, "were a painful experience. It was a period in limbo. I didn't know who I was and what I was. Yes, I wasn't hunted anymore. But was it a tranquil interlude—for better or worse? I was a lonely boy, eager for love and understanding, wanting recognition, and, above all, wanting to be the master of my own destiny. The experience living behind the fence was so painful that I put it behind me for thirty-five years."

It was the reunion at the camp thirty-five years later that had broken the dam. For the first time, when Walter shot pictures of the dedication of the monument, Celia learned the details of her husband's life as a child survivor.

NADA and RUDOLPH SELAN settled in Buffalo. In Yugoslavia, Rudolph's family had mined coal in their own coal mines and exported it on their own coal barges. "When we left the camp," Nada told me, "everybody was frightened. We had no money. I walked out the first day in Buffalo and said, 'I'm going to get work.' I went on the main street, walked into a dress shop called Darling and talked them into giving me a job selling. I knew almost no English, but the first days I sold a thousand dollars' worth of dresses."

Rudolph worked as an upholsterer and interior decorator, the trade he had learned in the ORT course in the camp. After one year, they moved to New York, where Nada worked for ten years for Saks Fifth Avenue and for the next eighteen years as a fashion coordinator for Bergdorf Goodman. In 1976 Rudolph died. Nada lives in Queens, an active member of the Yugoslav group. Her son, William, who was six years old in the camp, is now an architect in New York and won high praise in redesigning St. John's Hospital in Queens.

*   *   *

SONJA MERCER, living in the Bronx, came for tea one afternoon with Olga Maurer, International Harry's mother. Sonja reported that the oldest of her three daughters, YVONNE FRACKMAN, works for the Singer Sewing Machine Company in Long Island, her second daughter, LILLIAN JAGID, owns a dress boutique in New City, New York, and her youngest, BEATRICE YORMARK, born in the camp, is a computer scientist with a large accounting firm in Washington, D.C.

CLARA GAON's husband, SALOMON, died in the camp in the summer of 1945 and was buried in the Riverside Cemetery in Oswego. Clara supports herself in New York as a manicurist in a beauty salon. Her son JACK, who was seven years old in the camp, is married and is a welfare worker in New York's City's Human Resources Administration.

In Baltimore, ESTHER DANON KAIDANOW, who had been a devoted follower of Esther Morrison and the Quaker group, told me how it was she who had discovered there was nothing at Fort Ontario to show that it had once been a haven for refugees. Esther, now married to a successful businessman and the mother of two children, is the former president of the Anne Frank Chapter of Pioneer Women.

"We were on a vacation, driving to Canada," she explained, "and I begged my husband to take me to Oswego. For my family and for me the memories of the camp were very good. Coming as we did from former suffering and deprivation, the camp was our first taste of the American way of life. We had adequate lodgings, we had good and certainly abundant food, and, more than that, we had school, friends, recreation and clubs.

"I wanted to show it all to my husband. It was like showing him our personal 'Pilgrims' Landing.' We went inside the old fort, and there were pictures of the part Fort Ontario had played in American history. But nothing about us. I was terribly disappointed.

"Then, a little later, I met some of the members of the Syracuse Council at a Pioneer Women's convention in the Catskills. When I told them the story, they said, 'We're going to do something about it.' That's how the reunion at Fort Ontario got started."

SHARY and LEON KABILJO came to the Baltimore reunion with their daughter SYLVIA SIMCHA. They had named her Simcha, which means a joyous celebration, because she was born in the camp nine months after the voyage of the *Henry Gibbins*. "That was our first real honeymoon," they told me.

RENA ROMANO BLOCK, whose father had chosen Baltimore for their home to be close to the sea, began to work when she was fourteen. After high school, she continued to work, married and supported her husband while he finished college and went to law school.

"I have very warm memories of P.S. 2 in Oswego," she told the group around the dining-room table. "Especially of my teacher, Mrs. Murphy. She really inspired me and she gave me a good introduction to the English language. For years, until she died, she sent me a card every Christmas."

Rena has two adopted sons, Adam and Jeffrey. After sixteen years of marriage, she was divorced and returned to work. "All of us who came to Oswego," she says, "work hard, as our parents taught us, to give our children the advantages we missed in our war-torn childhood and to pass on our Sephardic European ideals and culture."

"My son, Ronald," FLORA KALDERON FRIEDMAN, who had attended P.S. 2 with Rena, told us, "just graduated at the head of his class of five hundred students. You should have heard my father stand up in front of his close friends, boasting, 'Every one of you should be proud that one of our Yugoslav children from the camp has a son who is graduating first in his class of all Americans.' "

SIMON KALDERON, Flora's brother, is now president of Advanced Packaging, Inc., which he founded in 1963. He manufactures and distributes material for packaging products, including sophisticated logistic systems, both for the government and for private industries. Their father, AVRAM, who owned a department store in Yugoslavia, started working as a laborer in Baltimore and eventually became a foreman at an upholstery-manufacturing company.

SILVIO FINCI struggled hard in Baltimore to forget his war experiences. In Sarajevo, Silvio had managed a large lumber mill; now, at seventy, he is a buyer for one of the largest mill and lumber companies in the city. Silvio and his late wife, RICKI, worked hard to put their two children through school. Following in his father's footsteps, their son, MIKE, who became a soccer star at the University of Maryland, owns a successful insurance company in Rockville, Maryland, and is a philanthropic member of the Jewish community. Silvio's daughter, SONYA SETREN, works as a secretary and paymaster with the Department of Public Safety in Baltimore, helping her husband send their three children through college.

"They are all good citizens," Silvio says. "I am happy that I could stay in the United States and give a good life and a good education to my children."

What they had lost in Europe they found in America.

In Philadelphia I found SYLVAN BONI, the former Boy Scout who had answered all of Congressman Dickstein's questions with a resounding "*Yes!*" Sylvan was at a Jewish Federation meeting for teachers when he heard a speaker talk about Roosevelt and Oswego. He stood up. "I am one of those Oswego refugees," he said. Sylvan now teaches philosophy of religion at Central High School, the honors school of the city. He has just received his Ph.D. in philosophy from Bryn Mawr.

His father, who had bought a boat and rescued one hundred refugees fleeing Bulgaria, is dead. His mother, BELLINA, and his brother, CLAUDE, who is in real estate, both live in Philadelphia.

SAMUEL FRAJERMAN, who came to Oswego at four, heard from a friend of my search for survivors and telephoned me from Philadelphia. I met him there soon after and learned that he is a graduate of Temple University, works as a management analyst in the Defense Logistics Agency of the U.S. Department of Defense, is married and has three children. His sister RACHEL GOLDFRAD is married and the mother of four children; his younger brother, JACOB, works for Eastman Kodak in Los Angeles, and HARRY, who was one of the babies born in the camp, is a driver-salesman for a large dairy company.

The process of finding survivors, once begun, became like a family gathering where each day more and more welcome relatives turn up.

In Nashville, Tennessee, after a speech at a Hadassah luncheon and a radio interview, I was told, "One of your Oswego refugees lives here in Nashville."

In the city's West End Synagogue I found EVA LEPEHNE ROSENFELD working as the bookkeeper. For a few minutes she stared unbelievingly. Then she began to speak. "I was seventeen when you brought us, but I was really like a child of eleven. I had lost all those years from the time we escaped from Germany. My mother died while we were running; my father was killed by the Nazis.''

On the day the quarantine was lifted, the frightened, traumatized orphan met her grandmother who lived in Rochester. ''I couldn't talk to her. I just wanted to run and hide.''

Oswego helped heal some of Eva's trauma. She went to school; she worked as a nursery-school aide in the camp, acted in plays, and when the camp closed she moved to Rochester with her grandmother. She married a printer there and later moved to Nashville, where she raised their four children.

A newspaper story about the 1981 reunion in the camp brought a letter from the Virgin Islands. JULIET LOWRY, part of the Czech group, wrote that after crossing the Rainbow Bridge at Niagara Falls she had settled in Syracuse with her husband, GEORGE, and their young daughter, MARIA RUTH. ''We got a cold-water, share-bathroom room, and on the second day we both started to work at the Onondaga Pottery,'' Juliet described their first experiences. George worked at the pottery for thirteen years, retired and died in 1969. Juliet, who found no future in the pottery plant, worked for thirty-one years for an air-conditioning firm until she moved to the Virgin Islands. Their daughter, Maria Ruth, a graduate of Syracuse University moved to Oregon with her husband. After twenty-two years and four children, they were divorced.

''Considering our start in Fort Ontario,'' Juliet wrote from St. Croix, ''it is an American miracle that my life here is not much different from the very rich, especially when you remember what we were.''

Kansas City, Missouri, was so hospitable to LIESL and CARL NEWMAN that when their son PETER turned thirteen the Jewish community celebrated his Bar Mitzvah, underwriting his year of studies, his prayer shawl and phylacteries and even his Bar Mitzvah party. I flew to Kansas City to help Peter celebrate. He is now a certified public accountant.

In San Francisco, MILIĆA and ZLATKO HIRSCHLER, whose sister had come from Tennessee the day the quarantine was lifted, are the lively center of a group that meets almost every week. Zlatko runs an electric-shaver repair shop and has written his own story, called ''The Flight: A True Story of Life in Hitler's Europe as

Experienced by Fred Z. Harris and May M. Harris, Formerly Zlatko and Milića Hirschler.'' Their son PETER is a social worker.

KITTY KAUFMAN, who had found security in the sight of the Oswego fence as the train pulled into the siding, is one of the regulars of the San Francisco circle. In the camp her husband, BRANKO, a photographer, began to take pictures of the refugees who wanted photos to send to their loved ones overseas. A small darkroom was set up for him in their barrack, and soon the staff and people from Oswego prevailed upon him to take their photos too. Professor Romney from the State Teachers College so admired his pictures that he loaned Branko his camera.

The Kaufman's were settled in New York with their little daughter, EVA. Professor Romney visited them several times and found them struggling hard to survive. Romney urged them to return to Oswego; he would help them find a studio and a house. In September 1946 they moved back to Oswego. ''We had a great success in our photo studio on Bridge Street,'' Kitty says. ''Besides our photo customers, Branko was photographing weddings and celebrations and made the yearbook pictures for the high school and college and for sororities and fraternities. After a few years, we were even able to buy a ranch house.''

But the ferocious winters on Lake Ontario made life difficult. In 1955 they moved to San Francisco and opened a photo studio in Daly City. In July 1968 Branko died of a heart attack. Their daughter, EVA KAUFMAN DYE, is an elementary-school teacher in Millbrae, California.

Others in the close San Francisco circle are MARY SPITZER, who wept when she held her first bedsheets in the camp. Her daughter, MARGARETA SPITZER FISSE, and her husband, Bob Fisse, built their home themselves in La Honda, California. Her son, ERNEST SPITZER, who attended Oswego High School, as did Margareta, and who played the accordion on the ship and in the camp, is now a lithographer in Fresno.

Also part of the San Francisco enclave are NADA and WILLIAM LOW—he was president of the Austrian group—who met in the camp and were married in New York in 1946; Nada's brother, WILLIAM SCHOENWALD, who ran a dry-cleaning store until he retired; ANNA SCHWARZENBERG, who has changed her name to Stassen; and GISELA TUSAK, who recently moved to West Lafayette, Indiana. Gisela now lives with her daughter, EDNA TUSAK LOEHMAN, who was a one-year-old when they arrived at the camp, and who now teaches environmental economics at Purdue University.

EDWARD KAISER, who had worked in a lumber factory in Yugoslavia, found work as a bookkeeper in a lumberyard in America, while his wife, MARGRITA, worked as a cosmetologist. BRUNO, their sixteen-year-old son, who had attended the Oswego High School, became an electrical engineer and now runs his own company, called Sentry Technology, makers of burglar and fire alarms. He too never talked about Oswego to his daughters until he took them on a trip in 1968 and showed them the camp.

The LEVITCH family moved to California, where LEON, the gifted young composer and pianist, continued studying music and composing while he tuned, repaired and rebuilt pianos and harpsichords. He has written a variety of chamber music, much of which has been recorded on the Orion record label, a cantata called "Of Plants & Humans," based on his own text, and a symphony. The symphony has had a number of performances by local community orchestras and served as Leon's thesis for his master's degree in composition in 1970 under the late composer Roy Harris.

In 1971 Leon founded a department of piano technology at UCLA Extension, where he taught what he calls a "paramusical art." In 1979 he moved the program of piano technology to the California State University at Northridge Extension, where he teaches now. "I have learned to love this technology which has earned me my living," he told me in Los Angeles, "as much as I love composing music. Because caring for musical instruments is really making music at the very grass roots. I like to think of my students as the next generation of 'servants of Music.'" Leon and his wife, Ruth, live in Pacoima, near Los Angeles. His dream, he says, "is to put some of my late father's poems to music; he saved a few of them, the rest were burned by the Nazis."

EDWARD, Leon's older brother, his younger sister, MANON, and FORTUNÉE, their mother, live in the San Francisco area, where Eddie is a builder, a licensed general contractor and a registered architectural designer.

"I am a builder of houses," Eddie told me, "because Tom Crabtree taught me the meaning of excellence."

For their father, JOSEPH, immigration meant strife and disappointment. In Yugoslavia he had been a well-known pharmacist;

he was called "Herr Doktor." In Los Angeles he opened his own drugstore. A few weeks after the grand opening, he was held up by a gunman who took everything from the cash register, cleaned the shelves of much of the drugs, and left him lying face down on the floor in shock. The trauma of old wounds inflicted by the Nazis returned, especially the memory of hiding from the Gestapo in the early days of the Nazi occupation. Disguised in peasant clothes, he was chased down the path of a small brook in the town of Mladenovać and was caught by two Gestapo men. One put a gun to his temple while the other shouted, "Shoot him." To save his life, he distorted his face and body to look mentally retarded. "It's a waste of bullets," one of the Nazis said, "to shoot someone *so verrückt,* so crazy." They let him go.

The mugging in Los Angeles reawakened the trauma; once again the Nazi gun was at his head. Joseph disposed of his drugstore at great loss and looked for work. Chain drugstores wanted young men; smaller stores could give him only part-time work. He had always loved working with his hands; now he became a handyman, fixing people's fences, cabinets, even their plumbing. He hid his depression from his family, while his health deteriorated. One day he was found dead in the basement of his home in Berkeley. Ironically, he had ended his life using the method he had taught his family to use if they were caught by the Nazis and slated for deportation to the death camps.

There were also other tragedies. RABBI TZECHOVAL left the rabbinate and with his wife, MINDLA (who had been able to get the *mikvah* built against all odds), entered the diamond business in New York. A few years later, their bodies were found in the water in Lakewood, New Jersey. Some diamond dealers who knew them well insist they had been robbed of their valise filled with diamonds and then murdered. Others call it suicide. Their deaths are still a mystery.

LEA HANF FRANK, highly efficient, managed a large textile business in New York and in 1965 spearheaded a twentieth-year reunion of the high-school students with Ralph Faust, his wife, Dorothy, and two of the teachers, Frieda Schuelke and Gladys Baker. Lea and her husband, Alexander, were killed in an automobile accident. They left a young daughter, Denise, who married recently and invited several of her mother's high-school friends to her wedding.

But RENÉE BUCHLER TANNENBAUM, the widow of ARPAD

BUCHLER, who was killed shoveling coal in the camp, has remarried and is living happily in Brooklyn.

ZDENKA RUCHWARGER, the tall elegant nurse who worked side by side with her physician husband, ABRAHAM, was first settled in New Jersey and later moved to Washington, D.C. But Abraham was restless, took Zdenka to Israel and finally returned to Washington, where he died of a heart attack in 1968.

Zdenka returned to New York and worked for years in a doctor's office. Recently she resettled in San Francisco to be near her children, while she works again in a doctor's office. Her daughter, Mimi, is married to Peter Haas, the president of Levi Strauss, the originators of blue jeans. Her son, Gary, is the financial counselor of the University of California at Berkeley.

DAVID LEVY, who enlisted Eleanor Roosevelt's help in getting the State Teachers College opened to the camp students, also lives in San Francisco, where he is a clothing salesman. His son, Robert, and daughter, Norma, are both lawyers.

IVO LEDERER, whose first English words were the slang he learned from the sailors on our ship, is now a well-known historian whose English is impeccable. He has a Ph.D. from Princeton and has taught Russian and East European affairs at Yale, Princeton and Stanford.

Of all the books and articles he has written and edited, he is proudest of the award-winning *Yugoslavia at the Paris Peace Conference: A Study in Frontier-Making,* and *Russian Foreign Policy; Essays in Historical Perspective.*

Divorced, the father of two sons, Ivo lives in New York, travels constantly and works as a consultant in both the U.S. and Europe.

"My life has been an extraordinary voyage for which I am profoundly grateful," he says. "The teachers in the high school were fantastic; I still have something I made under Mr. Crabtree, our shop teacher. Oswego was a very positive experience; so many of us who came out of the camp have had full and useful and rewarding lives.

"At sixteen, I wanted to go into international relations to make the world a better place. At fifty-two, I suppose, I'm still at it, but with a bit more salt and pepper. At one point you ask yourself, Why all this brutality; why do nations do these things to each other? I don't know. I'm persuaded that Western Europe has not run out of creativity; but it has run out of inspired principles, out of positive ethos. I don't feel that about America. A great many Americans have begun to lose faith. Yet faith is what has forged this society.

"Whatever inequities there are, and they exist in every country, the thing that makes America different from Europe is that here, if you've got the stuff in you, it will come out. Here you are promoted, not because of family or wealth, but on merit. But of course there are clouds and these mustn't be ignored."

Suddenly Ivo laughed. "What a motley group of ragamuffins we were when you brought us over. We were the dregs of World War Two, and look at us now.

"In Yugoslavia my family were assimilated Jews. The first time I really became aware that I was Jewish was when a local fascist in my very own hometown slapped a yellow star on my chest and spat in my face.

"That's perhaps why I feel so strongly about America. Only a foreign-born can understand the nature of the trunk of the tree on which he's grafted. Only a foreign-born can truly appreciate what America is."

I had never forgotten the haunted face of EVA BASS, the singer who had captivated the soldiers on the *Henry Gibbins* with her sad dark eyes and her ink-black hair cut like a boy's. Like Edith Piaf, whom she strangely resembled, she had come up from the streets, and like Piaf, she had sung in Paris in nightclubs before the night of Nazism descended.

In those early Oswego camp days, I would seek her out in her barrack; she sat pregnant, forlorn, a wounded sparrow, using her spent energies trying to cope with a headstrong thirteen-year-old, JOACHIM and a two-year-old blond toddler, YOLANDA. A third child, SUSANNA, had been born to her six months after our arrival in the camp, but the camp authorities had decided she was too fragile to care for the baby and she had been persuaded to give it to a childless Jewish couple in Buffalo. She never forgave herself.

Could she be alive? What of the children?

One morning the phone rang. "I'm calling from Minneapolis," a man said. "My name is Joe Fredkove. Somebody in my office gave me your book. My wife is in it. We haven't slept for a week."

"Your wife is—?"

"Her name was Yolanda Bass."

"Yolanda! Is her mother—?"

"Her mother is dead. But here's Gloria."

"Gloria?"

"Her mother was so grateful to America for taking her in, that she changed her name to a more American one. It was a way of showing her gratitude."

My talk with Gloria was long and emotional. "After we left Oswego," she told me, "we moved into a fourth-floor walkup on Columbia Street in New York's Lower East Side. My mother was totally wiped out, physically and emotionally. She took a few jobs, but she had a weak heart, and eight years of climbing all those stairs worsened it.

"Her only joy," Gloria said, "came from singing and playing the guitar. She would go to Greenwich Village, to the fountain in Washington Square. Often I would stand behind the crowd and watch their faces. She mesmerized them. In the summer there were lots of tourists in Greenwich Village from everywhere, and they would applaud her and follow her through the park. Once she wound up in a coffeehouse and about twenty-five people followed her and listened to her singing. I think she dreamed of singing on a Johnny Carson show, but she never made it. She never really recovered from what happened to her in those Nazi years."

Gloria's is a different story. She is happily married to her husband, a merchandising executive, and is the mother of nine-year-old twins, Jonathan and David. At forty, she is a legal secretary, and has gone back to college to get a degree in—music.

"What about JOACHIM?" I asked Gloria, remembering the little boy whose hand I held as we entered the camp the first day.

"He changed his name to Jack. He lives in New York, but he won't talk to you. He doesn't want to remember the past."

"Ask him."

"All right. I'll try," she said.

The next morning Jack Bass called. He came over that evening, and once he started talking, it was hard for us to end.

The undersized thirteen-year-old was now a robust, confident man of fifty-one, with his mother Eva's magnetism.

"It's true," he said, "I never wanted to talk to Gloria about the past. Why dig it up again? But I guess I am ready to talk about it now. Those early years, I lived on the streets—first in Philadelphia with a foster family, then in New York. I wouldn't go home for days, weeks, at a time. I couldn't stand all the fighting and bickering. I became a street vendor, selling ice cream in the summer, apples and pears in winter. I managed to finish junior high, though, and they sent me to a maritime high school. I couldn't see myself on a ship, so I dropped out."

He paused. "I love this country—more than anything I've ever loved in my life.

"Now I own my own limousine service—the 'Jack Bass Company'—with four limos and I'm buying two more. My way of paying this country back is this—whenever I meet somebody from another country or another city, I give them a sightseeing tour of New York they would never get otherwise.

"It's enough for me to know that this country opened its arms to a thousand people who needed it."

From the midwest came a letter and then a string of joyful telephone calls from EDNA SELAN—now Edna Epstein—who had been a spunky six-year-old in the camp.

A few weeks later, I joined her in her office high in a skyscraper in downtown Chicago. Edna—tall, zestful, strikingly handsome, talking and laughing as we raced through the crowded streets to her car then drove along the shore of Lake Michigan to her home—described the odyssey that had brought her to a unique role in the life of her city.

"I had a tempestuous childhood and adolescence. I went to Hunter Junior and Senior High School (one of the honor schools of New York). It was blissfully an all-girl's school in the mad 1950's when women were not supposed to have minds or ambitions. I received the English award, and for a refugee child who had learned English as a third language at the age of six, it seemed all the sweeter."

Edna's parents, LOTTE and CARL, were divorced in 1947. Lotte moved to Switerland with Mira, Edna's younger sister; Edna chose to stay in America with her father. She went to Barnard College, took her Ph.D. at Harvard in romance languages and taught at the University of Illinois. Then—married to Dr. Wolfgang Epstein, an internist and professor of bio-chemistry at Chicago University, and with two small sons, Michael and Ezra—Edna decided at the age of thirty-two that the academic life was far too passive and that "I liked the more practical and pragmatic world." She entered the University of Chicago Law School, and in her second year, gave birth to her daughter, Tanya. She made the Law Review and the Order of Coif cum laude at a time when women were just beginning to enter law schools.

After a stint in the local county prosecutor's office, she joined a major national and international law firm, Sidley and Austin, and is now one of its first women partners.

"I am active politically," she told me, "teach extensively, am involved in the American Bar Association, have published in the law, and am renewing my erstwhile academic/humanities interests by serving on the Illinois Humanities Council. I have a rich, full and happy life. This country has been good to me.''

Dining with us at Edna's, was Dr. NEVA SVECENSKI GOULD, who had been a teenager in the camp. Both women were unaware they were living in the Chicago area until our reunion. Neva—small, soft-spoken, sensitive—had gone to Hunter College, taken her M.D. at Downstate Medical School and is now a practicing pathologist at Michael Reese Hospital. She is married to Dr. Victor Gould, also a pathologist, and is the mother of three teenagers, Ingrid, Karen and Jimmy.

Neva came to dinner with her mother, Dr. LENKA SVECENSKI, a graduate doctor and dentist, who had worked in the camp hospital with her physician husband, EUGENE. They had both become accredited in New York State and for sixteen years were supervising psychiatrists at Harlem Valley State Hospital. Widowed in 1961 and later retired, Lenka moved to Chicago to live with Neva. At eighty-four, lively, tiny and energetic, she bowls regularly and works as a volunteer for senior citizen groups.

It was Neva's brother, IVAN STRONG, who had given me her address in Wilmette, Illinois. Ivan had telephoned after reading of our first big reunion in New York as guests of Mayor Edward Koch in City Hall. "Why wasn't I invited?"

"Because I couldn't find you."

Ivan, a graduate of City College and NYU Law School, is a successful attorney active in Democratic Party politics. He and his wife, Hannah, have a daughter, Phyllis, a *summa cum laude* graduate of Yale, now in law school herself, and a son, Ted, at the University of Pennsylvania.

In Chicago, talking of her grandchildren, Lenka said, "I see them growing up as excellent students, all possible because of Oswego. It was our haven from the horrors of war and persecution. Now, in my old days, I pray for peace in this troubled world."

For GEZA BLEIER, whose wife, KAROLINE, had been found dead on the banks of the barge canal, the first years in New York were filled with grief and heartbreak.

His daughter-in-law, Audrey, hearing me on a television program, wrote, "I was sure that your book told the story of my father-in-law. Sure enough I found him mentioned. Geza is now seventy, looks wonderful and is still active—he works full time as a salesman and plays tennis every week."

Audrey listed Geza's address in Brooklyn, and I phoned him

there. "My life is fine now," he told me, "but when the camp ended and we came to New York, it was awful. I couldn't take care of little RONALD and GEORGE. I had to work, and had no one to look after them. I put them in an orphanage in Brooklyn, and then worked repairing shoes and even bought a little shoe repair store. But I was so unhappy without the children that I took them home.

"In 1948, I married a Turkish girl from the camp, RAQUELA OVADIA. Unfortunately she didn't get along with the children, and I had to give them away again to another orphanage. The marriage ended. Then I found a young couple who were willing to live in my apartment and take care of the boys, so I was able to bring them home again."

Despite the shuttling back and forth, the two boys finished high school and were graduated from Brooklyn College. Ronald is now a high school teacher and George a guidance counselor in an elementary school. Geza, happily married to Doris, an American woman, is a successful salesman for a woolen mills firm, and not only plays tennis each week, but chess and soccer.

Like families who lose and then find each other, we reveled in our discoveries.

In the McKee Art Gallery on New York's East Side, RENÉE CONFORTE MCKEE, surrounded by paintings of American and contemporaries, talked of her mother, SALLY and her late father, ISAAC CONFORTE, one of the Yugoslav leaders in the camp, who had established the Manhattan Import and Export Company.

Renée, a graduate of Mount Holyoke, moved to Paris, where she did graduate work in philosophy at the Sorbonne. When she returned to New York, she married David McKee, and together they operate the gallery that bears their name.

On a blistering cold Saturday night in late fall, DORRIT REISNER OSTBERG, (sister of the late Renée Reisner Margulis), a math teacher in Kennedy High School in Long Island, sat in my living room sipping hot chocolate. Dorrit, youthful and attractive, with huge gray-green eyes, had earned a B.A. degree in comparative literature at Queens College, and a master's in math at C.W. Post. Married at nineteen and later divorced, she has a twenty-seven-year-old son, DANE BRIAN WESLEY, a graduate of Fordham Law School who works in New York City's Human Resources Administration.

"We young people," she smiled, "we had a magnificent time in Fort Ontario; we ran in the races; we performed in the plays, and though we all bear scars, I consider coming here salvation. I owe this country my whole education, my whole life."

The photographs on the ship and in the camp became another key to the past. FLORENCE SCHILD MILLER, who had taught French at the Hebrew Institute of Long Island for sixteen years, found her brother, IRVING SCHILD, in one of the children's pictures. Irving, a commercial photographer, now teaches fashion photography at the famous Fashion Institute of Technology in Manhattan and is chairman of the department.

In a letter to the publishers, LIANA KRAMER BROWN, wrote that she too had recognized her mother REGINA and herself as a three-year-old in the photo waving at the Statue of Liberty. After graduating from Brooklyn College she became a schoolteacher. Married to Robert Brown, a businessman in home improvements, she has three sons, Howard, seventeen, now spending a year in Israel, Ari, fifteen, planning to go to Israel next year, and Mordechaí, fourteen. "There is a plaque in Israel when you enter Yad Vashem, the Hall of Remembrance," Liana wrote me; "it says, 'Forgetfulness leads to exile, Remembrance is the secret of redemption.' This has become the goal of my life— always to remember—never to forget."

One day, IRENE LEVI, the widow of JUDA, the white-haired leader of the Yugoslavs in the camp, called to tell me she had lived for several years in Tel Aviv and now was settled in New York. Her older son, SIDNEY LEE, is a practicing attorney in New York; her younger son, ERIC LEE, lives in California, where he is a gastroenterologist, director of medical education in the huge Kaiser Permanente Medical Group in Bellfower, and associate clinical professor at UCLA. Eric, who lives with his wife and two children in a suburb of Los Angeles, wrote me that their daughter Linda is studying animal husbandry in college, and David plans to study marine biology.

"The war and the fight for survival," Eric wrote, "have taught us all to struggle, sacrifice and strive for a better future. In what country other than the United States would any of my accomplishments have been even remotely possible?"

Some of the people had tried to deny the past and had never told their children of Oswego. "I don't want to swim in sorrow," Jack Bass had said.

But others were convinced their children must know of the

years of flight and the courage to survive. In Detroit, JOSEPH LANGNAS read a review of the book in the *Detroit Jewish News* and wrote a long letter identifying himself. Joseph had been our first Bar Mitzvah in the camp and the president of Class 7B1 in the Fitzhugh Park Junior High School. ("In Austria," his proud mother had told me, "Joseph couldn't even go to school, and here he's president.")

In the warmth of his suburban home, surrounded by his family and friends, Joseph sat at the head of the dining room table, his face eloquent with joy at the reunion. Now a physician and teacher, he teaches pathology at Botsford Hospital in Farmington Hills near Detroit. With his father, IGNAZ, a jovial man who had worked in the commissary in the camp, his mother, DORA, an equally jovial, life-loving Viennese, and his ten-year-old sister, BETTINA, Joseph had come directly from Oswego to Detroit, where he finished high school, attended Wayne University, and in 1957, received his D.O. (Doctor of Osteopathy) from the University of Allied Health Sciences in Kansas City, Missouri.

Bettina, who joined us at dinner with her husband, Bernard Lis, the owner of a computer service, had attended a Yeshiva elementary and senior high school and worked as a secretary. She and Bernard have three sons, Lance, Steven and Kevin.

Bettina took turns with Joe telling me how their father had struggled for years in Detroit, taking odd jobs until, in his late sixties, he became a super-salesman of wines. But it was too late; ravaged by illness, he died in 1972. Dora, who had worked for twenty years as a seamstress in J. L. Hudson Department Store, married Berish Stock, a Canadian, in 1978, and now divides her time between Montreal and Miami.

In the Langnas family, there was no self-induced amnesia. As their children were growing up, Joseph talked with them and his wife, Frieda, a refugee herself from Danzig, of his feelings about the past and about America. The second generation has already begun acting out the tradition Joe had started—that of healing the sick: Alan, his first-born, is a resident in surgery and is married to Shari, a computer programmer; Gary, his second son, is a junior in medical school; Michael is a junior at Michigan State University, and Susan, at fifteen, "will be," Joseph smiled, "whatever she wants to be."

"Maybe I should have talked to them even more," Joseph reflected, "telling them more details about the war years and what it was like to be a kid and see your father get arrested and seeing people getting killed. Now I know we're going to be doing a lot more of this. He looked around the table at his American children.

"If America hadn't brought me here . . ." His voice trailed off, as though he were thinking of over a million murdered children who would never go to school, who would never become doctors or be whatever they wanted to be.

"Oswego," he said, "was one of those experiences by which we measure our lives."

Because I had been so much a part of their lives, it was hard for me for many years to form a single view of the total experience.

How to stack up the frustration and anger of some of the old, obsessed by the fence, against the exciting vistas opened by the Oswego schools to the young?

How to weigh the bitterness at the insensitivity of so much of official Washington against the gratitude for the noble and determined caring of people like Harold Ickes and Eleanor Roosevelt?

How to forgive FDR, my idol, for proving to be "a politician first and then a humanitarian"? And how to understand his need to tread carefully even though this meant anguish and uncertainty, for so long, for so many?

Now, after the search and the rediscovery of the people, I felt I had attained that final, single view. The people themselves helped me attain it. I was stunned and delighted by the record of their lives.

They had helped give back to America the kind of confidence that had made it great. Whether it was genes, heritage, an inborn passion for learning, or their strength as survivors, they absorbed with relish and enthusiasm what America offered, and in turn made their own unique contribution.

How grateful my country can be for having given them haven. And how worthwhile was the struggle.

INDEX

253

About the Author

Ruth Gruber is a renowned journalist, author and foreign correspondent. Born in Brooklyn, she became the world's youngest Ph.D., at 20, winning her degree on an American exchange fellowship at the University of Cologne, Germany, where she became eyewitness to Hitler's savagery as he rose to power.

At 24, working for the *New York Herald Tribune,* she became the first foreign correspondent, male or female, allowed to enter the Soviet Arctic. She made two trips to the Arctic where she lived among prisoners in the early Gulag of Stalin's "iron age." She covered this story, her German experience, and growing up in Brooklyn in her recent autobiography "Ahead of Time."

In 1941, Secretary of the Interior Harold L. Ickes sent her to Alaska to make a social and economic study to help open our vast northern territory to settlers.

In 1944, while war and Holocaust raged, Secretary Ickes sent her to Europe as a "simulated general" on a secret mission to bring 1,000 refugees to haven in Oswego.

In 1946, she left the Department of the Interior and returned to journalism. She was the only journalist to cover the voyage of the famous ship "Exodus 1947." Both the book and movie "Exodus" were based on her eyewitness accounts in the *Herald Tribune* and later in her book "Destination Palestine: The Story of the Haganah Ship Exodus 1947."

She continues to cover Israel, the Middle East, war zones and the rescue of refugees in articles, photos and books. In 1974, she traveled to Vietnam and Korea for her book on adopting orphans called "They Came to Stay" and brought back 10 orphans from Korea. In 1979, her book "Raquela: A Woman of Israel" won the National Jewish Book Award as the best book on Israel.

She covered the Camp David Peace Treaty between Israel, Egypt and the United States for 150 newspapers. She was the only correspondent permitted to witness Operation Moses, the rescue of the Ethiopian Jews, made two trips to Ethiopia, and described the historic liberation in her book "Rescue: The Exodus of the Ethiopian Jews."

She lives in New York City and is the mother of Celia Michaels-Evans and David Michaels and the grandmother of little Michael and Lucy.

Books by Ruth Gruber

Haven: The Unknown Story of 1,000 World War II Refugees
Ahead of Time: My Early Years as a Foreign Correspondent
Rescue: The Exodus of the Ethiopian Jews
Felisa Rincon de Gautier: The Mayor of San Juan
Science and the New Nations
Puerto Rico: Island of Promise
Israel Today: Land of Many Nations
Destination Palestine: The Story of the Haganah Ship Exodus 1947

Raquela: A Woman of Israel
They Came To Stay
Israel on the Seventh Day
Israel Without Tears
Virginia Woolf: A Study
I Went to the Soviet Arctic

UPDATE

Fifty years have passed.

In August 1994 a major reunion was held in the Fort Ontario Camp itself commemorating both Oswego and the lives of those to whom Oswego gave safe haven.

In these 50 years, there have been several milestones and reunions. Our first was held in 1981 when a memorial stone was placed in the camp grounds overlooking Lake Ontario. In 1984, we celebrated our 40th anniversary in Joseph Papp's Public Theater in New York with Governor Mario Cuomo as the keynote speaker.

Two years later, on January 27, 1986, the New York State Museum in Albany opened a permanent Holocaust exhibit called "Bitter Hope: From Holocaust to Haven." More than a thousand people came to the opening and since then thousands of school children and adults visit each year.

In 1993, HAVEN inspired a musical play, "OSWEGO" which was given a first workshop performance by the California State Summer School for the Arts in Valencia, California. Its authors are Jerome Coopersmith, the playwright, Joseph Darion, the lyricist, and William Goldstein, the composer.

Since HAVEN first appeared, those former refugees have continued to make extraordinary contributions to life in America and abroad. Here are a few:

> ROLF MANFRED (formerly Kuznitzki) recently spent three years in Indonesia teaching its engineers American uses of energy. He is now advising our government on energy-related matters in Central Asia.

> DR. DAVID HENDELL was so concerned by the dental work he saw among immigrants to the US from the former Soviet Union, that he is preparing to establish a Moscow clinic with teams of American dentists to teach American techniques to Russian dentists.

CHARLES STEVENS as a child was hidden with his little sister Lili in a monastery in Bruges, Belgium by Father Bruno Reynders, a resistance fighter, who changed Charles' name from Camille Silberman. Charles, a nuclear engineer, is one of the co-founders of a high-tech company, Science Applications International. Today it employs 17,000.

IVO LEDERER is the director of a prestigious management consulting firm, Global Business Policy Council of A.T. Kearney. He directs the programs that provide political analysis for chief executives around the world. He is also president of the West West Agency, a forum for European and American policy leaders.

From global contributions to gourmet pleasures, DORIS BLUMENKRANZ SCHECHTER, who was five years old when she ran barefoot through minefields in Italy to escape German soldiers, is the owner of a highly successful bakery- restaurant café on Manhattan's Upper East side, "My Most Favorite Dessert Company."

Once again, as I wrote in the first edition of HAVEN, I am stunned and delighted by the record of these survivors' lives.

How grateful my country can be for having given them haven. And how worthwhile was the struggle.

Ruth Gruber

Safe Haven Inc. is a not-for-profit organization in Oswego, NY devoted to tracing the lives of 1,000 people given haven from the Holocaust in the only American refugee center during World War II, and to exploring the meaning of that "great experiment" in the context of broader refugee issues.

Through photographic materials, audiovisual exhibits, a research library, periodic cultural events and travelling exhibitions, Safe Haven aims to spur educational research, address tough questions and prompt personal reflection on any event in which one group of people forces another out of their homes, out of their livelihoods or out of their lives.

The lives of the refugees at Fort Ontario became mirrors for those human destinies destroyed in the Holocaust. They must not be forgotten.

Dr. Ruth Gruber, the author of HAVEN, has graciously set aside the income for the sale of this book to help Safe Haven in its efforts to develop a school curriculum and travelling exhibit about the Fort Ontario experience. The all-volunteer group also plans to create a high-caliber permanent museum and research facility at Fort Ontario Park in Oswego.

Scott Scanlon

President
Safe Haven Inc.

✂ - - - - - - - - - - - - - - - - - -

Order Form

I wish to order the book HAVEN: The Unknown Story of 1,000 World War II Refugees, as below.

Please send me _____ copies of the book to the address below. Enclosed is a check or money order for $_____.
   (Each book costs $10.00 + $2.00 for shipping and handling)

Ship to:

Name:_____

Address:_____

City:_____State:_____Zip:_____

Please make checks or money orders payable to:
Safe Haven Inc., P.O. Box 846, Oswego, NY 13126

Please allow 4 to 6 weeks for delivery.